BLACK CULTURAL LIFE IN SOUTH AFRICA

AFRICAN PERSPECTIVES
Kelly Askew and Anne Pitcher
Series Editors

Unsettled History: Making South African Public Pasts,
by Leslie Witz, Gary Minkley, and Ciraj Rassool

African Print Cultures: Newspapers and
Their Publics in the Twentieth Century,
edited by Derek R. Peterson, Emma Hunter,
and Stephanie Newell

Seven Plays of Koffi Kwahulé: In and Out of Africa,
translated by Chantal Bilodeau and Judith G. Miller
edited with Introductions by Judith G. Miller

The Rise of the African Novel:
Politics of Language, Identity, and Ownership,
by Mukoma Wa Ngugi

Black Cultural Life in South Africa:
Reception, Apartheid, and Ethics,
by Lily Saint

Black Cultural Life in South Africa

Reception, Apartheid, and Ethics

Lily Saint

University of Michigan Press
Ann Arbor

Published in the United States of America by the
University of Michigan Press
Manufactured in the United States of America
Printed on acid-free paper
First published September 2018

A CIP catalog record for this book is available from the British Library.

Library of Congress Cataloging-in-Publication Data

Names: Saint, Lily, author.
Title: Black cultural life in South Africa : reception, apartheid, and ethics / Lily Saint.
Description: Ann Arbor : University of Michigan Press, 2018. | Series: African
    perspectives | Includes bibliographical references and index. |
Identifiers: LCCN 2018011120 (print) | LCCN 2018023035 (ebook) | ISBN 9780472124244
    (e-book) | ISBN 9780472074006 (hardcover : alk. paper) | ISBN 9780472054008
    (pbk. : alk. paper)
Subjects: LCSH: Blacks—South Africa—Social conditions—20th century. | Blacks—
    South Africa—Social conditions—21st century. | Popular culture—Moral and
    ethical aspects—South Africa. | Apartheid—South Africa.
Classification: LCC DT1758 (ebook) | LCC DT1758 .S25   2018 (print) |
    DDC 305.8960968—dc23
LC record available at https://lccn.loc.gov/2018011120

COVER CREDIT: James Barnor, "Ghanaian Indian, Accra, Ghana, c. 1955."
Courtesy Autograph ABP.

To David, reader extraordinaire

ACKNOWLEDGMENTS

Writing a book can be a solitary endeavor, yet each sentence in these pages bears witness to innumerable conversations that provided the real substance of this project. I am fortunate to have found so many interlocutors willing to discuss what may have frequently seemed an idiosyncratic undertaking. Often merely recalling these exchanges sustained my writing and attention during the project's less social hours. In the book's embryonic days when I was a graduate student in English at the Graduate Center of the City University New York, I was, and remain, deeply indebted to Peter Hitchcock and Nancy Yousef, as well as to my exacting and kind outside reader, Mark Sanders. Certain other individuals I met at this time have remained essential readers and true friends, and these include Christopher Ian Foster, Matt Tomás Lau, Nicole Rizzuto, and Bhakti Shringarpure.

I am particularly grateful to my students during those years, whose trust and compassion allowed me to take pedagogical risks so that I might begin to explore the ethical stakes of teaching. At Baruch College, especially, as well as at Hunter College, Medgar Evers College, and the Gallatin School at New York University, my students' willingness to engage with the more violent legacies of human existence regularly reminded me, as South African poet Keorapetse Kgositsile puts it, that "cynicism would be a reckless luxury." I trust students will continue to be my most exigent interlocutors. At the University of Pittsburgh, and more recently at Wesleyan University, my students continue to demonstrate how reading produces encounters with difference that just might lead to more thoughtful forms of social relation. For their attention and their faith, I remain thankful.

A number of fellowships gave me necessary time to write, and I am greatly appreciative of the semester I spent in the autumn of 2016 as a Faculty Fellow at Wesleyan's Center for the Humanities. A travel grant from the CUNY Graduate Center enabled me to spend some much needed time in the fabulous Michigan State University Library Comic Art Collection in Lansing. I am particularly grateful to the librarians and archivists for all their guidance during my stay there. Librarians at the New York Public Library also made study rooms available to me, and much of this book was written in the sedate quiet of the Wertheim Study and in the Shoichi Noma and the Frederick Lewis Allen Rooms.

During my brief but happy time at the University of Pittsburgh, it was a great pleasure to meet and befriend Nancy Glazener, Shalini Puri, and Gayle Rogers. Since then, at Wesleyan University, I have been blessed to find myself in a department full of hospitable and accomplished peers. Among the many kindnesses I have received as a newcomer to the department, I must single out the guidance and friendship of Douglas Martin and Sean McCann. Other individuals who have encouraged and advised me at various stages of this project include Magalí Armillas-Tiseyra, Rita Barnard, Eckson Khambule, Tsitsi Jaji, Fiona Lee, Stephanie Newell, Michael Staub, and Andrew van der Vlies. Miles Parks Grier and Grégory Pierrot are to be thanked, too, for their careful readings of several of the book's chapters. I am also most grateful to the manuscript's two thoughtful and patient anonymous readers and to Ellen Bauerle and Susan Cronin at the University of Michigan Press. Parts of certain chapters have appeared in different versions and are reprinted by permission: "Reading Subjects: Passbooks, Literature and Apartheid" was published in *Social Dynamics* 38.1 (2012), http://www.tandfonline.com (chapter 1); and "Not Western: Race, Reading, and the South African Photocomic" was published in the *Journal of Southern African Studies* 36.4 (2010), http://www.tandfonline.com (chapter 3) and reprinted in *Print, Text and Book Cultures in South Africa* (ed. van der Vlies) (2012).

To the many others who have helped me to live life outside the book, I am humbled by your friendship. Without all the wonderful women in my life—Jennifer Downing, Tess and Angie Munro, Tanya Rubbak, Paula Szuchman, Katherine Wolkoff, and Ute Zimmermann—this book would not be here. To my family, also, both new and old—Katy Leopold; Ellen Leopold; Andrew Saint; Beatriz de la Torre; Jed, Barrett, and Laura Freedlander; La and Justin Scheu; and the little blisters whose mother can't quite believe she pulled it off—ngiyabonga kakhulu.

CONTENTS

Introduction

Ethical Theory Is Postcolonial Theory

What happens as we read?[1] Do we disappear,[2] transforming into someone or
something else?[3] Is reading the discrete act of solitary individuals, or does it
also play a role in transforming the social worlds we inhabit?[4] Do we become
ethically engaged with others *as* we read, and if so, what about afterward,
when we stop reading? If we do somehow change along ethical lines, is reading the only avenue to these kinds of transfigurations?

An intellectual history interrogating the relationship between art and
ethics extends back to Aristotle's famous discussion of tragedy, continuing
today with current work in literary studies by "New Ethicists."[5] What unites
these philosophies and theories across this long historical period is the
claim that encounters with unfamiliar subjects, literary forms, or narratological structures allow readers and spectators to transcend the specifics of
their own geographic and historical contexts, momentarily suspending their
selves to become more receptive to and attuned with difference. Peter Brooks
and Hilary Jewett epitomize this line of thinking in their recent panegyric
on the humanities: "The practice of reading itself," they write, "pursued with
care and attention to language, its contents, implications, uncertainties, can
itself be an ethical act."[6] While practices of reading have radically, if unevenly,
transformed across the globe in recent years, the questions about the effects
of these new forms of engagement remain remarkably consistent and relevant, as we continue to attempt to know how cultural practice intervenes in
individual, communal, and global life.

For Frantz Fanon, however, the universalizing claims of most ethical criticism ignore how much a reader's response depends upon the reader's position. Writing in *Black Skin, White Masks*, Fanon notes that when colonized

children read comics, "there is always identification with the victor," even when other characters might more closely resemble the reading children. Through readings in mass culture, he writes, "the little Negro, quite as easily as the little white boy, becomes an explorer, an adventurer, a missionary 'who faces the danger of being eaten by the wicked Negroes.'"[7] Though Fanon's central point here is to show how reading practices produce a self-alienating Du Boisian "double consciousness" in colonized black children, his comments also draw attention to the ethical stakes of identification.

As Fanon's observations suggest, reading practices interpolate differing ethical subjectivities in the disenfranchised than in the privileged, a point almost entirely missed in ethical theory's long engagement with literature. The writer Chimamanda Ngozi Adichie recalls how her formative reading practices led her to pen stories populated by "white," "blue-eyed" characters who "played in the snow . . . ate apples," and "drank ginger beer," even though she lived in Nigeria, where they "didn't have snow," they "ate mangoes," and she "had no idea what ginger beer was."[8] While context has largely been overlooked in studies of "ethical criticism," both Fanon's and Adichie's observations highlight the way that geographic, cultural, historical, and racial particularities also determine textual and ethical responses, producing unstable, slanted identification practices like those José Muñoz calls "disidentifications."[9] By ignoring readers and spectators in the Global South, ethical theory has missed out on salient ways that such interlocutors complicate ethical criticism's foundational suppositions. While white schoolchildren during apartheid read canonical literary works with greater frequency than their black counterparts, they paradoxically seemed less able to transform their reading habits into a practical ethics in operation beyond the classroom. My book thus forces us to ponder whether we should give credence at all to instrumentalist theories linking cultural consumption with ethical being. Do our forays into reading and watching film, in fact, do anything to make us more just or more ethically responsible human beings?

Édouard Glissant affirms that aesthetic engagement does produce ethical effects in the world, though they may be infuriatingly intangible. "No imagination helps avert destitution in reality," he writes, "none can oppose oppressions or sustain those who 'withstand' in body or spirit. But imagination changes mentalities, however slowly it may go about this."[10] Following Glissant's line of thinking, this book also accords cultural works a kind of nebulous, gradualist influence. I build on existing arguments from ethical criticism but place them under scrutiny by testing the limits of their applicability to genres and geographic spaces largely left out of their considerations. Through an examination of widely read, highly popular, but largely untheorized texts (visual as well as written) this book insists we recognize the ethical potential that subtends all cultural activities, however fragmentary, however "lowbrow," however fleeting. Furthermore, I argue that it is imperative we take into account the material, historical, and social contexts involved in each act of "reading," since there are no neutral or objective stances from which a reader or viewer approaches a work. Indeed, those conditions best described as "oppressive" can be more conducive to the production of ethical being through cultural engagements than the more complacent and comfortable subject positions of hegemonic belonging. The more slanted the orientation to the text is, the more likely it is to produce ethical effects.

WHILE LIMITED ATTENTION has been paid to readership in the Global South,[11] the twentieth century's literacy boom produced a surfeit of debates about the effects of reading, both pernicious and beneficial, on individual and social development.[12] As literacy rates soared, printing became simultaneously cheaper and simpler, transforming reading practices, too, as new reading materials flooded world markets.[13] Given these massive revolutions in global reading practices it is curious that scholars interested in the links between reading and ethics rely on literary works as their primary source of evidence.[14] This tendency to read literature as the exemplar at the nexus of ethico-cultural engagement problematically excludes most other cultural forms from discussions of how works produce ethical response. This necessarily keeps most global readers out of the discussion, too, then, since literature has not been the primary source for most worldwide literate encounters for quite some time.[15]

This book takes up precisely those reading publics and audiences that are both underrepresented in official state archives and unexplored in studies of ethics and aesthetics.[16] At the same time, this study begins at the tail end of a considerably long history of ethical criticism to redirect attention to the substantial, if unconsidered, relationship between ethics and popular culture. By looking at literary production alongside other forms of cultural production, I aim to democratize considerations of the ethical value of cultural texts, to present a challenge to literature's long-assumed position as culture's moral arbiter.

In so doing, I draw significantly upon that very ethical criticism that takes literature as its paradigmatic form, since its arguments, with some modifications, can also help us understand the production of ethics in nonliterary forms, genres, and media. The introduction addresses key theoretical insights from ethical criticism that are relevant for the rest of the book. Furthermore, by historicizing the relation between ethical theory and postcolonial theory, I show how we might better notice the aporia in ethical theory, with its general disregard of readers in the Global South. I go on to suggest that there are important political ways that ethical theory might benefit from being put into a conversational framework with postcolonial studies.

IN *The Company We Keep: An Ethics of Fiction*, Wayne Booth likens our relation to books to a series of friendships we have with the works' implied authors. Like true friendship, as Booth defines it, these relations lack a clear instrumentalism; as we read we are living *in* friendship with these authors, becoming, through everyday acts of reading, "some more a person."[17] For Booth, reading is not an emptying out of the self, but an expansion.[18] One becomes "more" than one was before the act of reading, and that new, excess self is more replete with humanity, "more a person," or to put this in terms of relation, more ethical.

Booth values texts that "open" "the reader to new experiences of otherness . . . narratives that raise questions, that are open-ended and leave the reader unresolved." He argues that these works are most likely to produce an expanding, generous self that is more receptive and hospitable to alterity.[19] For him, the metaphor exemplifies how literary devices establish "intimacy" between readers and texts. Metaphors operate through comparison to shed light on previously unnoticed connections, mirroring the associative relation that exists between the reader and the otherness encountered in the book's thematic, narratologicial, and formal structures.[20]

While Booth's emphasis on metaphors values an ethics forged through observing similarities between the self and others, he also admires readings that elude readers' complete understanding. Praising a more indeterminate relation to otherness that seeks neither to subsume difference into the self nor to annihilate it by designating it as absolute and therefore unfathomable, Booth makes a further claim: "Successful narratives," he writes, "are constructed not of ideal total indeterminancy or total resolution but of *limited determinacies* that by their vividness create strong suspensions or . . . 'instabilities.'"[21] Thus unlike some other ethical theorists, Booth finds works most "successful" when they expose readers to the destabilizing effects of alterity all the while adhering to certain *expected* discursive, formal, or thematic arrangements. Works should not *only* destabilize a reader in order to produce ethical effects, but must in fact also make use of recognizably familiar effects and expected structures. This notion that ethical texts are composed of "limited determinacies" undergirds my arguments about popular culture, since its forms, especially, depend upon well-known, formulaic, and even cliché determinacies. When Fredric Jameson suggests that texts "possess some autonomous force" that can negate the very ideological context out of which they arise, he anticipates reception studies' assertion that texts can produce an otherness opposed to their intended meanings.[22] It is thus possible for works with retrogressive and even dangerous ideological import to communicate messages at odds with their own intentions. This tension between a work's formulae and its types of difference and strangeness is central to this book's treatment of popular culture as ethical form.

Published the year before Booth's book, J. Hillis Miller's *The Ethics of Reading* likewise considers ethics' "peculiar relation to that form of language we call narrative."[23] While Booth's and Miller's emphases on formal effects are important, I go further, as we shall see, in insisting also upon the role played by social context in the production of ethics through acts of reading. Miller's work aids in this as he moves from analyses of particular texts to the "acts" of their cultural consumption—to the audience, in other words—an imperative refocusing of the problem of literature and ethics.

The word *act* is central to his project as it emphasizes the characteristics of reading that are its live, agential, material, corporeal, and affective instantiations, in lieu of understandings of reading and spectatorship that figure readers as passive or detached.[24] Such descriptions tend to imagine audience members and readers as homogenous receivers of transmitted cultural ideologies who are unlikely to have heterodox interpretations or responses. By accepting reading's active, engaged properties, we can imagine actual readers and spectators who play a role in determining their own moral place in life, even as they are being conscripted by other social formations that structure and impose rule over their lives.

For Derek Attridge, the term "event" is preferable to "act" when it comes to his theorization of reading. Like Booth, however, he argues in *The Singularity of Literature* that the specific character of the *literary* "event" is an ethical one that "opens a space for the other . . . [and] invites an ethical response."[25] Attridge is aware of the problem implied by his term of choice—the literary. He writes: "It is only by an artificial and often arbitrary act of separation [from an art form other than literature] that the qualities of the literary can be discussed."[26] He continues: "It would not, I believe, be an especially difficult task to extrapolate from the main points of my characterization of literature to the wider arena, including . . . developments in electronic media" recognizing that "some varieties of cultural studies include an overt argument against making any distinction between literary and other works, and this is an argument that has to be taken seriously—indeed, it is one that I wish to grant almost in its entirety."[27] Admirably, then, he admits that

> the designation "literature" [should not] be construed as applying only to the productions of "high" or "elite" culture: inventive literary works, like inventive films or inventive songs, may be very popular indeed. . . . In fact, one of the ways in which a literary work can be inventive is by operating at the unstable limits of the literary, and reinventing the category itself.[28]

Yet despite this recognition of the literary's problematic political valences, Attridge's work, like Booth's and Miller's, remains bound in his examples to canonical literary genres, thus his book reentrenches literature as the quintessential ethical form even while conceding that it no longer should be treated as such. For my part I do not propose we jettison literature's ongoing relevance to the production of ethical life, but suggest we might do away with the types of claims that continue to reify its role in that process. Might it be possible for literature, or "great art," to allow for the presence of its others (including popular genres) while simultaneously making a case for its continued importance to human experience?

If we understand ethics to be a motile property, untethered to particular works, and mobilized instead through readerly and specular acts, we might more clearly recognize the ethical potential in *all* texts, from the popular to the literary. Ethics emerges through practices of reading and spectatorship formed at the nexuses of historical and geographic context, individual social position, materiality, and imagination and does not take up residence within texts. It arises at the intersection between the perceiver and the object perceived, a dynamic that comes into being between reader and text, filmgoer and movie, audience member and performer.[29] As Karin Barber writes, "If art is the construction of shared meanings, then the audience is as important as the artist in the process."[30] Ethics, therefore, emerges out of the negotiations, or to use Miller's term, the "transactions," between a reader and a text. There is a neat symmetry to realizing that an ethical life is one that attends most purposefully to relation, but also one that can only come into being through relation to others, be those other people or cultural objects such as films, pictures, narratives, and books.

Of course, if an aesthetically produced ethics is mobile, it is also ephemeral, with each act of "reading" eliciting a different intensity of ethical response at each "event." It is here we might recognize how related a text's "textualterity"[31] is to the *context* in which it is being "read"—in other words, a work may "test . . . and unsettle deeply help assumptions" in one place but not another.[32] In fact, I insist, the contexts of aesthetic reception determine whether or not a work generates ethical response. For Wolfgang Iser, it is precisely the "tension" or *incompatibility* between the author and the reader's positions and viewpoints that serves as "a precondition for the processing and for the comprehension that follows."[33] In other words, the discrepancy between the reader's position and the author's is what allows the experience to become meaningful and for an alteration to occur in the reader.

If we follow this line of reasoning, we might begin to see that a work's ethical potential is *most* palpable when read by readers whose sociocultural position operates at a distance from the work's intended ideological sphere of reference and reception. The more peripheral the position to the ideological message that the work intends to relay, the more likely the text is to generate a "misreading," foregrounding the work's difference, formally and thematically, thus allowing for the emergence of ethical response.[34] Judith Butler observes that when a person occupies a marginal social or political position, outside of the society's "moral norms," "this means only that the subject must deliberate upon these norms, and that part of deliberation will entail a critical understanding of their social genesis and meaning. In this sense, ethical deliberation is bound up with the operation of critique."[35] Such critique, Butler suggests, is more in evidence in those who operate at an acute angle to mainstream ideology. "*Over and against those who would claim that ethics is the prerogative of the powerful, one might counter that only from the viewpoint of the injured can a certain conception of responsibility be understood.* What will be the response to injury, and will we, in the language of a cautionary political slogan on the left, 'become the evil that we deplore'?"[36] Ethics, or at least the potential for ethics, originates in subjection almost automatically, and thus, without the necessity for its articulation, is lived as practice rather than obsessively theorized in absentia. Those least often considered by ethical theory and philosophy as exemplary readers and spectators have often been those most likely to practice an everyday, lived ethics, in part as a result of their aesthetic encounters. If we truly wish to understand how reading initiates ethical and political engagement, we must turn away from those readers in sites of privilege, who all too often have failed to make the imaginative leaps of sympathetic identification they profess to encourage, and look instead toward readers whose daily existence always already required acts of identification, deliberation, and interrogation. As this book explores, ethical critique and ethical consciousness are both more likely to emerge at this space of social disjuncture. Within the context of apartheid and postapartheid South Africa, the ethical prerogative becomes, furthermore, a site for the reimagining of politics.

CONSTITUTING THE ARCHIVE: READERS AND VIEWERS

Black Cultural Life in South Africa constructs a counter-archive out of everyday cultural materials that were in circulation during South Africa's *unethical* apartheid years (1948–94). While South Africa's black[37] inhabitants have always constituted the country's majority, they paradoxically occupy a marginal position in most historical accounts of South African readership and spectatorship.[38] Assembling a variety of widely read texts, including passbooks, memoirs, American B movies, literary and genre fiction, magazines, and photocomics, this book reconstitutes an archive of apartheid-era black South African cultural practice, conscious all the while of the partiality of such an undertaking. There are other popular media that would be well suited to my approach that I do not take up in this book, including television,[39] radio,[40] dance, popular music,[41] photography, theater,[42] and print journalism, among others. Subsequent work remains to be done on these reading and viewership practices during apartheid to supplement the important work that has already begun in all of these areas. Certainly the scope of this study could not claim to encompass the rich, complex array of cultural materials that was being consumed during this period particularly, but not uniquely, in urban South Africa. Nonetheless my approach to understanding the emergence of ethical life within situated political and social contexts should be applicable to all forms of popular cultural engagement.

This book is organized in a loose chronological order, looking first at passbooks and the cultural responses to passbooks emerging in black writing in the 1950s and 1960s, moving then to film reception practices during those same years, through to a consideration of photocomics and their audiences in the 1960s, 1970s, and 1980s. The final chapter examines literary works from the 1990s into our contemporary moment. The overlapping historical trajectory I trace helps to highlight the long history of black South African engagements with cultural objects as sites for ethical life, though the counter-archive gathered here mainly explores how such practices contributed to the formation of ethical consciousness and relation during apartheid.[43] As Leela Gandhi's recent book enjoins, we have to attend to the ethical life of colonized and oppressed subjects because their access to *politics* was severely limited due to the inequity underwriting legal and social avenues for political participation. Ethical thought and practice was, for many, the only available access point for political engagement, albeit through affective and everyday experiential circuits. Gandhi explains:

> A stringent disassociation of politics and ethics would not have been beneficial for the agents of radical democracy. . . . Many of them, such as the subject peoples of empire, had no substantive recourse to the domain of politics proper in which to air their grievances. The newly politicized terrain of the ethical, however, to which everybody notionally had free access, was readily available for appropriation.[44]

My book turns to this "politicized terrain of the ethical" to better understand how everyday cultural acts provide disenfranchised groups with pathways to taking part in political life. Such engagements necessarily involve small, or even gestural, modes of doing political work, and it is precisely this minor, discrete character of experience that constitutes ethical relation's value. As large-scale political undertakings continue to prove inaccessible, disappointing, and corrupt, particularly to those on the social margins, the more ephemeral sites of everyday ethical interaction provide alternate conduits for political being.

WHILE THE APARTHEID state's extensive bureaucracy intrusively reached into people's everyday working lives, there is little official archival data on black South Africans' leisure time activities. Nonetheless, a history of reading and film spectatorship can be reconstructed through other avenues that together provide rich descriptions of people's leisurely pursuits across the nation. Miners, reporters, photographers, maids, homemakers, skokiaan queens, farmers, prisoners, lawyers, singers, musicians, technicians, writers, pupils, gang members, doctors, shop assistants, university students, carpenters, washerwomen, community organizers, policemen, clergymen, nuns, messengers, and many others were all engaging in "acts of culture" in one way or another. And this despite the abysmal literacy rates among blacks, due to the state's severe and calculated underfunding of black education.[45]

There were other ways to read. As in many places, literacy among some allowed for the spread of information and entertainment to many. American missionary Ray E. Phillips, who spent the first part of his career screening films to South African miners, noted in 1938:

> A considerable section of the urban Native population is a newspaper-reading public. Men returning to the Locations after working in town are to be seen taking their newspapers with them. A news-stand at Pimville Township sells twenty-four newspapers daily to residents; more are carried out by train by returning workers. Native newsboys bring unsold papers back with them to their home communities. Articles in the European press influence Native opinion in unexpected quarters. *News widely travels and is widely known and commented upon even by non-readers.*[46]

Zakes Mda confirms Phillips's assessment in *The Madonna of Excelsior*, his novel set in a small apartheid-era rural town where its inhabitants read newspapers every day, particularly to find out information about a local interracial sex scandal. "*Die Volksblad. The Friend.* We ravished every page that had anything to do with immorality and miscegenation. Each issue circulated from one homestead to the next. Until it was tattered. Until smokers used the pieces to roll their zols of tobacco or dagga."[47] For these voracious readers, newspapers served their original function as conveyers of information and meaning and then were repurposed for a range of other recreational uses. As such, they performed a set of vital material and ideological functions in black everyday life.

For other forms of cultural engagement, and for those who were unable to read much, films and photocomics provided highly satisfactory alternative forms of entertainment. It is clear from cultural histories of the period that materials for reading and films for watching were available most readily in urban areas, but also, as in the case of traveling bioscopes, for instance, in more remote parts of the country. Blacks read books, magazines, comics, and newspapers; listened to radios; and watched movies, too, in all sorts of places—in segregated cinemas in townships, in private homes, at work, in schools, and on the buses and trains they rode endlessly between townships or rural "homelands" and their jobs on the mines, in city centers, and in white suburbs.

We are now turning, then, from the role played by the textual or aesthetic object in the production of ethical feeling to that other pole in the dialectic of cultural consumption: the reader/spectator. However, rather than accept the flattening out of difference that occurs in many ethical theorists' positing of a quasi-universal, equally literate reading subject, this book insists we pay attention to the ways in which marginalization alters reception. In line with much thinking on cultural practices at the fringes of hegemony, the archive constituted here makes it clear that black South Africans developed different "ways of seeing" mainstream cultural artifacts and that this difference was due to social position.

Such subjects approach the cultural material they consume from acute angles of both conscious and unconscious difference.[48] Chela Sandoval usefully examines the way that marginalization effects cultural response, designating the hermeneutic strategies of peripheral positions a "methodology of the oppressed." Founded on an ability to read dominant culture deconstructively, for Sandoval, such a methodology is unavoidable for marginalized subjects: "Social life under subjugation requires the development of this very process of semiotic perception and deconstruction," she writes.[49]

> Under conditions of colonization, poverty, racism, gender, or sexual subordination, dominated populations are often held away from the comforts of dominant ideology, or ripped out of legitimized social narratives, in a process of power that places such constituencies in a very different position from which to view objects-in-reality than other kinds of citizen-subjects.[50]

The development of this alternative hermeneutics is inevitable because it is structurally inherent to the position of marginality and may not be avoided even should avoidance be desired. In this regard, unlike the reader who chooses willingly to engage in a practice of ethical reading that cultivates, as Attridge does, an openness to alterity, for those groups Sandoval identifies, almost any cultural encounter is an encounter with otherness, willed or not.

Such encounters produce a "methodology" able to recognize the aporia in the world around the texts, to notice inconsistencies, hypocrisies, and moments at which self-rationalizations unravel. It is a heightened state of critique, as Butler has said.[51] But what kind of ethics might such a critically aware point of view generate? How does the encounter with hegemony-as-difference make new kinds of responses to cultural forms possible? One central way this marginalized critique operates, as other postcolonial theorists have discussed, derives from critique's reliance on intense, focused observation. For it is through the close attention to discursive and symbolic manifestations of power that subject groups begin to mimic and distort dominant cultural forms.[52]

Mimicry, of course, involves attentive scrutiny—it requires a process of close reading, in other words—to create detailed, careful reproductions of what is observed. In colonial settings as Homi K. Bhabha notes, while mimicry often works to solidify the rule and ideological dominance of colonial discourse, "colonial mimicry" also deforms the colonial project, exposing its artifice through the colonized's imitation of the colonizer. Yet colonial mimicry exists, for Bhabha, in a time of futility and impossibility, since the colonized may approach but can never become the colonizer. This impossibility serves to withhold the colonized from the colonizer, keeping the groups apart to maintain the colonial status quo, which is structured by unequal rights and relations.

But mimicry is also an agential, ethical structure of colonial subjectivity, and not just because it exposes colonial relations to be cultural constructions that can therefore be deconstructed. In its imitative performatives mimicry creates movement across entrenched subject-positions, involving transformations, however temporary, that in their approach toward otherness allow for contamination and exchange across the porous membranes of subjectivities. These subject-positions "threaten" or "menace" the colonialists' solid definitions of otherness, all the while never permitting for the total annihilation of discrete, situated selves. Ethical relation, conceived in this way, as a movement toward an imagining and mimicking of alterity, is always a process of becoming and never a teleological finality.

Bhabha's delineation of colonial mimicry focuses predominantly on its effect on colonialism and colonialists' self-perception, and pays less attention to the ramifications of mimicry on the mimics themselves. Mimicry, as a cognate of mimesis, returns us, of course, to the realm of literary scholarship and to the ethical critics.[53] J. Hillis Miller reminds us that

> in Aristotle's *Poetics* the function of mimesis is knowledge. Imitation is natural to man, and it is natural for him to take pleasure in it. He takes pleasure in it because he learns from it. He learns from it the nature of the things or persons imitated, which without that detour through mimesis would not be visible and knowable.[54]

Mimesis, then, for Aristotle, is a practice intimately linked to the desire to know others. It is a method for epistemological education and reorientation: by reenacting what are perceived to be the actions and emotions of another, one comes to know more about that other, and to understand more about alterity, more generally. Mimicry, or imitation, for Aristotle, involves a "detour" into the other's experience that necessarily depends upon a hospitality to difference, and consequentially produces self-transformation and ethical generosity.

As Bhabha notes, colonial mimicry never results in a colonized subject becoming a colonizer. Yet it is in the attempt to know otherness, to know and inhabit the world, the people, and the objects around us, that an ethics is produced, even while the attempt inevitably reaches a limit point of impossibility. Indeed, these flashes of connection, the momentary knowledge of others produced by imaginatively inhabiting unfamiliar bodies, thoughts and affects, also occurs through writing about others *and* through the process of reassembling reality through reading,[55] so that we become, temporarily, someone or something else, in some other space and time.

Even if attempts to approach otherness—through imitation, reading, realism, or whatever mimetic form we choose—may insufficiently permit access to that difference we careen toward, something occurs through the act of imitation, or as Aristotle notes, something is made known that was previously unknown. This knowledge, these fleeting moments of connection or transubstantiation, emerges through language, but also, as this book argues, in colonial and postcolonial and apartheid spaces, through the imitative reproduction of the mental, affective, and bodily projections of otherness. Ethics, then, is a formal mode of cultural knowledge making. It was practiced under apartheid most frequently by those who had to learn about the powerful other, primarily in order to survive. But then, perhaps almost as an afterthought, ethical knowing also becomes a way to render fully human a post-apartheid world that is still grappling to reinstate ethics after the inhumanity and cruelty of apartheid.

No treatment of ethics could responsibly proceed without addressing its own relation to the ethical. In particular, we must ask what the ethical implications are of the insistence that ethics is a *sui generis* characteristic of the experience of oppression. Why dwell on the fact that blacks under apartheid were conscripted into feeling their way—daily—imaginatively—ethically—into the experience of white subjectivity? How could the abomination of apartheid be the catalyst for a mode of relation that not only refuses racism but deploys new logics that are altogether distinct from the Calvinistic binarism undergirding apartheid?

I am not the first to suggest that at a society's ethical nadir new forms of relation become possible. These emerge to enable survival, certainly, but as a counter-logic, too, to a naturalized status quo that is as much a social and relational artifact as any that came before or will succeed it. Glissant writes of the slave plantation as a site that produced new progressive modes of relation, and Angela Davis observes, also, that under slavery black men and women related in egalitarian ways that Emancipation subsequently foreclosed. This point is not to rescue or extol those barbaric systems of human exploitation but to refocus attention on the openings within oppression for alternative social imaginaries.

What was black ethics during apartheid? While the word *ethos* suggests "the characteristic spirit, [or] prevalent tone of sentiment, of a people or community," such a definition is devoid of moral valence.[56] The central use of the term *ethics* in this book, then, refers more precisely to forms of relation characterized by doing good or living responsibly in the world. While an ethos may or may not be concerned with right living, ethical relation actively creates, maintains, or restores human relations within frameworks of responsibility. The two modalities of black ethics that interest me throughout this book include relations of solidarity between blacks and the murkier ethical terrain of interracial relation during and immediately after apartheid.

This second form of ethical relation requires some further clarification at the start. To be clear: the oppressed bear no moral obligation to their oppressors—indeed, those who foreclose morality have no right to expect it to work in their favor. Yet the experience of oppression almost universally necessitates and encourages *identifications* with mainstream, hegemonic ideology, an experience Du Bois famously encapsulated in the phrase "double consciousness"—"this sense of always looking at one's self through the eyes of others."[57] For Du Bois, such a state splits the psychic space that should ideally be whole or "true." He writes that these two ways of seeing the self, as "an American, a Negro," are forever "warring" with one another, in a permanent state of "strife."[58] I build on Du Bois's unforgettable formulation, arguing that the perpetually divided state of "double consciousness" might be thought to be a productive condition as well as one that can wreak extensive damage on material and psychic life. While the psychological effects of oppression are surely intolerable, these need not entirely obscure the fractures discernable within repressive, apartheid structures.

To be forced always to know and identify with a hegemonic white suprem-acist culture is to engage in acts of thinking one's way into otherness, thereby to develop a strong imaginative acuity that is not nearly as pronounced in dominant subjects. Chinua Achebe notes that social advantage actually erects a barrier to ethical being because the privileged are generally kept apart from that which might make them conscious of the unethicality around them. "Privilege," he writes, "is one of the great adversaries of the imagination; it spreads a thick layer of adipose tissue over our sensitivity."[59] In contrast, posi-tions of subjection produce affectively hyperaware experiences of the self and others, an imaginative capacity that is inescapable, to put it in Steve Biko's terms. Biko reminds us that, under apartheid,

> from time to time the liberals make themselves forget about the problem or take their eyes off the eyesore [that is white supremacy]. On the other hand, in oppression the blacks are experiencing a situation from which they are unable to escape at any given moment.[60]

This state of entrapment, while deplorable, engenders highly skilled acts of social perception and responsiveness to alterity, which is, by implication, and compared to the blind spots of white disregard, the more ethically advanced state of being. Postcolonial scholar Ashis Nandy insists that for readers of Hegel's parable of the bondsman and the master, we must "choose the slave . . . because he *represents a higher-order cognition* which perforce includes the master as human, whereas the master's cognition has to exclude the slave, except as a 'thing.'"[61] Such ethical capaciousness is precisely that which lit-erary critics accord to reading subjects, forcing us to think again about how ethical criticism should be reframed in light of postcolonial theory's insights.

While this book's archive certainly concurs with Du Bois's vision of an apartheid experience that damagingly splits the consciousness of black sub-jects, the ability to know and recognize alterity that apartheid engendered also permits for new post-apartheid assemblages of ethical being. The book's central claim is that the structures of relation that arose out of apartheid's worst moments of inhumanity appear, in writing of the post-apartheid moment, as the tentative articulation of new structures of human relation. Yet in addition to the conscious search for an alternative ethical approach that might welcome and embrace the full totality of difference present in the post-apartheid world, ethical relation has to be understood as a form of engagement with others that is precognitive and affective, bound to the body as much as to any form of rational subjectivity. Attridge argues that ethics emerges as a dynamic intersection between physical, rational, and emotional existence, noting that "in responsibility [for the other] I respond with much more than my cognitive faculties: my emotional and sometimes my physical self are also at stake."[62] Ethics, and ethical response (to cultural artifacts as well as people), is bound up in affective networks and is not merely part of a rational or moral regime of "doing good."

POSTCOLONIAL ETHICS

For South Africa's 1994 Truth and Reconciliation Commission (TRC), moral reconciliation was understood less fluidly. Indeed it was imagined to be a form of social relation that could actually be produced via mandate. Largely dependent upon acts of black sympathy, the TRC often asked blacks to identify with white affective experience in order to engage in acts of forgiveness.[63] Though it was never explicitly acknowledged, the compassion enjoined by the TRC built upon apartheid-era acts of imagining and sympathizing with whiteness that contributed to apartheid's very own structures of supremacy. Despite its appearance on the global ethical stage as a revolutionary form of transitional justice, the TRC did not introduce entirely new forms of intersubjective relation and in fact relied on those that helped apartheid's social dystopia to function relatively unimpeded.[64] Attunement to otherness— whiteness—already constituted black life under apartheid, if in no small part because blacks sought to make sense of the racist policies and everyday incarnations of apartheid.

Throughout the evidentiary archive of black experiences of apartheid we notice conscious efforts to understand what was largely incomprehensible, namely, the inhumanity of the apartheid *Weltanschauung*. Just as postcolonial theory sought to construct an ethics in the wake of the unethicality of colonialism, similarly, the incomprehensibility of apartheid gave rise to a series of imaginative, and frequently ethical, attempts to make sense of the injustice of apartheid. While "the youth of South Africa were finding it difficult to make sense of their existence," there was nonetheless an impulse, or imperative, to do exactly that—to understand the illogical and unjust cruelty of apartheid.[65] These attempts suggest the belief that a rationality actually existed—an insistence on a logic of the other and an attempt to know and understand her motivations, justifications, and actions. Endeavoring to understand the incentives and behavior of the unjust—to imagine their psycho-affective worlds—black South Africans engaged in a set of nuanced interpretive readings that, in their everyday practice of imagining otherness, precisely echoes the way that ethics is thought to function.

Resituating ethics' etiology in this space of subjection challenges descriptions of the ethical that have tended to rely on unidirectional models assuming one suffering body and one non-suffering body. An example of this reductionism can be found in Luc Boltanski's otherwise useful book *Distant Suffering*, where he argues that "to arouse pity, suffering and wretched bodies must be conveyed in such a way as to affect the sensibility of those more fortunate."[66] Boltanski and others rely on categories of the "more" and "less" fortunate, effectively reinforcing divisions between victims and perpetrators, a divide that this book understands as often pragmatic, yet unrepresentative of the instability of the two categories themselves. Such theories of ethics have implicitly denied suffering people's own ability to recognize the humanity of others, thus reinforcing imbalances in power by reducing descriptions of suffering others to monochromatic portraits of pure, passive suffering. While critics of postcolonial studies accuse the field of too starkly dividing the world into innocents and guilty, colonized and colonizers,[67] most work in the field recognizes the complicated terrain of colonialism and postcoloniality, acknowledging the agency of the colonized themselves, both in their complicities with colonial governments as well as in their resistance to colonialism.[68] In fact, recognition of this complexity has been a part of postcolonial studies since its emergence as a field of study[69] and has been treated with great sophistication, more recently in South African literary studies, particularly in the scholarship of Mark Sanders.[70] In 1983 (a relatively early moment in postcolonial theory), Nandy provocatively wrote that in colonialism "the victors are ultimately . . . camouflaged victims, at an advance stage of psychosocial decay."[71] While *Black Cultural Life in South Africa* is generally unconcerned with the ways this may be true, it *is* deeply invested in rethinking how the imagination and affect are mobilized among those so often pitied and victimized to the point of objectification. Indeed, how many black South Africans found ways to imagine a world other than that given them by apartheid, a world operating within an ethos of responsibility and justice, guided by an inclusive, ethical approach to difference, is the subject of much of what follows.

Central to my argument is the claim, made by many before me, that oppressed subjectivities be understood as complex and mobile, determined by contingencies, accidents, and contradictions, as well as by shared sets of political, social, and cultural affinities. Part of these shared experiences are, of course, those of oppression, alienation, racism, dispossession, sexism, prejudice, and marginalization; however, black subjectivities are not only, and should not only be, understood through the lens of victimization. Since such a unitary logic reinforces simplistic understandings of what have always been deeply complex experiences of injustice and relation, these shared experiences need to be understood alongside a wide variety of other aspects of psychological and social experience in order to recognize the complex agency and history of racial oppressions. A focus on a black ethics does not mean trying to encourage forgiveness of white wrongdoing. Rather, it attempts to paint a more nuanced, more accurate, and less divisive portrait of experience and complicity. To add affective ethical complexity to historical assessments of black experience under apartheid is to move toward an enriched, more accurate understanding of black life. This involves a turn away from the belittling and passive assignation of "victims" to a whole host of effective, angry, kind, cautious, curious people whose responses to life under oppression were more complex than is usually granted. To do justice to black history under apartheid is to make room for this intricacy in historical accounts and to recognize, furthermore, how central aesthetic acts were, and continue to be, in the production of a political and ethical post-apartheid world.

It behooves us to consider how sympathetic consciousnesses that challenge simplistic systems of categorization arise and how such potentiality might be channeled toward productive modes of ethical and political relation. Jacob Dlamini and Megan Jones have recently called for a reemergence of ethical imagining in South Africa. "The challenge is to place ourselves in the shoes of another," they write. "Try to understand, for example, what it means to live in a shack along the N2 on the Cape Flats. If there is a moral failure, it is this inability to put ourselves in the shoes of another—but how do we help engender a new sense of empathy?"[72] Dlamini and Jones explain how an explicit recognition of the intimacies, or entanglements, of apartheid— "where violence itself gives rise to the fractures and cracks that let the other in"—emerges in the post-apartheid period and might suggest a way to transform relation in the present.[73]

Their concern to resurrect an ethics after apartheid is explored in the book's final chapter. But concerns with ethical philosophy undergird the origins of postcolonial theory in its earlier incarnations as anticolonial and decolonizing writing and thought. These articulations countered the professed ethical aims of imperial rule (uplift, modernization, religious conversion, etc.) by exposing the contradictions and hypocrisies underlying such discourses. And inversely, European Enlightenment philosophy's emphatic obsession with moral life emerged contemporaneously with the unethicality of imperial doctrine and rule. The coincident rise of British and French imperialism with the sudden explosion in British and French theories of responsibility, interrelation, and sympathy[74] suggests deep anxieties about the colonial project that put, at least imaginatively, so many French and English in contact with unfamiliar peoples from all over the rest of the globe.[75] It is no stretch to argue that eighteenth-century moral philosophy emerges precisely out of the ethical crisis of colonialism. When David Hume uses the figure of a nameless Indian to emphasize the global reach of his theories of sympathy, he reminds us how present the colonial project was, even for those philosophers intent on articulating objective and universalist truths about human nature from Europe. In his *Treatise of Human Nature* Hume insists that "'tis not contrary to reason for me to chuse my total ruin, to prevent the least uneasiness of an Indian or person wholly unknown to me,"[76] thus in one eighteenth-century sentence predicting the Levinasian turn so compelling to recent theorists in its positioning of the fragile self as the only viable response to the existence of the other.[77] As a challenge to thinking in postcolonial studies that understands colonialism as the repressed other of Enlightenment philosophy, Siraj Ahmed shows that the period's central thinkers were aware of how the ethical crisis of colonialism enjoined them to seek philosophical solutions.[78] There is an important etiological link, then, between the colonial project and ethical theory, because the West's thinking about ethics is underwritten by its direct and indirect thinking about colonialism. Western philosophy (from Aristotle to Spinoza to Kant, to Nussbaum, Levinas, Derrida, and Butler) obsessively returns to theories of the ethical, *because* there is the constant need to reassert an ethical modus operandi in an imperial and neo-imperial world plagued by its absence.

While these ethical theorists differ in their assessments of how ethical being comes about, they universally agree that it cannot come about without recourse to the imagination. *Any* ethical act requires an individual to imagine the situation of another person in order to relate responsibly to that person. Hume suggests that merely the idea of someone else's sentiment (its imagined existence) may at times "be so inliven'd as to become the very sentiment or passion"—"'tis certain we may feel sickness and pain from the mere force of the imagination."[79] Similarly Jean-Jacques Rousseau tells us that pity, though innate, "would remain eternally quiescent unless it were activated by imagination," and he links sociality itself with imaginative capacity, pithily claiming that "he who imagines nothing is aware only of himself."[80] As these philosophers argue, along with numerous others, ethical relation is predicated upon imaginative acts or, to use a term from literary studies, upon the fictional.

Postcolonial theory itself positions imaginative explorations of otherness as an essential prerequisite of ethical action. Anticolonial and postcolonial thought promotes ways of knowing or responding to otherness that work against the failures of colonial ethical philosophy to disrupt its unethical ideological and practical instantiations. Leela Gandhi's recent book, for instance, examines various strands of anticolonial intellectual and political ethical thinking that respond to colonialism's own ethical aporias. Gayatri Chakravorty Spivak, another crucial figure in postcolonial thought, suggests that the imagination might help us avoid violent unethical acts. She recalls:

> When I was a graduate student, on the eve of the Vietnam War, I lived in the same house as Paul Wolfowitz, the ferocious Deputy Secretary of Defense who was the chief talking head for the war on Iraq. . . . As I have watched him on television lately, I have often thought that if he had had serious training in literary reading and/or the imagining of the enemy as human, his position on Iraq would not be so inflexible.[81]

Here, despite the "and/or" separator Spivak deploys, her quick shift from "serious training in literary reading" to "the imagining of the enemy as human" suggests that literary training is, if not synonymous with ethical imagination, then, at least, intimately connected to it.

Ethics, or rather a concern about its absence, is central to postcolonial thought from its beginning. While colonial regimes propagated universalistic ethical discourses of liberty, justice, and democracy to justify territorial expansion and the imposition of foreign rule, postcolonial thought relentlessly exposes the hypocrisy of these discourses. Fanon notes that in colonial discourse, on the one hand, "the 'native' is declared impervious to ethics, representing not only the absence of values but also the negation of values. He is, dare we say it, the enemy of values."[82] Yet, he explains, "All [the colonized] has ever seen on his land is that he can be arrested, beaten, and starved with impunity; and no sermonizer on morals, no priest has ever stepped in to bear the blows in his place or share his bread."[83] Thus, while the messengers of colonial discourse, figured here as the "sermonizer on morals" and "the priest," describe and promote a world of ethical ideals (recall Hume's statement about being willing to switch places with an Indian), the lived reality of colonial rule not only conflicted with circulating discourses of ethical responsibility but proved these very discourses to be, contradictorily, tools in the sedimentation of the unethical imperial project. Postcolonial theory, therefore, has sought from its beginnings to resuscitate ethics in a terrain most obviously damaged by its negation.

Recent writing by the New Ethicists agrees with postcolonial scholars and earlier ethical philosophers that "what is ethically, aesthetically, and politically at stake . . . is the productive power of conceiving of the self as other."[84] I contend, however, that South African blacks under apartheid were forced on an everyday basis to identify in this way with the dominant, white other, whether or not this was meant or felt to be "productive." Part of the experience of being marginalized or mistreated by a dominant culture like apartheid that denigrates or denies difference involves not only a perceptive awareness of the dominant mode but also its constant imagining. Survival within a system that excludes, ignores, or debases individuals both physically and psychically, positions those individuals in such a way that it becomes imperative for them to imagine the needs and requirements of the dominant group—imperative to imagine the drives and impulses of the powerful. But this experience of oppression may indeed, at times, generate productive ethical modes of subjectivity, as I have already suggested. Cornel West's recent work, for instance, coins the term "black prophetic fire," which he defines as "the hypersensitivity to the suffering of others that generates a righteous indignation that results in the willingness to live and die for freedom."[85] It is this "hypersensitivity to the suffering of others" born out of oppression that thus engenders ethical, or to use West's term, "righteous," being.

INTERMEDIALITY AND ETHICS

While much of the book delineates how black practices of *reception* led, during apartheid, to the formation of a counter-ethics resistant to apartheid's tyranny of relation, black apartheid writing and artistic production has also been the site of ethical articulation. This aspect of apartheid writing has been particularly overlooked in the historiographic focus in literary studies on black writing's relation to apartheid-era political commitments. In order to tease out the ethics of black writing from that period we need to apply that type of reading practice—close reading or symptomatic reading—that has recently been called into question in the American academy. Under apartheid, censorship forced authors to conceal their politically inflected opinions within seemingly innocuous "entertainments," though fiction of the period was often, of course, a direct engagement with apartheid's injustices. This necessitates that we read "suspiciously," in search of anti-apartheid critique, alert to subtle articulations of an alternative psychic order of things. In the case of a series of stories by South African writer Arthur Maimane, his fiction was also the site for clear expositions of the ethical primacy of various media in the lives of everyday black South Africans. A brief consideration of these tales exemplifies the centrality of popular media forms in black South African everyday experience, and helps foreground this book's focus on their role in the formation of ethical life.

In 1953 Maimane published two connected short stories in *Drum* magazine under the pseudonym Mogale. The stories' protagonist, a private investigator named Chester Morena or "Chief," blackmails criminals by filming their misdeeds using a movie camera hidden in a book. Then he screens the films back to the criminals in the rear of his car using a projector hooked up to the car's ignition. The law breakers are forced by this evidence to pay whatever Morena demands in order to avoid being turned over to the police.

This camera-as-book, a jerry-rigged and quintessentially multimedia device, relies on a commonly held view of the book as a simple symbol of literary entertainment, posing no threat to criminals. When people looked "at the big book I was carrying," Morena explains, "[p]robably they thought I was just another book-worm."[86] Hiding a camera between its covers, the book serves as a conduit for film, a medium that, unlike literature, is granted actual agential and evidentiary powers by the plot. Morena's homemade detective tool suggests that by the middle of the twentieth century books were viewed as only superficially instrumental, since it is film, not fiction, that enables him to capture and then confront criminals with their wrongdoing. Filmic evidence supplants written documentation and appears more successful at bringing criminals to account.

Yet since the camera-as-book is used to hold criminals accountable for their wrongdoing, the book is also positioned in Maimane's stories as an indirect instrument of ethical reckoning, a device used in tandem with film to expose the moral and ethical corruption within South African society. Books, in other words, aid in the process of uncovering and revealing social wrongs. In fact, for the subterfuge of the film to work, Morena *needs* the book, suggesting a more complex valuation of writing in Maimane's story than might initially appear. By replacing writing with film as the primary means to document and monitor misconduct, the decoy book seems impotent as a media of intervention. Yet its instrumentality and agency are merely masked from the crooks. Books appear harmless, yet can be transformed through the material use to which they are put into powerful agents, indirectly influencing the course of events on the larger social and political terrain despite their seeming ineffectiveness.

By placing books and other media within an economy of criminality, morality, and ethical behavior (Chief holds wrongdoers accountable, even if it is largely for his own benefit), Maimane's stories have thematic concerns that overlap with ethical theory's claims that books create, elicit, and modify ethical consciousness. Viewed this way, Morena's camera-book symbolically manifests the instrumentalism ethical theorists and philosophers accord literature or "the literary." The interdependence of film and written media in these stories, and the way they work together to bring wrongdoing out of the shadows to hold perpetrators accountable to others, foretell the intermedial compass of the rest of this book. Contemporary studies of cultural forms in Africa must acknowledge that we live in an

> era of radically mixed media, old and new, oral and mass-reproduced, broadcast and interactive, local, global and glocal, [in which] it is no longer possible to investigate one medium, even the historically privileged institution of cinema, without serious investigation of others, from broadcasting to pirate video to printing on clothing as well as paper, that enable the production, distribution and reception of visual narratives across Africa.[87]

While much important scholarship looks at nonliterary forms of cultural production in African and African diasporic contexts, nonetheless, by isolating generic difference in separate studies, such works tend to reproduce the hierarchical distinctions between literary and nonliterary forms long dominant in genre studies.[88] Following a more inclusive approach to studying cultural consumption on the African continent, this book reorients theories of ethics and aesthetics away from a focus on specific forms (literary) and specific media (writing). An ethical response is as likely to emerge in reaction to reading a work by Henry James[89] as it is to reading an apartheid-era comic book sanctioned by the apartheid state. Extant theories linking reading practices with ethical being transform when the textual material under consideration comprises not only works of so-called highbrow literature but also includes popular texts, such as the photocomic, the South African passbook, or a mass-marketed Hollywood film.

For blacks who read books and watched films during apartheid, their social and material positions determined the ethics that emerged through these textual engagements. Yet the form and content of what they read also influenced this. If reading instantiates ethical being, the ethos interpellated by texts varies according to the form, content, and genre of the text itself too. While John Docker detaches politics from form altogether, arguing that "being ideologically radical, or liberal, or conservative, is not intrinsic to . . . any genre,"[90] the will to affirm genre may itself be ideologically inflected.[91] And as Caroline Levine points out in her recent book on form, "in many cases, when forms meet, their collision produces unexpected consequences, results that cannot always be traced back to deliberate intentions of dominant ideologies."[92] It is in such a vein that Dlamini explains how black reception practices under apartheid often contravened the intentions of their creators. He points out "how the very instrument (the radio) that was supposed to be the government's propaganda tool actually had the opposite effect, awakening in me a political consciousness that saw me adopt a politics at odds with the political gradualism and religious conservatism of my mother."[93] For Levine, each form possesses a proscribed range of "affordances," or latent possibilities for use, and while these are often predictable, they can also be unforeseen or surprising. Because blacks were seldom the intended audiences of the works they most frequently engaged with, such "unexpected" affordances constitute many of the central examples of this book.[94]

Importantly, this book suggests that unpredictable responses to cultural texts were often generative sites of political consciousness and agency. Dlamini explains, for instance, that

> it was radio's effect on the apartheid conception of space that had the most positive benefit for black South Africans. In a political time and space that was coded in racial terms, with severe limits imposed on black mobility, *black people could move through radio in ways that the apartheid state could not curtail. Black people could enjoy a freedom of movement and being that the apartheid state could not take away.* Sure, apartheid censors could limit what one listened to, they could try to dictate what made the news. But *they could*

not determine how the listening public received the propaganda. They could not tell blacks how to listen.[95]

Working under the assumption that radio, newspapers, and other popular genres are, as Benedict Anderson theorizes, as much avenues toward the construction of "imagined communities" as self-consciously literary texts, this book turns to genres that have tended to escape consideration in studies of the relationship of reading to ethics. This reorientation of attention is necessitated not out of an academic drive for esotericism but because these were the cultural texts that *most* people read *most* often. That they have continued to elude inclusion in studies relating reading and consumption practices to ethical becoming represents a gross blind spot in ethical theory. In J. M. Coetzee's novel *Elizabeth Costello*, the eponymous narrator reflects on the reading practices she noticed on her trips to the African continent: "She has visited Africa. . . . She has seen Africans reading, ordinary Africans, at bus stops, in trains. They were not reading novels, admittedly, they were reading newspapers. *But is a newspaper not as much an avenue to a private world as a novel?*"[96] This book works from a cultural studies perspective to insist emphatically that it most certainly is.

The book's chapters explore how particular genres produce (and resist) particular ethics, through both formal affordances and local social contexts. If we return to Wayne Booth's thinking, for instance, we might note how he uses methods of close reading to tie metaphors, particularly, to the production of ethical being in order then to extrapolate from this an explanation of how texts influence social relation. This book does not eschew such methods and indeed engages intimately with them, at times, but with a reorientation to those formal techniques and styles promoting ethical response resident within popular genres.

All the same, as these chapters repeatedly show, it is largely through reception practices and the context of these practices that ethics comes into being, and less through any ontological characteristic of a specific generic form. The thread that links all the chapters is the exposition of the process of ethical becoming that works, or fails, dynamically through the experience of forms of popular culture in the context of oppression. Ethical becoming emerged time and time again through black practices of reading, watching, and writing in South Africa, and it is this network of interrelation, rather than the specifications and parameters of any singular generic form, that the book delineates.

CHAPTER 1, "BLACK BOOKS, White Bodies: Reimagining the Passcheck," looks at passes, the identification documents that blacks were required to carry by the apartheid state after 1952. While these represent an unusual archive for literary studies, I examine how practices around the reading of these books that occurred at roadblocks or "passchecks" could, on occasion, establish a space for ethical imagination and ethical relation. Suggesting that one of the most hated documents of state surveillance could produce ethical consciousness may well seem counterintuitive. But as Kirsten Weld writes, historians of state archives, such as these compiled by the apartheid state, must read state-produced materials "against the grain," with a different logic than that applied by the state and its ideological proponents. Looking at pass-books along with another black apartheid archive—literary depictions of the passcheck by black and coloured apartheid-era writers—helps us understand how the legal documents meant to police and control human movement produce, at times, semiotic practices that are not only antithetical to their intended purpose but ethical in tenor. These texts' ethical possibilities emerge *out of the material conditions set up by the state*. In this chapter, I show how this notorious genre of oppressive control could also operate within a realm of radical potentiality, and not merely as the clear, administrative agent of the state's white supremacist aims.

Chapter 2, "'Blood and Thunder': Popular Film and Black Spectatorship at the Midcentury," argues that black spectatorship practices during the 1950s and 1960s were largely constituted by encounters with difference, priming blacks for the kinds of ethical responses that ethical theorists have long associated with imaginative, aesthetic encounters. Because of South Africa's extensive censorship laws, the films blacks had access to were mostly American and European B movies. These had neither black South African actors nor directors and producers. Nonetheless, these imported movies were wildly popular. While racial, geographic, and national difference constituted these films' content and cast, blacks nonetheless developed strong affinities for white film actors at the height of apartheid's racist oppression, identifications that were capable of producing effects beyond the borders of the cinematic space. While black film consumption animated debates on both sides of the political spectrum, the chapter shows how actual reception and response frequently undermined expectations and intentions. I emphasize the variegated responses blacks had to popular films, refusing the approach so noticeable in writing about film during this period that thinks of black audiences as a naïve, passive, or susceptible spectating monolith. While black acts of cultural consumption may not have clearly operative functions in the world of politics or in the production of national, racial, or political identities and ideologies, they were not without effect or influence beyond the cinematic space. Following Frederic Jameson's urging that we read carefully in order to "unmask" "cultural artifacts as socially symbolic acts," this chapter considers how black practices of interracial identification were produced in "bioscopes"[97] and cinemas through encounters with popular American films and how these practices aided in the development of nuanced ethical thought and social relation.[98]

Turning in chapter 3, "Race, Reading, and the Photocomic," to the previously popular but now obsolete photocomic, I explore how the content and theme of specific photocomics, as well as the formal properties of the photocomic itself, contribute to a set of derivative ethical responses that defied the relational schema encouraged by the apartheid state. Focusing on the Western or cowboy photocomic, wildly popular among South Africans during apartheid, the chapter examines its function as an outlet for indirect expressions of racial anxieties. With its tropes of the expanding frontier and the indigenous "noble savage," the Western resonated strongly within apartheid South Africa, discursively producing and disturbing cultural, national, and racial subject positions. Cultivating the kinds of interracial identification remarked upon by Fanon and Adichie, these photocomics brought black and white readers in visual and textual contact with alterity, establishing ethical potential through literary and visual practices. This chapter argues that reading practices destabilized supremacist fantasies, despite the apparent visual apartheid embedded in South African photocomics' representational optics. The photocomic provides a strong case of a genre in which the otherness requisite to ethical theorists' notion of the "literary" inhabits genres overlooked by literary criticism. This attests to the utility of expanding theories linking literature and ethics to include mass-produced and popular genres alongside genres of "highbrow literature" to recognize the function of all acts of reading in the creation of ethical life.

"Writing Ethics After Apartheid," the book's final chapter, moves our consideration of the relationship between ethics and genre into the transition and post-apartheid period. It is at this moment when writing is freed from any urgent political agenda that the ethical emerges as an obvious central concern of black South African writing. The ethical question of how we live responsibly together in the wake of the gross abuses of legal segregation and apartheid is formally and thematically foregrounded in post-apartheid writ-

ing, in memoirs, and in works of literary fiction. While this shift may seem
to indicate a rupture between the apartheid and post-apartheid moral imaginary, what this chapter establishes, building on the previous chapters, is how
a concern with ethical relation went from being latent, or subtly and secretly
expressed in black practices of reading, watching, and writing, to finding
a public, interracial space for its explicit articulation and discussion in the
post-apartheid era. Yet through a reexamination of Biko's Black Consciousness philosophy, the chapter also emphasizes how withholding interracial
ethical relation in the post-apartheid moment appropriates power, producing
an ethics that keeps a more integrative, universalist ethics in abeyance. This
final chapter thus takes up writers whose works explore this liminal moment
of ethical concern between the apartheid and the post-apartheid future. In
response to the disappointments of the present, represented most violently,
perhaps, by the African National Congress (ANC) government's massacre
of miners at the Lonmin platinum mine in Marikana,[99] black South African
writers are reevaluating the function of writing in politics, constructing in its
stead an anti-instrumentalist and non-prescriptive ethics that itself constitutes a new form of political engagement.

CHAPTER 1

Black Books, White Bodies

Reimagining the Passcheck

Your documents, all neatly put together,
Are transferred from the living to the dead,
Here is the document of birth
Saying that you were born, and where and when,
But giving no hint of joy or sorrow,
Or if the sun shone, or if the rain was falling,
Or what bird flew singing over the roof.[1]

Between 1952 and 1986, during apartheid's most repressive years, black South Africans were required to carry passbooks. Read literally, passbooks—like driver's licenses, birth certificates, passports, and other identification documents—demand simple interpretive responses. As the excerpt above from Alan Paton's poem, "To a Small Boy Who Died at Diepkloof Reformatory" acknowledges, when read for basic personal information, state documents like passbooks reveal little on the surface beyond a few factual details about their bearers. They cannot, like poetry, tell us "if the sun shone, or if the rain was falling, / Or what bird flew singing over the roof." Paton laments the discrepancy between what official documents pay attention to and record as the meaningful details of a life, and the more changeable, varied, and individuated experiences of those whom such documents represent. For the inhabitants of Diepkloof Reformatory, especially, where Paton himself served as principal from 1935 to 1949, the reduction of individual lives to a few summary pieces of paper, "saying that you were born, and where and when," served to further erase the particularity of these boys' lives that were already so minimally represented in South African textual cultures. Despite Paton's valid complaint about the incompleteness of a historical record that condenses a person's identity into a handful of factual metrics, this chapter suggests that when we deploy a different set of reading practices to examine those same documents, eschewing their more official, governmental affordances, we may discern considerable more detail about the lives of passbook owners than Paton allows. Indeed, there is ample supplementary evidence on hand to allow for a reading of the apartheid-era passbook that shows it to be far more than a mere tool of oppressive summarization; indeed as this chapter explores, the passbook, as a lived, read document, was a powerfully symbolic reservoir of social and personal meaning.

Most famously, the passbooks were emblematic of apartheid's legalized racism. As such, they were clear targets for anti-apartheid activism so that many organized anti-apartheid gatherings were explicitly voiced as protests against the pass system. These notably include Mahatma Gandhi's pre-apartheid anti-pass demonstration in 1908; the 1956 multiracial Women's March against Passes in Pretoria; the tragic Sharpeville Massacre of 1960 during which the police shot sixty-nine people dead; and the passbook bonfires, which live on in photographs famously depicting protestors setting their passbooks alight.[2]

Since the abolition of the pass system in 1986, and since the demise of apartheid's legal instantiation in 1994, the passbook's symbolic resonance has inevitably shifted, even while it continues to be remembered as a figure of apartheid's injustice. From our post-apartheid position we read and interpret differently than subjects did in the apartheid era, and it is no longer imperative that we speak only of "passes [as] slavery," as one protester put it on a sign during an anti-pass campaign.[3] From where we stand today we can engage in counter-readings that refuse the "archival logics" of the apartheid state, which positioned the passbook as the symbolic manifestation of a highly bureaucratized national surveillance system.[4] Passbooks unwittingly told life stories, albeit ones quite distinct from those narrativized in biographies, poems, or novels. Though an unintentional consequence, calling identification documents *books*—passbooks, reference books, and, in Afrikaans, *Bewysboeke* (books of proof)—encourages alternative readings of the passbook that permit us to see it as a genre in possession of its own set of shifting discursive properties. The genre's name asks us to examine the passbook as a book in possession of its own attendant material and aesthetic properties that call forth its own particular practices of reading and consumption. We are now able to reconfigure the archival narrative of the passbook, locating an alternate history coextensive with that more oppositional one initiated by apartheid policy but taken up, too, in the Manicheanism of much anti-apartheid ideology. This refocus intends, following Alexander Weheliye, to recognize

> the importance of miniscule movements, glimmers of hope, scraps of food, the interrupted dreams of freedom found in those spaces deemed devoid of full human life. . . . [These] represent alternative critical, political, and poetic assemblages that are often hushed.[5]

Such an approach orients us toward creating apertures in the historical archive to allow for multiple, overlapping narratives of the past that cannot be, and indeed should not be, collapsed into one dominant narrative order.

Passbooks, I suggest, were symbolically malleable even at the time of apartheid's most heightened policing. A small booklet carried in the pocket or purse apportioned space in the same way that the segregationist signs at public facilities did and could be read to signify far more than a mere set of practical instructions. While passbooks were authored by the apartheid state to aid in the functioning of apartheid law and ideology and were thus largely intended for readers who were functionaries of its vast bureaucracy, they were also read by others, including, importantly, the passbooks' bearers themselves. *These* reading practices, and the network of other reading practices opened up by encounters occasioned at the passcheck form the central preoccupation of this chapter. Surprisingly, perhaps, as I shall show, black representations of the passbook bestow it with a certain hermeneutic multivalence—a series of ways of responding to the passbook not limited to seeing it only as a loathed stand-in for the racist state.

Furthermore, the occasions for reading passbooks that occurred every day because police set up randomized passchecks on city streets, in private homes, at work—anywhere they wanted to demand a person's pass—led, ironically, to a series of other unintended readings. These inadvertent readerly acts included acts of reading the bodies and faces of the police, as well as those black faces and bodies under surveillance. Thus, as I explore, the passcheck occasioned a series of sequential and overlapping readings that surprisingly set the groundwork for imagining social relation in ways that differed considerably from that structured by apartheid policy and thought. Such readings were, I argue, ethical in tenor, though the material circumstances of apartheid meant they were rarely expressed, let alone transformed into ethical action. They were, however, precursors to the more explicitly theorized ethical writing and thinking that have emerged in the twenty-first century, as this book's final chapter explores.

Evidence of counter-readings of passbooks comes primarily here from novels and memoirs written by black South Africans during the period. Alongside the textual practices of statecraft epitomized by the passbook was the writing of black and "coloured" apartheid novelists, playwrights, journalists, and poets who also participated in "writing the world" or, as Gayatri Spivak neatly emphasizes, in explicit acts of "geo-graphy."[6] While the apartheid regime made it nearly impossible for black writers to consciously elaborate any interracial ethical agenda to restructure the polarized race relations of the time, the presence of such passages within the texts I examine here brings into being—through writing—the acknowledgment and articulation of alternate responses to alterity than those imposed by the state and reproduced by its henchmen. This chapter emphasizes how nonliterary genres such as the passbook produce unexpected acts of reading that could be described as ethical. In an examination of this unlikely genre that seems least liable to produce an ethics, and aided by evidence culled from literary sources, it becomes evident that even under the most restrictive of generic circumstances, practices of reading might call forth moments of ethical becoming. As my final chapter suggests, when contemporary black South African writing began to shift its attention away from its former anti-apartheid imperatives, its new preoccupations often concerned a series of affective-ethical positions with precursors in prior apartheid-era hermeneutic modes, such as those explored here. While this chapter largely focuses on the ways that practices of reading enjoined under oppression provoked ethically charged imaginative forays that nonetheless were limited in their options for expression, the final chapter in this book looks at how such daily acts of ethical reading were transformed into a clear *thematic* of ethical relation in post-apartheid writing.

Literature serves less in this chapter as the genre through which ethics arises and more as the source of information that indicates how blacks read otherwise. Realist novels, short stories, and journalism from the period provide insights into the everyday experience of living and moving under a surveillance system regulated through the written form of the passbook. Certainly one must be cautious about *only* reading literary works "ethnographically," especially within African contexts. To ask literature to work to discern "factual" representations of actual "real" people, events, and places, particularly when the works are explicitly fictional, is to deny literature many of its other properties, including its ability to provoke encounters with difference and elicit ethical response.

Yet fictional portraits of black responses to the pass system greatly enrich the more quantitative data provided by economists and social scientists about how the pass system operated. Those more empiricist records constitute the predominant archive of the pass system, and they provide important information about its implementation, process, and reach; yet they generally forgo detailed explorations of the pass system's lived effects.[7] My turn to works of fiction highlights, of course, a problem of archival retrieval and methodology, drawing attention to the prevailing absence of representations of black experiences of apartheid's legal manifestations. Novels and short stories individualize experiences of the passbooks, imagining characters with a range of specific emotional and material experiences that refuse any univocal "black experience."[8] While these works expose the shared brutality at the center of black lives regulated by the pass system, the fictional portraits under consideration also map out detailed and varied responses to passbooks and their administrative and legal expressions.

Though mostly fictional, these are works of realism that ask to be read as accurate depictions of actual pass control encounters. Indeed, an engagement with the real world was the direct intention of many of the authors discussed, who saw writing as a confrontation with history geared toward effecting change. As Kelwyn Sole remarks in his discussion of South African Black Consciousness writers of the 1970s and 1980s:

> [Its adherents] rarely perceived what they did as limited to the printed page or performance podium. Literature was regarded as a transformative practice, stirring its practitioners and readership to fresh insights and values . . . a form of activity which could, through various textual and performance strategies, spread knowledge and truth to its putative black audience.[9]

Like passbooks, then, fictional works might be read "factually" and need not always be subject to the "deep" hermeneutic analysis of literary criticism. Derek Attridge's work on literary ethics defends such instrumentalism. "There is no contradiction," he insists, "in saying that, as testimonies, [literary works] witness in a powerful manner and at the same time, as literary works, they stage the activity of witnessing."[10] And if novels can serve as documentation, the contrary move is also possible—namely, reading passbooks for content other than their intended surface meaning. Might it even be possible to imagine that passbooks, like literature, could elicit ethical reaction? What follows begins with a brief chronicle of the history of passbooks in South Africa. Thereafter, I turn to an examination of how passbooks were experienced: first, as manifestations of apartheid's near-total control over space, time, and life; and second, as more physically and semiotically malleable texts.

PASSBOOKS IN CONTEXT

> Write down!
> I am an Arab
> And my identity card number is fifty thousand.
> I have eight children
> And the ninth will come after a summer
> Will you be angry?[11]

The history of human confinement using passes and their equivalents extends back as far as we have documentary evidence, suggesting that freedom of movement may be the exception rather than the rule. Using a system of passes to control movement was hardly apartheid South Africa's sole purview—under slavery in the United States, for instance, slaves were required to carry passes written by their owners whenever they left the confines of the plantations to which they were tethered. But the apartheid state's version of the pass system has particularly strong historical resonances, explicable, in part, because of its unlikely duration within a period of mass decolonization on much of the rest of the African continent. In addition, its exceptionally bureaucratized nature, while prone to administrative setbacks, made it "the first universal biometric order . . . unprecedented in the twentieth century."[12]

Blacks in South Africa were long subject to forms of surveillance that relied on textual documentation, as Alan Paton's famous poem, "To a Small Boy Who Died in Diepkloof Reformatory," demonstrates in its contrast of the sparseness of a child's life in documents with that child's far richer lived experience of the world. But arguably the most important moment in the history of that form of documentation known as the pass, in South Africa, occurred in 1952 with the passage of the misleadingly titled "Abolition of Passes and Co-ordination of Documents Act."[13] The shift in policy ushered in by this act was dictated both by the desire to reduce bureaucratic costs (though it failed to do so) and by the apartheid government's "panoptic fantasy" of omnipotence.[14] Designed by the "architect of Apartheid," the then Minister of Native Affairs

Hendrik Verwoerd, this law standardized the pass system, establishing the bureaucratic machinery to register every black adult as "African." When this registration process began in 1953, subjects' fingerprints were taken and their names; tribal ethnicities; places of residence and work; tax and marital statuses; and "rights" to live, work, and/or reside in certain areas were assigned by a whole range of state-appointed functionaries. This new system assigned a reference book number to each person in order to monitor black subjects "from registration to death."[15]

Keith Breckenridge notes how ironic it is that contemporary democratic South Africa may be the first nation to produce an electronically based population surveillance system to monitor employment, criminal, medical, tax, credit, and travel histories, all through one simple card. One particularly sinister implication of South Africa's current Home Affairs National Identification System (HANIS) is its involvement with companies and banks that, with the express approval of the ANC government, are encouraged to use the identification cards to extract profit. Troublingly, while the "New South Africa" may be the first democratic country to implement such a process, its whole system of identification rests on the archival resources and administrative networks left behind by the apartheid state. The fantasy to "grasp the identity, and history, of its elusive citizens" continues to define South African governmental agendas, despite the injustices promulgated in the name of such a fantasy and despite the system's structurally inefficient and blatantly incompetent failures.[16]

Unfortunately, then, the pass laws cannot be relegated to the past or written off as ways of state control best left behind us. Nor is this discussion relevant alone in South Africa. Document policing still forms a central component of states' control over racialized bodies the world over, and thus the modes of relation produced through apartheid's pass system remain a crucial lens through which to examine racial policing today in a wide variety of locales.[17] While the use of biometric surveillance techniques to monitor national and international populations has drawn considerable protest in recent years,[18] it is disturbing to note how normalized such processes have become. What was once only South Africa's Benthamite dreamscape of state control—thought of as the *exception* of apartheid—looks normal today to subject-citizens, migrants, and refugees worldwide. Today, the parallels made with increasing intensity between Israel's treatment of Palestinians in Gaza and South Africa's programmatic apartheid regime mean that we cannot stop looking at how state-driven ideology works through the tight policing of textual borders as well as geographic ones, emphasized in Palestinian poet Mahmoud Darwish's apostrophe in 1964 to an administrative official—"Write down!" he insists.[19]

THREE DECADES EARLIER, in 1938, a black South African man described everyday movement in the country of his birth as an endless series of checks on his mobility:

> There is no authoritative department where an African does not have to produce his pass. He takes his money to the Savings Bank: a pass is demanded. He takes a walk in town: a pass is demanded. He goes to the station to take his ticket for a journey: a pass is demanded. He arrives at his destination: a pass is demanded. There is a pass to produce here and there until he feels no better than a prisoner.[20]

Thirty-five years later, when Alex La Guma wrote *In the Fog of the Seasons' End*, the system described here had been standardized and implemented nationwide and was also well recognized as a quintessential apartheid injustice. La Guma's narrator describes the process of registering for a passbook that each sixteen-year-old black man was forced to submit to under the 1952 laws:

> When African people turn sixteen they are born again or, even worse, they are accepted into the mysteries of the Devil's mass, confirmed into the blood rites of a servitude as cruel as Caligula, as merciless as Nero. Its bonds are the entangled chains of infinite rubber stamps, and the scratchy pens in the offices of the Native Commissioners are like branding irons which leave scars for life.[21]

Here the link between the violence of the apartheid state and the materiality of textual production is made explicit, reminding us that writing is neither inherently ethical or unethical but can be put to the service of ethical or unethical ends. The ritualistic inculcation at "the Devil's mass," where young black men were required to go when they turned sixteen to be assigned a passbook, "confirmed [them] into the blood rites of a servitude as cruel as Caligula," where the state began the life-long subjugation of its subjects through the violent tools of writing: "the scratchy pens in the offices of the Native Commissioners are like branding irons which leave scars for life."[22] As if searching for the right metaphor to encapsulate the horror of the pass system, La Guma deploys mystical imagery of devils, despots, and enslavement, because none is sufficient alone to communicate the scope of the state's bureaucratized cruelty. La Guma reminds us here of the inseparability between writing and violence in apartheid's trademark regime of domination.

La Guma's novel is one of several key apartheid-era works that repeatedly returns to the encounter between police and black South Africans at the passcheck. Such works draw attention to both expected and unexpected responses that the passbooks provoked in their bearers. I take seriously the deeply felt antipathy to passbooks and the pass system that these works repeatedly express. Such moments allowed authors to communicate their anti-apartheid sentiments (rage, depression, horror, frustration), thus insisting on the existence of counter-discourses in print that could circulate to audiences within and outside of South Africa. As such, scenes decrying the injustice of the pass system make the moniker "protest lit" an appropriate designation for these texts. Yet at the same time, following Eve Kosofsky Sedgwick, I find it useful to allow for surface readings to coexist alongside less apparent readings of these texts, not so much to assert "close" or "paranoid" readings as necessary or essential critical methodologies, but because these literary texts themselves demand alternative readings to those that are strictly Manichean. Descriptions of encounters between police and their targets at the passchecks in these works certainly denounce the political structures of the day; however, they also suggest other, more complex ways of thinking about alterity and difference, providing useful guides for examining how ethics emerges through readerly acts, particularly under conditions of inequality.

The central texts in what follows include Peter Abrahams's pre-apartheid novel *Mine Boy* (1946); Bloke Modisane's 1963 fictionalized memoir *Blame Me on History*, banned in 1966; Can Themba's collection of short stories and essays *The Will To Die* (1972), banned preemptively in 1963 by a complete ban on his writings; and Alex La Guma's *In the Fog of the Seasons' End* (1973). Except for Abrahams's novel, the works all appeared after the standardization of the apartheid state's pass law program, and as such, each responds to an already firmly established set of surveillance practices. The three decades between the publication of Abrahams's novel and La Guma's, and the negligible differences between their descriptions of the encounter at the passcheck, remind us that the apartheid pass system was such a normalized component of daily life for black South Africans that it must have, at times, felt permanent.

"PASSES ARE SLAVERY": READING DOMINATION

The pass laws were implemented first and foremost to regulate black movement. As such, the government aimed to create a comprehensive, Foucauldian form of control in which time, space, speech, and the body could all be rigidly disciplined. La Guma's novel bleakly parodies the discourse of the pass system in a scene that takes place at a pass office where a white policeman addresses a black man who is there to have his pass validated. "You are a good kaffir," he says, demeaningly:

> You understand, of course, that you are not allowed to travel from here to take up residence in another place without first having permission to leave here and arrive there? And to remain there, take up residence, to work, to go to work and to return from work, to walk out at certain times, and so on and so forth also requires permission.[23]

Here the policeman serves as a mouthpiece for the tragic absurdity of the system's dictates. In its comprehensive totality, the pass system regulates virtually all aspects of a person's life, surveying the body's every move, so that life is in fact synonymous with life under a pass system, synonymous with enforced immobility. Indeed, under apartheid, the word *pass* came counterintuitively to signify *not* being able to pass, its etymological meaning so distorted as to represent its antonym instead—the pass as a hindrance to the act of freely moving through space.

This type of discursive control over bodies could be communicated even without recourse to spoken language, for encounters between blacks and policemen at passchecks were normalized through physical obedience as much as through verbal exchange. The main character in Peter Abrahams's 1946 novel, *Mine Boy*, does not even need to be spoken to in order to know what is expected of him when he is stopped outside a bakery where he is standing gazing at cakes through a vitrine. "He stopped and looked at them. He felt a tap on his shoulder and turned. It was a policeman. *Without a word* he fished his pass from his pocket and gave it to the policeman. The policeman *looked at it, looked him up and down*, and returned the pass to him."[24] In this exchange, no words are exchanged; instead, communication occurs through a series of bodily gestures—a tap, a proffered passbook, a look at the book, a look at the body, and a return of the pass. Both bodies are transformed into vehicles for apartheid ideology. In Foucauldian terms, apartheid as a "disciplinary apparatus" exercised "infinitesimal power over the active body," over all movements, gestures, and behaviors.[25] Reducing humans on both sides of the pass encounter to automatons—in the figure of the disciplined policeman as much as in the figure of the black man called on to present his pass—produced Foucault's "docile bodies," apparently eclipsing, simultaneously, their potential for revolution and dissent.

So complete seemed the reach of apartheid doctrine in the creation of these conforming bodies that even internal organs were subject to discipline. When La Guma's narrator insists that the everyday fear induced by the threat of the pass control was so extreme that "palpitations of the heart had become a national disease," he positions that most internal, individual, and private human organ—the heart—as relentlessly subject to the nation's regime of legalized terror.[26] Sexual relations and reproduction were similarly controlled as well, since passes were required for couples to leave their designated areas of labor or residence to visit one another.[27]

Furthermore, as Foucault shows so well, the disciplining and construction of obedient subjectivities, maximized for utility, not only involves regulating the physical body in space. It also requires the control of the temporal. Under apartheid the hours of the day were regulated by curfews, but as Mr. Laxon Gutsa, "a relatively prosperous builder" in nearby Southern Rhodesia, explains, even the time one was legally allowed out of the home was constantly co-opted by the colonial state's order to see the passbook: "Each time you would move in the street, when you meet [*sic*] a policeman he would ask you for [the pass]; 10 times a day. 10 policemen a day, you would have to produce it."[28] The inevitability of this encounter helps to explain how the demand for and display of a pass came to be such an automatic part of black life under apartheid domination.

Can Themba's short story "Ten-to-Ten" further exemplifies the relationship between apartheid law and its regulation of everyday time. It tells the story of a black policeman nicknamed "Ten-to-Ten" by the residents of the neighborhood he patrols, because he begins his shift just before the ten o'clock curfew. In the opening passage, Themba shows that controls over time were as likely to create panic as controls over space:

The curfew proper for all Africans in Marabastad, Pretoria, was 10 p.m. By that hour every African, man, woman and child, had to be indoors, preferably in bed; if the police caught you abroad without a "special permit" you were hauled off to the battleship-grey little police station . . . and clapped in jail. The following morning you found yourself trembling before a magistrate in one of those out-rooms that served as a court, and after a scathing lecture, you were fined ten-bob. So it behove [sic] everyone, every black mother's son, to heed that bell and be off the streets at ten.

But it was strange how the first warning bell at ten-to-ten exercised a power of panic among us, really out of all proportion. I suppose, watchless at night, when that bell went off and you were still streets away from your house, you did not know whether it was the first warning—ten-to-ten—giving you that much grace to hurry you on, or the fatal ten o'clock bell itself.

However, there were ever women in their yards, peering over corrugated-iron fences and bedstead gates, calling in sing-song voices "Ten-to-ten! Ten-to-ten!" as if the sound of the bell at the police station down there in First Avenue was itself echoed, street after street, urging the belated on, homewards, bedwards, safe from the Law.[29]

The bell in this story tolls neither for a death nor for a marriage nor for people to congregate, but rather as a reminder of the depth with which apartheid rule penetrated and segregated private lives. Turning neighborhoods into prisons, homes into cells, and humans into the prisoners as well as the guards, this scene demonstrates how seamlessly spatial domination was internalized under apartheid regulation of the temporal. Ideology sings out in the bell and then in the women's voices—"Ten-to-ten! Ten-to-Ten!" By a subtle act of substitution, the women become the very messengers and instruments of apartheid discipline, while the guard's individual identity—his name—marks him as nothing but the physical embodiment of state oppression.

Examples of other manipulations of temporal experience can be found in novels of this period. Passes, for instance, tended to be issued for relatively brief stretches of time, so trips to the Office of Native Affairs were common interruptions in the normal course of a day, in addition to the random pass-checks Gutsa describes above. "Thank goodness," the narrator of R. R. R. Dhlomo's early novel *An African Tragedy* observes, "there was no necessity for him to go to the Pass Office and spend half a day there waiting for his pass to be endorsed."[30] In an article written for *Drum*, Themba recounts what actually happened at these pass offices, explaining that class distinctions between black subjects were quickly rendered obsolete under the gaze of the apartheid state. After being X-rayed, you pass into an inner room where you are curtly told to drop your trousers, all of you in a row.

You may be a dignified businessman, a top-class lawyer, a jeweller, a wood merchant, or anybody. You will find yourself naked. Well, you wanted a permit to work in Johannesburg didn't you? The official world is not finicky about your embarrassed modesty.[31]

The omnipresent gaze of the "official world" worked, via humiliation, to produce as vulnerable, and thereby as docile, a subject as possible. One man Themba interviewed for the article, John Raditsebe, a watchmaker, explains: "This pass . . . is so precious that one shuts one's eyes and goes through with the miserable experience."[32] Raditsebe's comment exemplifies the way in which the gaze of the all-seeing, ever-vigilant state could actually annihilate its subjects' ability to see for themselves, even askew. Literally, he "shuts [his] eyes [to] . . . the miserable experience," and in so doing relinquishes his ability to observe the state's operations of control, and metaphorically, he succumbs to this control becoming a docile participant who poses no threat to its continuation.

Lifespan, too, was subject to pass laws. Elias, a fictional member of the anti-apartheid resistance movement in *In the Fog of the Seasons' End*, notes that his pass incorrectly reflects his age:

So they made me older than I really am, Elias thought, and smiled to himself. They have command of everything now, even the length of time one is entitled to lived [*sic*] in this world. If they do not do it with the gun or the hangman's rope, they can easily write it out on a piece of paper, ending days, years, life, like a magician he had once seen at a concert, making playing-cards disappear.[33]

As in the novel's earlier scene in the Office of Native Affairs, writing is directly accused of enacting violence, but La Guma has also added an important comment here on this violence's infuriating inexplicability: the state works "like a magician," choosing, at whim, which "playing-cards" to keep and which to erase. Within this necropolitan apartheid structure, *black life and death itself* constitute white state power, becoming most manifest in the state's exceptional ability to take and give life at random, contravening the strictures and rationalities of ordinary law.

The pass laws thus exerted control over time, space, and also social relations. Following Foucault, power consolidated during apartheid meant "uninterrupted" and "constant coercion . . . exercised according to a codification that partitions as closely as possible time, space, movement."[34] The apartheid government aimed to establish an inescapable, totalizing reign of spatio-temporal-biological surveillance and control, though it did not wholly succeed. While literature of the period, as we have seen, describes a world bound tightly by the pass system's intimate and gross forms of social monitoring, these very same works also bear traces of other ways of living and thinking within the strictures of a world governed by passbooks.

Criticism often leveled against these literary works deems "protest literature" too concerned with the representation of apartheid injustices.[35] According to such assessments, these works exaggeratedly depend on reductive binaries of good and evil. As Njabulo Ndebele argues in his famous essay, "The Rediscovery of the Ordinary," protest fiction insufficiently attends to the details and affective moralities of everyday life, thus failing to address the larger systemic causes of inequality. "Writers of the fifties and sixties," Njabulo Ndebele writes,

> codified the predominant themes, characters, and situations which were welded into a recognizable grammar of what came to be called "protest lit" . . . thus unintentionally reducing actual experiences of poverty and oppression into types which deny the nuance and complexity of such existences.[36]

Ndebele's emphasis on nuance is key to my revisiting of these very texts he decries. Indeed, they contain evidence of other, more complex understandings of relation during apartheid alongside the more polarizing depictions he objects to. Though many of the novels of the 1950s, 1960s, and 1970s abound in stark Manichean representations of the relationship between the state police and their black and "coloured" targets at the passcheck, examined together, as a group of descriptions repeating the same basic scenario, more than one clear mode of relation is described. This suggests that the moment of the passcheck—when the black and white police asked for and read a black subject's pass—led to a more complex variety of interpretive responses, some of which, I argue below, were ethically inclined. Many, of course, directly reinforce the strict oppositionality Ndebele bemoans, yet some directly or subtly problematize these binaries, revealing fissures in their absolutist dedication to a solely anti-white stance. Taken together, the descriptions of relation extend beyond the rigid boundaries intended by the architects of apartheid laws and also beyond those usually attributed to "resistance literature." These same novels suggest that there were also other ways to approach readings of the passbook that contravened the state's authorial intentions. They thus deserve a closer look.

READING PASSBOOKS ETHICALLY

In a book documenting the making of his famous underground film, *Come Back, Africa* (1959), director Lionel Rogosin remarks: "Naturally, the Africans detest these passes." A moment later he adds, surprisingly: "They refer to [the passbook] as the 'bible.'"[37] This unlikely coupling of the passbook with Christianity's most sacrosanct book gives it a revered characteristic undetectable in the accounts examined so far. Of course, in South Africa, the Bible was not solely seen as an inviolable icon of Christianity, since the religion arrived along with the extensive violence of colonial expansion. Yet the ambiguity Rogosin identifies—passbooks are both "detest[ed]" *and* sacred—pinpoints the way the passbook provoked contradictory structures of feeling that were simultaneously bound up in networks of repulsion and desire (recall that Raditsebe calls it "precious"). As David Goldblatt's arresting photo "Young men with 'dompas,' White City, Jabavu, Soweto, November 1972" attests, the association of the passbook with the Bible suggests that the pass had a totemic or reliquary value for its holders, investing it with positive as well as repugnant qualities (fig. 1).

Goldblatt's photograph shows how relationships with the passbook were characterized by more than just alienation or disgust. In it a young man protectively encircles another while the smaller of the two holds up a passbook to show to the camera. Together they form a caring unit around the book, seeming at once to foreground its tyrannical centrality in structuring their lives while also tenderly recognizing its talismanic properties. Certainly with the correct stamps and signatures the passbook could guarantee its owner many advantages. South African artist Sue Williamson's 1990 installation piece, composed of copies of the forty-nine pages from one man's passbook, bears the title "For Thirty Years Next to His Heart," suggesting the double signification of the heart as both affective center and guarantor of continued life and survival.[38] In Goldblatt's photo, the young man on the right holds the passbook in the center of his body, and Goldblatt's choice to crop the image in this way, doubled by the frame of the men's bodies, positions the passbook

Fig. 1. © David Gold-
blatt, "Young Men
with 'Dompas,' White
City, Jabavu, Soweto,
November 1972." The J.
Paul Getty Museum, Los
Angeles. Purchased with
funds provided by the
Photographs Council.

as the heart of the photo.[39] To link the passbook with the heart is to stress the vital role it played in policing life. Goldblatt recounts the moment he took this photograph:

> These two young men, sitting at this coal yard, posed for me. I asked if I could take a photograph, and then the one pulled out his dompas, his pass. Now I think that was a very interesting gesture. It's partly defiance. He's telling me, "Whitey, you don't know nothing! This is me. I've got to carry this book." But he's also posing in the way that Africans, particularly in those times, loved to pose, with something that was precious to them. So if you asked a man in the street to allow you to photograph him, he might pull out his pack of cigarettes and display it, as though to say, "You know, I'm quite a cool cat. I smoke this or that." And I think in some degree, that's what this young man was doing.[40]

Passes, Goldblatt's photo confirms, held ambivalent qualities, since it could enable passage to a world of increased material and social privileges, render-ing an individual "a cool cat" if the book enlarged the realm of possibilities for its owner. In addition to being the manifest symbol of the racist limits of apartheid, the passbook was also considered a valuable text that opened up new avenues of mobility for its bearers. Within the reality of the pass system, a book with the best permissions was highly sought after. This meant, also, that people manipulated its contents directly, and a lively trade in forged and repurposed passes flourished.

Forgeries and "illegal" edits show how important passes were for those whose movement was dictated almost entirely by the book. Yet the very fact of such revisions positions the pass as a more instable tool of control than the state planned for, since the government could not stop its bearers from playing with their intended meanings. Jane Caplan and John Torpey caution against only understanding identity documents through the negative lens of fascist control. For them, this approach fails to

> capture the ways in which human ingenuity and recalcitrance have taken up the state's tools and turned them against themselves. This is not just a matter of forgeries and frauds, but of the creation of new identities and names, a parallel world of revised or resistant identities and relationships.[41]

While state-mandated oppression through a pass system severely limits human capacity to live outside the dictates of legal constraints, the forgery and tampering of passbooks reminds us that apartheid failed to eradicate all creativity, and this is again evidenced in the anti-apartheid literary output of the period.

In Athol Fugard's 1972 play *Sizwe Bansi Is Dead*, a character assumes the passbook and identity of a dead man. And Henry Nxumalo's 1951 short story "The Birth of a Tsotsi" illustrates how simple it could be to obtain forged passes. In the story, "a Coloured 'king' of Kliptown" tells another character,

> On the whole it is quite easy to get fixed up with a pass. In fact the real crimi- nal has nothing to fear on that score. It is easy to get either a Chinaman or an Indian to take out a pass for you so long as you are able to find the pass fees. Some African businessmen also help sometimes.[42]

Identity was therefore, to a certain extent, an exchangeable commodity in this shadow economy, determined by the material needs of the population. As we have seen, it was not only pass holders who saw identity as malleable when the need arose—the state, too, could assign or take it away. A character in La Guma's *In the Fog of the Season's End* explains that pass officers "could give you a name and an age, all nicely ready-made, like a hat or a coat out of a shopwindow."[43] Yet it was not *only* the state's prerogative to assign or do away with identities as individual pass holders also showed, at times, a shrewd awareness of the flexibility of identity. Despite the rigidity of apartheid's classificatory categories that were so firmly solidified through the pass system,[44] the manipulation of identity documents nonetheless exposed identity's more mutable qualities, even as the revisions and changes to documents relied on the pretense of permanence.[45]

Flaws in the pass system, such as these, undid the sturdiness of the racial classification system it sought to solidify, thus implicitly suggesting that there could be alternate ways to structure group identity and solidarities. For the remainder of this chapter I turn my attention to one further way the pass system facilitated anti-apartheid modes of thinking and relationality, focusing particularly on its unlikely role as the progenitor of ethical consciousness. Ethical thought attends to relation, but emerges first, most powerfully, out of actual relations. Encounters enabled by the pass system itself produced the possibility for alternate ways of relation that undid the logic of apartheid's racial separatism. In certain instances the passbook came to operate within a realm of radical potentiality, functioning as more than the administrative agent of the oppressive state. How then does the book betray the original intents of its creators? How does the passbook's complex array of affective associations permit for a reinvention and reimagining of the text itself so that it can be understood as able to elicit ethical response all the while remaining the representative of apartheid's unethicality?

IMAGINING WHITENESS

Alex La Guma's 1962 novel, *A Walk in the Night*, recounts a night in Michael Adonis's life as he walks around Cape Town's famous District Six. Throughout the narrative he is regularly stopped by police asking to see his passbook. Though the story focuses on Adonis, the narrative often shifts perspective to provide a sense of the varying and diverse people circulating in and through District Six. Among these are the policemen themselves. Chapter 6, for instance, begins by describing Police Constable Raalt, who "lounged in the corner of the driving cabin of the patrol van and half listened to the radio under the dashboard. . . . The other half of Raalt's mind was thinking, I'm getting fed-up with all that nonsense, if she doesn't stop I'll do something serious."[46] La Guma devotes another paragraph to Raalt's interior monologue as he muses angrily upon his wife and the disappointments his marriage has brought.

He sewed and mended his own clothes and often he had to do the housework, too, and that angered him further. His wife had been good-looking before they had been married but now she had gone to seed, and that irritated him, too. He sat in the corner of the van and nursed his anger.[47]

This anger is soon transferred in his conversation with the driver of the patrol wagon to his descriptions of the people they are there to "patrol." He refers to them pejoratively as "effing hotnot bastards," and then the story switches gears to return to the point of view of Adonis in a new chapter.[48] What are we to make of the eruption of this episode in the midst of a larger story about the final days of District Six and the destruction of a vibrant, if impoverished, interracial neighborhood? Why has La Guma written paragraphs on the domestic struggles of Raalt? If writers of this period were, as Ndebele charged, committed to portraying whites, and white police in particular, as emblems of unalloyed evil, what are we to make of this foray into a policeman's unhappy psychic interior?

To begin, what must be acknowledged is that life for black and coloured people under a system such as apartheid made it nearly impossible to avoid thinking about white interiority. Structurally determined though it was, blacks were forced to imagine white psychic life to survive or get through their day without incident. Ashis Nandy observes that in Hegel's master-slave dialectic, which serves as a useful analytic lens for certain aspects of the apartheid structure, the slave represents the higher order of cognition since he is able to imagine the master's psyche as well as his own. While very precise structural parameters dictated how and to what end the passbooks and their bearers should be read by the police in order to retrieve superficial "factual" information about people stopped at the passcheck, their owners read them, in contrast, in multiple ways: as carriers of information, as documents that either restricted or permitted mobility, and as a written manifestation of the state's racist ideological organization and power. Similarly, they read the police both as the representatives and enforcers of oppressive, unavoidable, violent control *and* sometimes, as La Guma's novel makes manifest, as complex human beings with a wide range of motivations and emotions.

Homi Bhabha coined the term "sly civility" to describe the way this additional level of consciousness could be put to strategic use by colonized or oppressed peoples. In Bloke Modisane's apartheid memoir, *Blame Me on History,* he explains how semiotic fluency and manipulation are requisite for surviving under an oppressive regime: "The shadow of apartheid spreads long over my life," he writes. "I have to be sane, calculating and ruthless in order to survive."[49] For Bhabha, despite the deeply disadvantageous and unequal social structures inherent to a system like apartheid, sly civility procures the colonized certain benefits in addition to mere survival, benefits that also involve destabilizing state rhetoric and rule. Surreptitiously, sly civility becomes a subversive way of using the hyperawareness about colonizers and their needs and desires that is inherent to the position of subjection, in order to distort colonial discourse without being detected by the unwitting colonizers. Such sly civility is thematized in one of Modisane's short stories, "The Dignity of Begging," published in *Drum* in 1951. The narrator, Nathaniel Mokmare, is being sentenced for begging. The judge berates him for returning to the court:

> "You beggars make it difficult for me to do my duty. In spite of my constant failures to rehabilitate you, I always believe in giving you another chance . . . a fresh start you might call it," the magistrate said. "But I am almost certain that you'll be back here in a few days!"
>
> The magistrate is getting soft, I can see my freedom at a distance of an arm's stretch, here is my chance to put on my act; a look of deep compassion and a few well-chosen words can do the trick. I clear my throat and clear a tear or two. . . . I can see from the silence in the court that everybody is deceived, the magistrate is as mute as the undertaker's parlour. I read pity spelled on the faces of all the people in the court; perhaps the most pathetic face is my own. I am magnificent, an answer to every film director's dream.[50]

Here Mokmare self-consciously, "slyly," appeals to white liberal sympathy, using "a few well-chosen words" to prevent a jail sentence. He "*read[s] pity*" in the courtroom faces, texts in which their sentimentality is "spelled" out as evidence of the success of Mokmare's feigned remorse.

Reading a text and reading a person are, in fact, similar *acts*, as Attridge argues when he makes the conflation: "any text we read—like any person we encounter . . ."[51] Booth also argues this when he proposes that books are like friends and also when he suggests "that we arrive at our sense of value in narratives in precisely the same way we arrive at our sense of value in persons: by *experiencing* them in an immeasurably rich context of others that are both like and unlike them."[52] What the passage from Modisane's story highlights is how much the subtle reading of others, and a heightened awareness of alterity's many guises, is characteristic of the experience of oppression. Mokmare's trickster-like manipulation of the audience in the courtroom hardly changes the system; indeed, it only really affects one individual's life, yet his actions are not entirely without political implication. For this method of responding to power assumes a relation of antagonism, which puts it at a considerable remove from those automatic, physical, discursive, and affective responses to power that characterize subjectivities of passive docility.

While encounters at the passcheck often produced responses of this nature, as I have already shown, by dint of the proximity forced upon both blacks and whites—even in this most unbalanced of situations—blacks were compelled, often against their wills, to imagine whiteness as an identity or subjectivity that could not be simply explained by resorting to polarizing bromides about pure evil. Structural inequity meant that blacks could not avoid considerations of white subjectivity and were thus forced into more imaginative explorations of otherness than those required of whites. Chela Sandoval's work on semiotics and power observes that

> social life under subjugation requires the development of [a] process of semiotic perception and deconstruction; it provides moments when . . . colonised or subordinated subjects perceive dominant ideology, and understand the distortion that power is capable of imposing on any form.[53]

This kind of "semiotic perception and deconstruction" creates the possibility for alternate, resilient readings and interpretations, cognizant of power's discursive manipulations and thus capable of reworking systems of signification.

For Sandoval, Barthes's science of semiology—sign reading—is a key "methodology" used by the oppressed to effect power relations. It is a methodology

> that allows one to read forms of domination as "artifacts" . . . a familiar behavior among powerless subjects, who early on learn to analyze every object under conditions of domination, especially when set in exchanges with the master/colonizer (what is his style of dressing? her mode of speaking? why does he gesture? when do they smile?) in order to determine how, where, and when to construct an identity that will facilitate continued existence of self and/or community.[54]

Citizen-subjects engage semiotics by continually gauging and redrawing their responses to signs in order to survive *and*, for Sandoval, "*to pursue a greater good*."[55] The ethical implications of this methodology differentiate it, then, from Bhabha's sly civility.

Following Frantz Fanon's recognition that the "values, morals, and ideologies of dominant Euro-American cultures . . . [are] 'artifacts'" we may say that semiology permits new possibilities for relation, since forms of oppression are recognized as products, or "artifacts," and not as ipso facto ontological conditions of existence.[56] Sandoval explains: "Such emancipation requires citizen-subjects to 'incarnate a new type' of subjectivity. Fanon describes this process as occurring through a 'slow,' 'painful,' re-'composition of my self in an ongoing process of mutation.'"[57] As these modes of subjectivity, new and old, are born from the ideological structures and counteractions determining them, so do they effect intersubjective relations in turn. While it is hard to identify *when* subjectivities emerge that escape mere ideological dictates— for Fanon, this process is "slow" and "painful"; indeed, it is *"ongoing"*—they can ultimately redefine intersubjective relations in addition to individual self-perception, thus opening the possibility of the introduction of an alternative or ethical form of interaction.

Sandoval's emphasis is on a mode of semiotic perception that carries the possibility of an ethically conscious relation. This form of interaction emerges out of necessity (survival), yet it also promises an imminent intersubjective relation characterized by productive, positive exchange. The excerpt from Abrahams's novel *Mine Boy*, referred to earlier, illuminates the complexity I am getting at. Here it is again, with the addition of one more line:

> He stopped and looked at [the cakes]. He felt a tap on his shoulder and turned. It was a policeman. Without a word he fished his pass from his pocket and gave it to the policeman. The policeman looked at it, looked him up and down, and returned the pass to him. *Xumas [sic] could see he was a kind one.*[58]

Previously in this chapter, this passage served to exemplify the way that the passcheck effected automated, bodily responses, ensuring the smooth functioning of power, without even recourse to speech. But with the addition of the next line, we are forced to wonder how it is that Xuma knows this policeman is "kind." Abrahams provides no further clues in the rest of the section. They are not necessary, anyway, since it is clear to the reader that Xuma, like Nathaniel Mokmare in Modisane's story, must have quickly gone through a semiotic process of assessment and interpretation, a process very much a part of daily life for blacks under apartheid. By *reading the signs* of the policeman's body, much as Mokmare read the faces of the courtroom audience, he comes to the conclusion that this particular officer would be agreeable and easy to deal with.

That a policeman—any policeman—working for the apartheid state can be deemed "kind" hints at a whole realm of ambiguity in which the agents of oppression are understood by the victims as complex human beings rather than as mere embodiments of aggression. That Xuma can find a "kind" police-man, and does not express further shock at so doing, suggests that this was not a surprise to him; that, in fact, there were other "kind" policemen work-ing for the apartheid state; and that intersubjective relations between police-men and the subjects they attempted to regulate were not all characterized by stark opposition and violence.[59] A passage such as this from Abrahams's novel challenges Ndebele's accusation that "protest lit" only simplified apart-heid oppression by relying on Manichean oppositions between good/bad and black/white, since, for this moment in the text, at least, we see that a virtue normally associated with goodness—kindness—is attributed to a policeman, the figure most often portrayed as the personification of evil.

Indeed, when a policeman (black or white) asked a black person to show his or her passbook, a series of reading processes were initiated. First, of course, the policeman read some of the information in the book itself. But even before this central act of reading, the bodies of the police were often sub-ject to scrutiny by those waiting in line to show their passes at a passcheck. Furthermore, the police were not only reading the books but interpreting the bodies of the bearers of the passbooks too. Some of these interpretive acts, producing both docile, obedient responses and subtly cross-grained counter-readings, suggest a repurposing of the original point of reading (that was the state's), as well as the creation of other sets of readers. The state, which wished to be the only reader, reducing the man in the street to the status of the only text to be read, could not prevent an inversion of this relation-ship in which the policeman-as-state-representative becomes the text and the interpretations more varied. This distortion of the state's intentions subverts the intended politics of the reading encounter as well. So then, if imagining oneself *as other* is the first step in initiating an ethics of responsibility toward difference, then blacks were more likely to exist ethically than whites. While such acts of imagining rarely resulted in ethical acts of interpersonal relation, these were not entirely absent during apartheid, and La Guma's articulation of otherness as a form of suffering (Raalt is unhappy in his marriage in part because he feels unloved) indicates an interest on La Guma's part to engage with the interior lives of white others in ways that extend beyond the instru-mental deployment of imagination as a mechanism for survival. Reading, we see here, always inevitably produces further, unexpected readings that can confirm but also derail the politics of the intended act of reading.

THAT THESE MOMENTS are infrequently depicted in "struggle literature" attests less to the infrequency of such sympathetic interracial encounters and more to the novelists' political motivations. Here Ndebele's charge that these novels fail to adequately depict the nuances of everyday life rings true, since their authors often expressly desired to influence political outcomes. Nonetheless, as I have been showing, such moments *do* emerge, however fleetingly, and hint at a range of intimacies and identifications rarely discussed in scholarly treatments of black apartheid literature.

These examples from La Guma's and Abrahams's novels (and there are others[60]) suggest that oppressed groups use ethical reading practices to transmogrify extant structures of inequality. I will discuss this at far greater length in chapters 2 and 3 as it relates to cinematic reception practices and to the popular photocomic genre. Here I argue that, counterintuitively, affective attunement with those who oppress and dominate is an additional mode of survival for subjected groups and provides—*at times*—a way for imagining and theorizing alternative forms of relation.

How such an ethical approach to relation is cultivated through reading and spectatorship practices is the subject of much of the rest of the book. And how this "sympathy for the devil" is taken up in the literature of the post-apartheid years is the focus of the final chapter. It is clear, however, with regards to the pass laws, that there was rarely room within the intersubjective encounter at the passcheck for such ambiguity. Despite the marked openness suggested by the passage in Abrahams's novel—an openness to a relation characterized by more than just strict opposition, possessing the potential for alternative conceptions of relation—the pass laws tended to severely limit this kind of reading. Within such rigid confines, relation was tightly circumscribed and seldom found ways to escape predictable antagonisms.

Nonetheless, these ethical textual acts refuse the narratorial absolutism that the apartheid state aimed to impose via the pass system. A consideration of such alternative historical trajectories resurrects the very polyvocality the state tried to erase from both public and private discourse. And while the novels I have touched on in this chapter were often banned within South Africa, they were still published and publicized abroad and then surreptitiously sneaked back in to South Africa, thus sharing the public space of signs that apartheid doctrine tried to monopolize, working as insistent gadflies to its monolithic fantasy.

These literary works operated as *anti*-passes insofar as they managed to transmit written ideas not entirely circumscribed by legal mandate. Censored, banned, and sometimes publicly maligned, these still made it into print, defy-ing the boundaries of township, Bantustan, and nation that prevented many human beings from similar forms of mobility. These books were passports into other places and particularly into a future imagined, if not perceived. The novel defied the limits imposed by its official other—the passbook—refusing its tethering to place and testifying to a South Africa unlike that revealed in the passbook's pages, and these black and coloured South African writers wrote despite the fact that the occupation "writer" was not a category ever stamped or written into the passes they carried. They understood that writing in English, Afrikaans, Xhosa, Zulu, or any of South Africa's other languages was not, and did not have to be, the monopoly of the apartheid state.

CHAPTER 2

"Blood and Thunder"

Popular Film and Black Spectatorship at the Midcentury

In Peter Abrahams's 1954 memoir, *Tell Freedom*, he describes cinema (the "bioscope") as being one of the most crucial cultural influences on twentieth-century black urban experience in South Africa. "The bioscope in Twentieth Street was Vrededorp's most powerful and direct link with the outside world," he writes. "Through it we kept touch with the scientific advances of our time. From it we drew our picture of the world of white folk. Our morals were fashioned there."[1] For Abrahams, film made possible a vernacular global imaginary,[2] forging the "most powerful and direct link with the outside world."[3] This chapter explores how cinematic representations of the foreign places, ideas, languages, objects, and people, all beyond apartheid's geographic and ideological ken, positioned films—and specifically popular American Hollywood films—as harbingers of alternatives to apartheid's social organization and logic. It focuses on the reception of the films that were most popular even though they depicted people and places at a considerable remove from everyday black South African life. Indeed it was this distance itself, between the images, narratives, and lives depicted in these films, and the lives of black South African viewers, that helped activate various forms of ethical response.

Certainly, while American movies provided black South Africans with a set of alternative visual economies to apartheid's racial-social order, they often also echoed South Africa's own white supremacist visions. Eliciting a range of spectatorial (dis)identifications, American popular films nonetheless presented a differently structured, but no less racially coded, society, showing racialization, though this comparative lens, to be a process of social construction rather than a fixed characteristic of human identity. Through the recognizable and yet dissimilar racial structures on display, these films undercut the seeming intransigence of apartheid.

Furthermore, in South Africa's physical cinematic spaces, affective, material, and intellectual encounters with American films distorted and reshaped the practices of identification necessitated by apartheid's political and aesthetic exigencies. In consequence, the social and aesthetic experience of watching movies was also one that restructured the parameters of ethical being. As Abrahams put it: "Morals were fashioned [at the bioscope]," not just in the extra-cinematic space outside.[4]

THIS CHAPTER EXAMINES how ethical being is initiated by engagements with popular culture by looking at moviegoing practices during the middle of the twentieth century, beginning around 1931 and continuing through the earlier years of apartheid rule. Though films were in distribution earlier than 1931, and subject to censorship as early as 1910, this date marks the passage of the Entertainments Act, which mandated that all films be reviewed by a state-appointed censorship board before being either released, edited, or banned.[5] As such, it is an important moment in South Africa's history of spectatorship since it inaugurated nationwide interventions in black film consumption. Anxieties about the ideological influence of film culture thus preceded the legalized racism ushered in by the National Party's election in 1948, suggesting that mass culture was identified early on as a particularly potent site of sociopolitical indoctrination.

Excellent studies on the history of film production in South Africa already exist.[6] Yet scholarly work on South African film is primarily concerned with films as aesthetic and discursive objects, and these mostly glance over discussions of film audiences.[7] My focus is instead on the relationship between black spectators and the films they *loved* to watch rather than on individual films, actors, or directors. Following Lindiwe Dovey and Karin Barber, "I see author and audience as two sides of the same coin,"[8] insisting that "if art is the construction of shared meanings, then the audience is as important as the artist in the process."[9] While film audiences are generally acknowledged to be as instrumental in the production of meaning as directors and actors, when it comes to studies of interpretation, film studies continue to overprivilege *auteurial* intent. This is no exception in African contexts.

As Rosalind Morris points out, in order to understand film's role in the production of black South African modern subjectivities, "the history of cinema's effectivity has to be understood less in terms of production than through reference to the forms in which it was received and by which it was taken up into everyday life."[10] This chapter thus pays only passing interest to films made within South Africa since the most popular films among black South African film audiences were foreign, and usually American.[11] In this chapter I seek to understand the appeal of these films in order, first, to theorize the ethical implications for black spectators of such an abiding preference for American popular films and, second, following Morris's injunction, to tease out some of the effects of filmic consumption in the wider social sphere.

Critical responses to American films' popularity are generally polarized along ideological lines, casting Hollywood films as racist and dangerously pro-capitalist on the one hand or as threateningly interracial and modern-izing on the other. In both of these guises, Hollywood films are thought to *damage* their audiences in some way; the films, such logic goes, deliver infor-mation and aesthetics that are inherently propagandistic, producing audi-ence responses that are largely objectionable in the eyes of their detractors. Both of these positions rely on a marked delineation between the keepers of knowledge and those who are knowledge's objects. In other words, there is a condescending reentrenchment of the power of the critic-scholar in such assessments and a refusal to recognize, instead, how independent forms of consciousness and knowledge production occur "from below," in response to moviegoing experiences. Against this emphasis on filmic content as neces-sarily deforming its audiences, this chapter largely avoids direct engagement with the films as texts themselves in order to focus more consistently, instead, on the viewers and on their capacity for independent interpretation, even under psychological and ideological duress.

Arguments that treat popular films as ideologically defective mistakenly ignore the wide variety of possible responses audience members can have, denying the way that audience members, both as individuals and as group participants, resist propagandistic appeals possibly as much as they are swayed by them.[12] Furthermore, audience members are likely to develop unpredict-able responses to works of cultural production when they are not the films' target audiences.[13] This is especially so when spectators' geographic, tempo-ral, linguistic, and racial experiences differ vastly from those of the places and people depicted in the films. Certainly, black South Africans' lives were con-siderably removed from those of average American audiences. While char-acters and locales in Hollywood-produced "A" and "B" films may have often also appeared distant to American audiences (along lines of gender, ethnicity, race, and class, for instance), the *degree* of difference or alterity that such films highlighted for urban black South Africans was more extreme, warranting an examination of these films' popularity, since identification along lines of nationalism, race, or even language cannot satisfactorily explain their success.

And successful they certainly were. Film director Ramadan Suleman remarks upon the active interactions that South African audiences have with the films they watch:

> Historically we all know that Africans or Third World people have the tendency, if they like something, to see it two or three times. . . . We have even experienced in movie houses that the audience knows movie dialogues by heart. They memorize; they even tend to talk to the screen characters![14]

Hortense Powdermaker's 1973 study of film culture in a mining town in colonial Rhodesia recounts that "the African audience was never passive; it was always actively participating and with emotion."[15] "During [the cowboy] film," for instance, "men, women and children rose to their feet in excitement, bending forward and flexing their muscles with each blow the cowboys gave. The shouting could be heard several miles away."[16] Powdermaker transcribes the outbursts she hears: "Wheoo! He is intoxicated with a blow!!" and "I know this cowboy."[17] Missionary and film zealot Reverend Ray A. Phillips observed in the 1920s that "'Wild West' films are reported as being most popular, with the Western hero in any film given the name 'Jack', and audiences shouting 'we want Jack' when films they did not like were screened."[18] Such vocalized engagements ruptured any pact between viewer and film narrative central to "classical cinema,"[19] which usually aimed to heighten film's "reality effect" by diminishing audience awareness of its technical, mechanical, and directorial artifice. Viewers who spoke with, or reacted to and against, on-screen depictions were not willing participants in that illusion of diagetic absorption that increasingly became the dominant way to consume films among audiences in the United States.

In part, these differing reception practices owed something to the spatial arrangements of movie theaters, where blacks were either quarantined in inferior seating arrangements above and behind whites or only permitted to watch films in a few specially designated black-only or coloured-only theaters. In her work on black American film audiences, Jacqueline Stewart notes that "for Black spectators the practice of segregated seating complicated the process of forgetting one's social self and becoming completely absorbed into an increasingly self-enclosed narrative."[20] "Black spectators at the dawn of the classical era," she writes, "were not meant to be fully integrated into the developing narratives on screen, in large part because they were not fully integrated into American theater audiences."[21] Black South Africans' relegation to the periphery—in terms of the physical space of the cinemas, in terms of plots and actors in the films they watched, and in terms of their geographic position in South Africa as well as within the world at large—positioned them at an acute angle to the medium, a position that, for Edward Said, is crucial for the production of intellectual critique. This more disjunctive experience of Hollywood films meant that, as in the United States,

> black spectatorship did not revolve entirely around expectations or experiences of complete "identification," uninterrupted narrative engagement, or visual mastery, cornerstones of classical practices and psychoanalytic film theory. Instead, it may be more useful to regard the cinema as a field for the continuous interpretation of the Black subject's highly contested public roles, rights, and responsibilities.[22]

Cinema was, thus, as in South Africa, not only a space for the experience of private interiority but as much a venue for the articulation of, and response to, each individual's interconnectedness with others. Cinema, to invoke Glissant, was a space for relation and, as such, an ethically charged zone.

That the South African cinemas in black and coloured areas were also used for purposes other than film screenings suggests, too, an association of the cinematic space with communal political and social critique.[23] The Odin cinema in Sophiatown, for instance, was the location for political meetings between Nelson Mandela and the South African Indian Congress secretary Yusuf Cachalia, who was subsequently arrested on the platform of the cinema's stage.[24] In Sophiatown, Don Mattera recalls people going into a cinema to see anti-apartheid activist Trevor Huddleston speak at an ANC rally, noting that "the people were entering like thick black syrup with specks of whites, Indians and coloureds."[25] Mattera's portrait of the community reminds us that the politically conscious anti-apartheid movement was composed of people from across the racial landscape, a heterogeneity sometimes replicated in the cinematic audience.

While Stewart astutely notes that Hollywood films failed to produce the same kinds of identifying spectators in black audience members as in white ones, because blacks were less able to transcend their own specificities in order to meld, *passively*, with the film—a central aim of "classical cinema"—

passivity may not be the only state that enables cinematic identification. Miriam Hansen suggests that outspoken, active spectatorial engagement of the
kind Powdermaker, Phillips, and Suleman point out need not be read as a
failure of "complete 'identification.'" While vocal ejaculations and physical
responses to films may be culturally or socially anathema to the "middle-class
standards of silence and passivity that were becoming the mark of the cinema's respectability," these engaged viewers often still imagined themselves as
those very characters they admired, or fought with, on screen, thus "*chal-
leng[ing] the conceptual coupling . . . of narrative identification with spectatorial passivity.*"[26] As Karin Barber notes in her work on "popular arts," cultural
forms shared together by an audience can "dissolve the distance between performer and crowd by establishing a relationship of intimacy and immediate
response. Popular, that is, is defined by the relationship between perform-
ers and audience, not by the medium through which the performance takes
place."[27] Extending Barber we can see that even in the absence of a live actor or
performer, audience members' responses to films—to their settings and plots
as much as to their actors—might also be experiences of intimacy, immediacy, and identification. In the South African context, film viewing could
generate personal emotional and affective responses in semi-private spaces
that were often also marginalized public and political spheres of interrelation.

Though what was depicted on screen was foreign, even alien, to the viewers in South Africa, aesthetic encounters with radical difference, as ethical
theorists have long argued, can be the precursor for ethical identification and
for thinking of the self as unique both within a wider community of like-
minded and similarly structured others and *also* within a world of difference.
In the contrasts and dissimilarities highlighted by viewing American films, in
the disjunctive, misaligned sequences of identifications (identification with
white subjectivities *as well as* identification with all that is foreign and strange
to hegemonic racial identities), a kind of ethical intimacy emerges that is akin
neither to the total absorption of classical cinema nor to the self-annihilation
of false consciousness.

Abrahams's memoir provides a striking example of how patterns of relation modeled in the cinematic space bled out into the world beyond it. He
recalls:

> The young men of Vrededorp slapped their girls as they had seen men slap
> girls on the screen. The girls modelled themselves on the ladies of the screen.
> Once a Vrededorp murder was modelled on a murder we saw on the screen.
> People wept bitterly at screen tragedies; more bitterly than at their own, real-

life tragedies. Often the illusions of the screen became the reality of some frustrated boy's or girl's life; and drab Vrededorp became the illusion. There was a boy who became Douglas Fairbanks. He jumped off roofs, leaped on fast-moving cars and leaped off before the shocked drivers realized what was happening. He drowned in one of the mine dams. He was trying to get into the pipe that pumped the water up from the bowels of the earth.

Illusion and reality often merged at the bioscope . . .[28]

For Abrahams, identification worked so well that individual spectators actually "became" the characters and actors they met on screen, as the films permitted heightened states of emotional feeling—"people wept . . . more bitterly than at their own, real-life tragedies." Abrahams's suggestion here calls into question claims that black audiences found little to identify with when faced with movies featuring all-white casts. Indeed, as Abrahams makes clear, for *many* people, film produced experiences of the self as other. While these transmutations were desirable in part because they afforded escape from "real-life tragedies" and "drab" life, spectatorship practices such as these also mirror the dynamic of a self held in suspension that ethical theorists deem most crucial to the development of ethical feeling.

What is hard to gauge is the way these moments might translate into ethical practice. Yet Stuart Hall notes that the "decoded meanings" spectators take from encounters in popular culture do "'have an effect', influence, entertain, instruct or persuade, with very complex perceptual, cognitive, emotional, ideological or behavioural consequences."[29] Similarly, for J. Hillis Miller, "the ethical moment . . . is genuinely productive and inaugural in its effects on history, though in ways that are by no means reassuring or predictably benign."[30] Despite the degree of intangibility Miller and Hall admit to when it comes to assessing the effects of cultural engagement on our relations with others, such influences, of the cinema in particular, were readily discernable in audience members' responses to those films which relayed projections of global modernity.

CONSUMING MODERNITY AT THE CINEMA

American film's function as a conduit for various forms of modernity partly explains its considerable appeal. These movies showcased "modern" material cultures (dress, technologies, goods) and introduced plots and characters that diverged from more traditional narrative models. Many urban black South

Africans cultivated modern sensibilities because this positioned them outside apartheid discourses that located blacks on a lower rung than whites on development's presumed teleological ladder. Such racist thinking meant blacks were frequently referred to as ignorant, tribal children, still yet to achieve the full, modern adulthood of white South Africans.[31] For urban black South Africans, a fluency in filmic conventions and American forms of dress and dialogue contravened such arguments, conveying, instead, the sophistication of a subject cognizant, fashionable, and cutting edge. Film, much as in other parts of the world, revolutionized South African modes of subjectivity, conscripting its spectators into various lived forms of globalizing modernity. As elsewhere, film's popularity was often synonymous with the popularity of all things American. Anthony Sampson, the English editor of *Drum* during its early years, recalls interviewing a man who expressed his dismay that an early issue of *Drum* focused on African tribal cultures instead of on American popular culture:

> "Ag, why do you dish out that stuff, man?" said a man with golliwog hair in a floppy American suit, at the Bantu Men's Social Centre. "Tribal music! Tribal history! Chiefs! We don't care about chiefs! Give us jazz and film stars, man! We want Duke, Satchmo and hot dames! Yes, brother, anything American. You can cut out this junk about kraals and folk-tales and Basutos in blankets—forget it! You just trying to keep us backward, that's what! Tell us what's happening right here, on the Reef!"[32]

Echoing the colonial ideology equating African tribal practices with "backwardness," this man expresses a clear preference for "anything American," eschewing a sense of ethnic loyalty in favor of the symbolic trappings of Western modernity. He equates "what's happening right here, on the Reef" with American culture, making it clear that life "on the Reef"—in Johannesburg— was already a life rich in American-inflected ideas, practices, and objects.

Peter Davis's *In Darkest Hollywood* documents the United States' appeal for "the generation of urbanised Africans . . . which was particularly obsessed with American demotic culture, with American clothes, as with jazz and movies."[33] South African poet Don Mattera recalls, too, that

> almost everything we wore or ate was fashioned after American styles. Some gangs and gang members chose the names, habits and mannerisms of film stars such as George Raft, John Garfield and John Wayne, who was nick-

named *Motsamai* (swaggerer). Some fashion shops actually overpriced these clothes on the recommendation of the American gang who wanted—and were supposed to pay for—the exclusive privilege of wearing USA imports such as Florsheim, Nunn Bush and Jarman shoes. . . . "Made in the USA" became the sole criterion and any rubbish that carried the USA label was desirable for that alone. . . . Even the traditional African herbalists used brightly painted signs to advertise their USA aphrodisiacs, blood mixtures, and lucky charms. And if you rejected the American fad, you would quickly be dubbed *moegoe* or greenhorn.[34]

As Mattera observes, American imports were not absorbed into black South African culture without adjustment—instead, they were incorporated to form parts of black South African life. In Sophiatown "the Americans" are a gang that forms one part within a whole network of township-specific aesthetics and criminality; John Wayne is refurbished as a Sotho "swaggerer"; and the herbalists' use of the moniker "American" to sell traditional medicines literally reverses the meaning of the word by making it serve as a synonym for the best, or most exceptional of traditional, local cures. South African blacks thus used the term—the U.S.A.—and all its many associated referents with considerable interpretive and semiotic flexibility. In a similar passage Lewis Nkosi recalls that

young boys were actually writing to America. They got hold of the catalogues showing special shoes like Florsheim shoes. And when these boys were going to parties, they would pull up their socks and show you these shoes, because you couldn't get that shoe in Johannesburg, they said. "This one comes straight from New York, man it's a Can't Get!" *And it was all the influence of the films, and watching people who were very much like you, who were black like you.*[35]

As Nkosi's comment accentuates, American films sometimes elicited identifications with *sameness*, and the all-black casts in films such as *Stormy Weather* and *Cabin in the Sky* must have provided a welcome break for midcentury black South African audiences mostly exposed to films with white actors. Racial solidarities across widely separate spatial zones often enabled blacks to disregard or overlook dissimilarities between spaces and experience of blackness, so that, as here, black South Africans could find an image of themselves in the screen projections of American blackness.

Yet while blacks mostly saw films with white actors, these still produced shifting, recombinant identification practices that should be understood not only via Du Bois's "double consciousness" or, indeed, through Engel's "false consciousness." Hansen agrees that "classical cinema" sought to conscript spectators into clearly controlled patterns of identification, what she calls "the codification of spectatorship." But she notes how counter-identification occurred as well, so that identification with people "other" than the self might at times enable the viewer to resist conscripted patterns of identification:

> The codification of spectatorship offered a mechanism to regulate and contain forms of scopic desire, to channel it into scenarios of conformity and consumption. However, since the desire had to be ceaselessly renewed and redefined according to the frontiers of the market, it also harbored the risk of reproducing some of the same tensions and contradictions—within and against the classical codes designed to minimize them.[36]

These kinds of divergent modes of response and identification arise particularly when a film's audience is markedly *not* the same as its intended audience. Stuart Hall says this in a discussion of how audiences "decode" ideological messages when he remarks that "codes of encoding and decoding may not be perfectly symmetrical."[37] While dominant ideological paradigms (or what Hall calls "naturalised codes" or "preferred readings"[38]) press themselves upon audiences and are often hard to avoid, discrepancies between intended and received messages exist and have "a great deal to do with the structural differences of relation and position between broadcasters and audiences," or, in this case, between white American producers and filmmakers and black South African audiences.[39] Umberto Eco refers to this mismatch between the intended and the received message as "aberrant decoding," suggesting further that polysemic readings have become more frequent as media forms have transformed. Though Eco and Hall both recognize the existence of such "aberrant" readings, little scholarly work exists examining the implications of such alternative modes of reception. Apart from the work of Miriam Hansen, Jacqueline Stewart, and bell hooks, few studies examine the types of spectators that elude complete ideological conscription.[40]

Though much scholarship on popular culture challenges the negative reputation of "the culture industry," it often continues to accept Theodor Adorno's links between popular films and capitalist indoctrination, Americanization, and Westernization/globalization.[41] But films are purveyors of heteroge-

neous meaning, and as such they produce equally complicated viewing subjects who are less Adorno's frightening automatons or Kracauer's "vaporized
beings" than complex, agential spectators involved in negotiating ambivalent acts of identification, indoctrination, subversion, and transformation.[42]
Reception practices are a matrix of shifting responses within which viewers
adapt a variety of subject positions. All media, however "base" they might
seem to more rarified audiences, however simplistic they might appear from
our more technologically sophisticated position, tend to produce ambivalent,
sometimes contradictory, often hegemonic, yet also transformative responses
in those who engage with them as spectators and readers.

In what follows I present a brief overview of the history of black film
spectatorship in South Africa in order to allow for a consideration of the ways
filmic practices produced these "aberrant decodings," especially unexpected
ethical ones. Certain forms of identification with otherness allowed for the
imagination of other lives and other structures of social formation and by
so doing proposed more ethical worlds. Open and responsive to difference,
this very practice of imagining otherness exposed the myriad and complex
ways that people inhabit the world both as individuals and members of social
groups, and, in so doing, made it possible for them, also, to imagine the end
of apartheid.

LOCATING BLACK RESPONSES

Descriptions and details found in novels and short stories written by South
African writers during this period, as well as in newspapers, interviews, and
other miscellany, substitute an everyday black cultural archive for the more
formal trappings of a state-produced one. There are few firsthand sources
documenting black South African responses to the films they saw in the movies. The sources I draw on here are motley, but no less so, perhaps, than the
experience of viewing films under apartheid or the movies themselves, which
had either passed the censor's approval or been edited or excised in order to
gain that approval. I turn to the literary archive as well as the limited historical one, not only as a source of factual evidence but also because literature
is well suited to an examination and instantiation of the complexity of black
audience spectatorship during this period.

Black audience members shared many experiences, and this could be
strongly felt inside of cinemas by the time the apartheid system implemented

more methodical limitations on the number and types of films blacks could be shown. Yet audiences are always composed of heterogeneous individuals, each bringing to bear the particularity of his or her geographical and historical experience, these in turn coloring interpretations in various hues.[43] As Hansen puts it, the cinema is "a medium that allows people to organize their experience on the basis of their own context of living, its specific needs, conflicts, and anxieties."[44] In tension, however, with this claim that each individual draws unique interpretations is a belief that "media imperialism" is what actually determines audience responses.[45] Subscribers to this line of thought believe that

> we never really confront a text immediately, in all its freshness as a thing-in-itself. Rather, texts come before us as the always-already-read; we apprehend them through sedimented layers of interpretations, or—if the text is brand new—through the sedimented reading habits and categories developed by those inherited interpretive traditions.[46]

Yet what Fredric Jameson fails to account for in his understanding of how cultural texts function as a mechanism for ideological conscription is how they transform when they travel beyond the orbit of their intended audiences. In such instances, works are consumed in ways acutely different from and even antithetical to the "inherited interpretive traditions" anticipated by their authors. Indeed, cultural *misreadings* occur not out of a failure of the reader or viewer to pick up on the signs that the text interpellates but because what is being read or watched has an ideological message targeting a very different group from the one actually consuming it. What hermeneutics arise when the audience of a film is not the film's intended audience? As Karin Barber asks: "What exactly [does] an African audience gets out of . . . a film in a foreign language, about culturally remote people who perform a series of actions almost invisible to the naked eye on a dim and flickering screen?"[47] What did South African blacks think and feel about Hollywood films intended largely for an English-speaking American audience? Hansen argues that for immigrants entering the United States, these films Americanized them;[48] but what effects did they have on South Africans, some of whom could hardly dream that they would even leave their own Bantustans, let alone come to America? Though films were often edited for overseas audiences,

> as systematic as the effort to conquer foreign markets undoubtedly was, the actual reception of Hollywood films was likely a much more haphazard and

eclectic process depending on a variety of factors. . . . To write the international history of classical American cinema, therefore, is a matter of tracing not just its mechanisms of standardization and hegemony but also the diversity of ways in which this cinema was translated and reconfigured in both local and translocal contexts of reception.[49]

In South African studies, attention to film reception should be equally specific and nuanced, since interpretive practices were often radically unfaithful to films' original aims. The mere act of going to the movies was, as Tsitsi Jaji notes, "not merely an escape from, but a means of coping with, racist apartheid policies." She writes: "By preserving the time and space of the cinema as an imaginative vista that stretched beyond the windows of opportunity which apartheid was rapidly shuttering, black South Africans used cinematic viewing to assert and revel fully in their humanity."[50] Much as Janice Radway understands acts of reading sexist harlequin novels as avenues for women to temporarily elude the sexism regulating their lives outside the books, Jaji understands cinematic consumption as a practice that contravened life under apartheid, regardless of whether the film material was itself liberating. The act of aesthetic consumption is linked, for Jaji, with the fullest expression of humanity, for in the cinema (as in the theater), in conjunction with those around us and those on screen, we are made aware of ourselves as discreet individuals who are also quintessentially linked to others physically and, through the imaginative and projective space, emotionally and psychologically too.

A BRIEF HISTORY OF BLACK FILM AUDIENCES

In her famous essay "Living in the Interregnum," Nadine Gordimer recalled how easy it was, during apartheid, for whites to forget about the existence of blacks altogether. Using an unusual ophthalmic metaphor, she writes:

> The weird ordering of the collective life, in South Africa, has slipped its special contact lens into the eyes of whites; we actually *see* blacks differently, which includes not seeing, *not* noticing their unnatural absence, since there are so many perfectly ordinary venues of daily life—the cinema, for instance— where blacks have never been allowed in, and so one has forgotten that they could be, might be, encountered there.[51]

This altered vision Gordimer identifies enabled whites to avoid what Steve Biko called the "eyesore" of apartheid, an apposite term describing the poverty and suffering caused by the system's blatantly unjust visual organization.[52] Nor did the films whites consumed much expose them to black characters and actors, unless, as Fanon observed in 1952, they appeared on the periphery, as servants or as occasions for cheap, racist derision. Yet Gordimer's observation that blacks were "never allowed in" white cinemas does not account for South Africa's long history of black cinematic viewing practices and is thus itself somewhat of a blind spot in her own reckoning.

As early as 1910, the first "Electric Theatre" for "Coloured People Only" opened in Durban showing scenes outside the mosque in Grey Street (SAHO).[53] While the preeminent historian of early film in South Africa, Thelma Gutsche, notes that the number of movie theaters for nonwhites was relatively small compared to that for whites, black audiences were nonetheless large in number as films were available for viewing outside as well. Film screenings on mining compounds were widespread as part of government-sponsored leisure-time plans.[54] In a 1920 newsletter Ray A. Phillips, the American missionary who supervised the Mines' Compound Cinema Circuit, describes one of his regular visits to the mining compounds. When he arrives,

> a thousand men have already seated themselves on the ground and are waiting for the performance to begin. I quickly arrange my projector while other thousands gather around. "Tulani" I shout, (meaning that I wish the babbling in a dozen different languages to cease). Silence reigns supreme. I explain what the first picture is going to be. Then the whole happy crowd goes off on a trip around the world. They hob-nob with the crowded folks of China or India, see the surf-riders of Honolulu and the reindeer drivers of Lapland, laugh with the immortal Charlie, and applaud the rescue of the small heroine by her faithful dog. At the end of an hour and a half or two hours I leave with the shouts of delight changed to good-by greetings, "Hambakahle, Mfundi-si," (Go in peace, missionary). As I puff away I am followed by a crowd who always extend a cordial invitation to me to come "every evening." A week is too long to wait.[55]

Phillips's account, while grossly paternalistic, does give a sense of the density of film audiences, as well as providing important details about the global scope of the subjects miners were shown in the early traveling bioscope shows.

Because these films were easy to bring into institutionalized settings, "[the mines' screening] program expanded to include leper houses, reformatories, jails, police barracks, hospitals, orphanages, and the like. Films were transported via rail to Natal to be shown in African Reserves and sugar mills."[56] Ntongela Masilela and Bhekizizwe Peterson have written about other early traveling bioscopes, including those run by the writer, translator, and intellectual Sol Plaatjie, who screened films about black American life, including those on "New Negroes" made at Booker T. Washington's Tuskegee Institute. Harriet Gavshon points out that "because of the venues, a large proportion of the audience are children who [are] more vulnerable to the contents of the films."[57] I return to the relation between films and cultural anxiety for both black and white critics in a moment, but here it is sufficient to note how quickly the medium of film proliferated in black life once the technical necessities for transportation and projection became manageable.

Moviegoing practices also operated outside of governmental dictates about spectatorship. Indeed, in the early days of film, blacks were often able to watch movies that had been censored. One early 1917 censorship law, for instance, applied largely to the Cape alone despite much clamoring for a National Censorship Board.[58] In the Transvaal, "there is sometimes only one policeman entrusted with the duty of inspecting films and . . . sometimes the police authorities there judge a film merely on the general report it receives from the Press."[59] Phillips recalls an equally lax manner of applying early film censorship policies:

> Before exhibiting films which have been banned for showing to Africans, the exhibitor is instructed to post a notice: "Natives are Not Admitted to this Performance," and to refuse admission to them. The writer discovered that this provision was ignored. He visited two of the Non-European theatres while they were exhibiting banned films and failed to find such notice posted. The proprietor of the third theatre said: "This censorship is a farce. We don't exclude anybody. The educated Native is a better patron than many Coloured or Poor Whites." It is expecting a good deal of exhibitors that they shall turn customers away who come with money in their hands asking for admission. The writer obtained printed programmes from the four Non-European theatres, advertising the names of feature films scheduled for future showings. No indication was given on the programmes whether shows were to be open to Natives or not. The proprietors of all four theaters displayed little sympathy with the classification of desirable or undesirable by means of the racial

label. "Why shouldn't we admit a well-dressed Native? Isn't he as good as an Indian or a Chinese?" seemed to be the attitude. This attitude was explained by the Manager of the distributing agency: "The position is complicated by the fact that Indians, Chinese, Coloureds and Natives are classed under the one category to all intents and purposes, and this is distinctly unfair when you realize the tremendous gulf between the educated Hindu or Chinese, or even the educated Native, as against the lowest type of Native. This makes the whole question most difficult as far as the audiences in the larger towns in the Union are concerned."[60]

As with all official policies, on the ground, in practice, things never run as smoothly as state historians and policymakers would like the public to think. While blacks were often able to see films the state refused them, it seems whites were also engaged in transgressions against segregationist law, not only because there were profits to be made from widening the circle of possible ticket buyers but also because theater owners were equally attuned to class and educational difference as they were to race thinking. At least in this earlier period, some whites were not as limited in their approach to understanding blacks as the apartheid state came to insist upon.

South Africa's 1931 Entertainments Act was a response to the increasing presence of visual media in everyday life. Establishing a film censorship board meant that the state recognized film to possess considerable ideological content, and this was subsequently confirmed by its use of film as a tool of apartheid propaganda, particularly in its production of "B Scheme" films targeting black audiences.[61] Yet the films black and coloured spectators watched also presented the occasion for the development of alternate, *sometimes* resistant, expressions of individual and group identity. These arose from unusual and unexpected sets of identifications as well as *refusals* to identify, so that the film-viewing experience produced individual and group affective and cognitive interpretive responses that operated inside and outside of state control.

Resistance, of course, is a complex word, and it is not meant here to suggest any organized form of political insurrection. For Jacques Rancière, the social order is challenged simply through workers' engagements with the consumption and production of culture, because these acts disrupt the ordered time of the worker, which might otherwise be devoted to activities like working, sleeping, and eating that merely reproduce capitalist hegemony. "These *gains in time and freedom*," he writes, for entertainment and pleasure, "were not marginal phenomena or diversions in relation to the construction of the workers' movement and its great objectives. *They were the revolution,* both discreet and radical."[62]

For film scholar Lindiwe Dovey, filmic engagement need not be revolutionary in order to disrupt the social order, as spectators' responses that are politically or socially *critical* may be equally necessary in order to challenge the structures of rule. In an essay on filmmaker Ousmane Sembène, she argues that Sembène's "use of cinema [was] to critique, summon reflection, or forewarn," exposing "his belief in the medium's critical potential"; he is "the exemplar and inspiration of an African cinematic mode that concerns itself with critical awareness rather than with revolutionary action."[63] While Dovey contrasts awareness with action, critique can itself be understood as an active form of engagement with and opposition to the world's unequal structures of organization. For in addition to the opposition to apartheid made explicit through the channels of organized groups such as the ANC, the Pan Africanist Congress (PAC), and the South African Communist Party, other forms of critique occurred daily through more subtle practices. Some of these oppositional modes may appear, superficially at least, to have enabled rather than to have refused apartheid's ideological underpinnings. Some practices, for instance, were simultaneously anti-apartheid *and* pro-capitalist. Apartheid and global capitalism, often thought of as complicit partners, could also be in tension with one another since certain consumerist-driven choices (purchases in sartorial or reading materials, for instance) permitted the manipulation and reframing of social consciousness in direct defiance of the apartheid state. Occasionally, in fact, the critique of apartheid is expressed in blatantly pro-capitalist modalities.

Rosalind Morris's work on the popularity of film noir among urban black South Africans, and its sartorial reincarnation in the form of the zoot suit, suggests ways consumerist practices inspired by American film undermined apartheid doctrine. She references Njabulo Ndebele's comments on the derivativeness of black and coloured ways of looking and living to highlight how seemingly benign imitations "concealed the 'growing confidence' of 'sophisticated urban working and petty bourgeois classes.' No doubt, black audiences discerned," writes Morris, "that Hollywood cinema was not addressed to them, and for this reason their purpose was to radicalize the discourse they received through overhearing."[64]

So while donning a zoot suit may signify a conscious desire for inclusion in capitalist modernity, it also allows us to theorize participation in American demotic culture as a form of political, or anti-apartheid, resistance. Like the popular magazine for black readers of this period, *Drum*, which "appeared to function as a political instrument in spite of its tawdry, irresponsible air," with "its commercial guise somewhat bel[ying] its importance as an articulator of the black experience and black aspirations," complicity in the symbolic project of capitalist modernity may also have allowed for the emergence of resistant possibilities in black cultural life.[65] Everyday negotiations with various forms of popular culture provided strategies and methods for existence as an oppressed apartheid subject that could stand outside the ideological conventions that the state sought to calcify.

ANXIETIES OF INFLUENCE: THE STRUGGLE OVER CINEMA

In 1952, a group of black and white schoolboys met in Johannesburg to debate whether "the coming of the bioscope has been a major disaster to modern culture." Pupils from St. Peter's Non-European Secondary School and St. John's European Private School engaged in a series of interracial dialogues that did not, at least on this occasion, adhere to apartheid's segregationist education policy. Organized by Trevor Huddleston, the well-known anti-apartheid activist, the debate took place in the library of St. Peter's and was featured in an article in *Drum*'s June 1952 issue as part of its regular "Teachers' Talk" column.

The article's layout assumes the divided format of a debate, simultaneously replicating on the page the spatio-racial partitioning of apartheid. A photo on one side of the text features a white speaker, Mr. Buchanan, and to its right is a photograph of Mr. Mofokeng, a black speaker. Other presenters are quoted at length throughout the article that begins by summarizing the debate:

> Opening for St. John's, Mr. Foot accused the bioscope of having reduced reading and degenerated our minds. In reply, Mr. Cingo said "You pay 2s. to be educated in half an hour" by seeing films of masterpieces like "Hamlet." The first half-hour only got as far as "Mickey Mouse," Mr Bull retorted.[66]

At the cinema, Mr. Buchanan argued, in English,

> We only watch the quick changes of scene without time to digest seeing them. As the chances of seeing a good film were few, it is not true that every visit to

the bioscope was of educational value. Unlike what his opponents said, films like "Hamlet" were of no value, as many parts were cut out, and the film only Olivier's interpretation—which might not be ours.[67]

Here Buchanan alerts us to South Africa's busy censorship apparatus, which cut scenes, even from films one might imagine less susceptible to the censor's splicing tool. But in his pained observation that "Olivier's interpretation . . . might not be ours," Buchanan also displays an anxiety about interpretative instability that leads him to argue against film altogether. Of course, he mistakenly assumes here that this problem of interpretation could somehow be avoided in readings of the play. For Buchanan, "the intellect can only be developed by thinking," a process he assumes anathema to the act of *looking* involved in film consumption. The distinction between reading books and watching films is highlighted, then, through a twofold anxiety that contrasts scopic consumption with intellectual rumination and bristles at film's "infidelity" to canonical texts like *Hamlet*.

On the other side of the debate, Mr. Mofokeng insisted:

> "It is not true that films reduce the reading of filmed books." . . . [Mofokeng] claims that many boys read *Cry [the Beloved Country]* only after seeing the film. *The bioscope was our greatest art*, needing months of skillful preparation and the making of correct costumes. Only after seeing a film on soil erosion had people taken steps to prevent it, for the methods were clearly shown without one having to read difficult books.[68]

Mofokeng thus sees filmic adaptations less as degraded representations of classic works than as spurs that encourage engagement with "great works." He also recognizes, however, the central role film plays in the lives of the busy or illiterate, who have neither the time nor the skillset to "read difficult books." Film, for Mofokeng, has different uses for different audiences under apartheid, some of which are aesthetic and intellectual and others of which, as his example of the film on soil erosion highlights, are significantly more instrumental.

After the debate was over, everyone cast a ballot, and "about 80 per cent of the house voted in favor of the bioscope."[69] The vote confirmed film's popularity, proving that people across the racial divide recognized it to be as capable of fulfilling pedagogic aims as written texts. The deliberations that took place highlight the stakes for black and white filmgoers in Johannesburg in the middle of the century and attest to the seriousness with which cinema was treated by educators and students alike. But the debate also highlights the palpable anxieties brought about through the mass dissemination of film. As Phillips remarked, "If Plato was right in saying that he who makes a nation's songs exerts a greater influence than he who makes a nation's laws, then it will certainly not be far wrong to say that he who controls a people's films exerts a greater influence for good or ill, than he who makes the country's laws."[70] Indeed, film was frequently held accountable for producing undesirable behaviors, as when, for example, political unrest on the Rand in 1949 and 1950 was attributed, in part, to "the evil effects of 'bioscope films.'"[71]

Phillips, though a proponent of films' possibilities for moral uplift, also worried about the consequences of black practices of identification with white characters, suggesting that some films blacks watched "did not convey an elevating or ennobling picture of western civilized life to the spectators, many of whom have scant experience of the ordinary home life of the European."[72] In a section headed "*The Recognition of a Different Purpose in Exhibiting Films to Africans from that in Showing to Whites*," Phillips writes: "While programmes for the African must have entertainment value, it must be recognized that the man viewing the films is advancing from a primitive environment. *He has much more to learn of the world about him and his fellow human beings than has the White man.*"[73] Phillips's assumptions ignore how blacks' understanding of their "fellow human beings" and "the world" were often more adept than whites', because subjection, as I have been arguing, produces this epistemological difference. The dissolute depictions of white life that, for Phillips, does not show "[the African] enough of the finer side of the life of the White man to enable him to form a true estimate of his Western civilization and standard of morals and conduct" may have been more accurate than Phillips was willing to admit. We witness here that oft-repeated contradiction between white discourses evincing a certainty about their own intrinsic moral probity, and the evidence—filmic, here—of white irresponsibility and ethical failure.

Interestingly, while Phillips believed film dangerous enough to unduly affect black audiences, he also described it, in the newsletters he wrote back to his friends and colleagues in the United States, as a medium with a salvific function, capable of protecting black South Africans from the more insidious evils of drink and sodomy. He describes a mining compound in Johannesburg as "a regular Clearing House of Evil, where boys from one section of the country exchange evil for evil around the blazing coal fires at night and in the quiet of their rooms. The white man provides the work, and the Devil provides the recreation for these fellows."[74] For Phillips, the films he brought into the mining compounds provided a healthy distraction from these more "fiendish" pastimes.

This ambiguity in his estimation of film's influence on South African miners (in his accounts they are alternately sources of good or evil) reminds us again of all films' semantic instability. But whites were not alone in feeling anxious about the influence of Hollywood films on black African viewers, and several important debates took place among filmmakers across the continent aiming to assess American films' powers of persuasion. In 1974, for instance, Malian filmmaker Alkaly Kaba joined his voice to a growing opposition to Western "cultural imperialism" in Africa, lamenting that "our peoples have been more uprooted by the Western cinema than by the 'white school.'"[75] Given that a few years earlier Ngũgĩ wa Thiong'o famously equated imperial education with military domination, Kaba's accusation accords a relatively unprecedented degree of influence to these imported cultural forms. For Ghanaian independence leader Kwame Nkrumah, American films were akin to the billy clubs and guns of policemen and the army, as they also were liable to reproduce colonial structures of rule.

> Commercial cinema, he argued, functions as a weapon of the West to pacify Africa's colonized populations. "Even the cinema stories of Hollywood are loaded. One has only to listen to the cheers of an African audience as Hollywood's heroes slaughter the red Indians or Asiatics to understand the effectiveness of this weapon. For, in the developing continents, where the colonialist heritage has left a majority of illiterates, even the smallest child gets the message contained in the blood and thunder stories emanating from California."[76]

That the masses were somehow more "susceptible" than themselves to the messages of Hollywood film was a feeling shared by the Third World filmmakers who gathered in 1973 to produce "Resolutions of the Third World Film-makers Meeting." Among these resolutions is the following statement:

> Imperialist economic, political and social domination, in order to subsist and to reinforce itself, takes root in an ideological system articulated through various channels and *mainly through cinema* which is in a position to influence the majority of the popular masses because its essential importance is at one

and the same time artistic, esthetic, economic, and sociological, affecting to a major degree the training of the mind.[77]

Like many white opponents of the bioscope, these filmmakers believed that through their own interventions they could directly control audiences' ideological responses. Like Phillips, they saw the purpose of film in the Third World entirely through the lens of possible political instrumentalism, though, of course, seeking different outcomes.[78] Divesting cinema of the historical and geographical contingencies of its reception, Third World filmmakers largely understood ideology to inhere in the materiality of the form and not in any practices of reception, though on occasion they admit that "films [are] a social act within a historical reality."[79] Overall, for these filmmakers, as for Nkrumah, the (il)literate masses were deemed capable only of detrimental identifications that solidify colonial rule, while other forms of identification were overlooked. While these black thinkers and filmmakers working to liberate African subjects lacked the racism of whites who tended to "attribute to black South Africans an especially acute aptitude for and tendency toward mimesis," they nonetheless still believed colonized subjects to be most susceptible to film propaganda.[80] There is an irony in the echoing condescension of these elite intellectuals whose social positions as educated and literate blacks led them to decry their compatriots' "addiction" to Hollywood films as evidence that average spectators cannot decipher for themselves the complexity of films' messages and their ideological cues. They were unable to recognize what Jacques Rancière, in his critique of the Left, repeatedly calls the "equality of intelligences," characteristic of all cultural, gendered, national, ethnic, racial, and economic groups.[81]

Despite their varied and often contrary political vantage points, all these concerned cultural critics—Phillips, the anti-bioscope crusaders at the school debate in Johannesburg, Nkrumah, and the Third Cinema filmmakers— assume that a film's ideological message is both singular and fixed. Each fails to recognize that meaning making occurs in the negotiation between filmic content and audience members' reception practices and contexts of consumption. Revolutionary or oppositional ideologies might inhere in spectatorship practices even when films convey anti-revolutionary, static, or conservative agendas. And conversely, revolutionary aims can belie other oppressions.[82] South African writer H. I. E. Dhlomo rebuts the notion that there is a direct causal relationship between bad behavior and film-viewing practices. He writes: "A healthy mind in a healthy body in a healthy home in a healthy environment can see hundreds of gangster films and think of them as exciting or dull entertainment, without once thinking of emulating them. It is the social conditions that produce the criminal."[83] Films certainly influence spectators, then, but not as direct transmitters of pure ideological meaning embedded in the films themselves, but at the intersection of the material, social, and historical positions of the spectators; the material and social contexts of the screenings; and through engagement with the images, stories, plots, and characters of the film too.

How might we then quantify these more slippery forms of influence? And how, particularly, might our understanding of reception practices in the Global South shift through a consideration of the affective, emotional, and psychological effects of cultural practices? Until now, influence has largely been understood via a distinct preoccupation with its problematic or worrisome forms, with critics placing undue emphasis on how cultural artifacts *harm* audiences. While spectatorship practices for black South Africans certainly came about through moralizing impulses, both in the form of Plaatjie's presentation of American "New Negroes" as Christian exemplars and in Phillips's proselytizing missionary films, "it was the specular pleasure afforded by narrative film that drew audiences," and it is therefore to the felt, emotive, or affective spheres that we might find the best ways to reorient our understanding of influence.[84]

POPULAR FILM AND "THE NEW SENSORIUM"

Film contributes to the ethical consciousness of viewers, though in ways noticeably different from other media. While textual forms might be read unpredictably—flipped through, lingered over, skimmed, and dog-eared—film is less directly malleable, and as viewers in movie theaters we watch the sequence of images as we are directed to do so. Yet film consumption practices need not be thought of as proceeding only in a strictly linear fashion. For Walter Benjamin and Siegfried Kracauer, "cinema . . . achiev[ed] through the strategies of montage and suture what fiction accomplished with the gesture of the 'meanwhile.'"[85] That film can represent time and experience nonlinearly is, of course, one of the reasons the medium has become so irreparably linked to those breaks in social structure constitutive of modernity and a modernist aesthetics.

Crucially, in South Africa as elsewhere, film played a significant role as the purveyor of innovation, producing and then relying upon new forms of affective and sensory response. As Hansen writes, "In a very basic sense, *even the most ordinary commercial films* were involved in producing a new sensory culture."[86] Mass-marketed films produced "new modes of organizing vision and sensory perception, a new relationship with 'things,' different forms of mimetic experience and expression, of affectivity, temporality, and reflexivity, a changing fabric of everyday life, sociability, and leisure."[87] These emerging forms of cognition in turn produced new forms of subjectivity and are a defining component of what it means to be a modern subject and, importantly, one made more conscious of one's role in political transformation. The restructuring of subjectivity that film enacts, Hansen argues, suggested to audiences the possibility of restructuring social formations. She writes, "It was not just *what* these films showed, what they brought into optical consciousness, as it were, but the way they opened up hitherto unperceived modes of sensory perception and experience, *their ability to suggest a different organization of the daily world*."[88]

In South Africa, Jacob Dlamini also emphasizes modernity's role in the production of new affective experiences for South African blacks—what he calls a "new sensorium." Calling for the reassessment of the history of black South African modernity along more "sensuous" lines, Dlamini demands that scholars move away from dominant quantitative historical accounts of black apartheid experience. He explains:

> The urban experience worked itself in the senses. It was, to put it another way, felt—a felt experience. *It is not often that writers and thinkers take seriously the descriptions that Africans gave of their feelings*, their sense of what it meant to be urban. More common is to treat Africans as hapless victims of a mechanical process of proletarianisation. I do not dispute the profound changes that took place in southern Africa as more and more Africans entered the market economy. However, I question historical accounts of this process that treat it only and simplistically as a materialist development. *The point is urbanization had a sensuous as well as a material dimension to it.* It was as much about material conditions as it was about how people felt it and, dare we say, felt about it.[89]

Dlamini insists we work to understand the vital role aesthetic consumption played in the restructuring of affective life and to consider, for instance, how unexpected practices might have brought about coextensive shifts in political imaginaries and agency. Arjun Appadurai's influential scholarly work on modernity tellingly opens with the author recalling that his earliest experiences of modernity were aesthetic encounters with magazines and movies. "The experience of modernity was notably synaesthetic and largely pretheoretical," he writes. "I saw and smelled modernity reading *Life* and American college catalogs at the United States Information Service library, seeing B-grade films (and some A-grade ones) from Hollywood at the Eros theater."[90] Appadurai, Dlamini, and Hansen enjoin us to consider the ways in which knowledge of modernity happened at the bodily level before becoming explicitly rationalized. As Appadurai explains, the first subjective experiences of modernity were "pretheoretical," and for Hansen, these new ways of perceiving, feeling, and being could produce new forms of response that were politically productive and even liberating. "We have to understand," she writes,

> the material, sensory conditions under which American mass culture, including Hollywood, was received and could have functioned as a powerful matrix for modernity's liberatory impulses—its moments of abundance, play, and radical possibility, its glimpses of collectivity and gender equality.[91]

Morris concurs with Hansen, contending that, in South Africa, film created visions of the world that contrasted with apartheid's hierarchies of racial distinction. The formal rupture of modernism

> enter[ed] into black vernacular space . . . most productively in and through cinema, which not only provided the medium for apprehending and reflecting upon the material transformations accompanying industrialization and urbanization, but also *for resignifying the corporeal world* on which basis apartheid had been elaborated and naturalized.[92]

Indeed, it is America's foreignness vis-à-vis South Africa that permitted for alternative readings and responses: "Cinematically concretized objects," Hansen writes, "function differently in different films and film traditions, and are bound to have different meanings and affective valences in different contexts of reception."[93] This "aesthetics of contingency" explains how films, set loose from their original geographic moorings, produced widely divergent interpretive, affective, and material responses. It is worth quoting Hansen at length here:

If classical Hollywood cinema succeeded as an international modernist idiom
on a mass basis, it did so not because of its presumably universal narrative
form but because it meant different things to different people and publics,
both at home and abroad. . . . We must not forget that these films, along with
other mass-cultural exports, were consumed in locally quite specific, and un-
equally developed, contexts and conditions of *reception*; that they not only
had a leveling impact on indigenous cultures but also challenged prevailing
social and sexual arrangements and advanced new possibilities of social identity and cultural styles.[94]

For Hansen, these cross-cultural encounters are generative because they produce new identities and "styles." Following Kracauer, she notes that the cinema encourages identification with a range of people and objects across space
and time. Cinema's "mobilization" of the gaze, which "*transcends physical
laws as well as distinctions between subject and object, human and nonhuman
nature, promises nothing less than the mobilization of the self, the transformation of seemingly fixed positions of social identity*."[95] Jacqueline Stewart sees
such transformed identification practices as modes of "black reconstruction":
"This range of spectatorial contexts and potential responses suggests how
Black spectatorship is better characterized as a set of numerous complicit and
resistant possibilities for Black agency and activity, and *for the reconstruction
of the negated Black viewing subject on psychic, social, and public levels.*"[96]

Hansen and Stewart thus alert us to an individual's potential to deploy
scopic engagements to transcend socially determined identities and, thus,
also to film's potential for extra-theatrical social transformation. The colli-
sions with alterity that occur in the cinema—formally, thematically, socially,
and materially—are equally relevant for their ethical effects. While Hansen's
interest is largely in the liberatory potential film provides for the individual
subject, as an avenue for transcending the particularities of her confining
social milieu, the "polymorphous projection" that occurs in movie theaters
is also a way of opening the viewer to affectively and cognitively feel what it
is to be someone or something else, not only as an antidote to her own situation but as a gesture toward acknowledging the primacy of alterity in the
experience of both the individual and the social self.[97] Film critics who are
interested in race studies note the importance of these acts of identification.
With language directly echoing Kracauer's, James Snead points out that "it is
not true that we identify only with those in a film whose race or sex we share.
Rather, the filmic space is subversive in allowing an almost polymorphically

perverse oscillation between possible roles, creating a radically broadened freedom of identification."[98] Additionally,

> Michelle Wallace suggests that African American spectatorship can be heterogeneous and complex, even in relation to "mainstream" products. Recalling her own childhood admiration of white movie stars, Wallace suggests that Black fandom "may have been about problematizing and expanding one's racial identity instead of abandoning it. It seems crucial here to view spectatorship not only as potentially bisexual but also multiracial and multiethnic."[99]

Such identifications, as Du Bois famously observed, do not occur equally across racial, economic, gender, or sexual difference. They are contingent: dependent on sociocultural context and more likely to occur in the disempowered and dispossessed members of a society than in its beneficiaries. For after all, while blacks were often exposed to films with all-white casts, the reverse was seldom if ever true, and continues to be rare.

The forms of identification elicited do not thus always need to be understood as disadvantageous, despite the endless expressions of anxieties of influence from critics, scholars, politicians, journalists, and film buffs alike. In an echo of Hegel's philosophy of recognition, Peter Davis notes how,

> in a peculiar sense, in the rough scrimmage of cultural confrontation, subject people have a distinct advantage over their oppressors—they have a measure of access to the dominant culture that is denied in reverse. That is to say, while a Zulu may have to learn English in order to survive economically, his employer has no incentive to learn Zulu. So the master, in his conviction of racial superiority, remains culturally limited, even if the limitation is voluntary. By having to deal with European culture in all its aspects on a daily basis, the African has a sophistication automatically denied to whites, an extra dimension.[100]

This "extra dimension" or "sophistication" is of an ethical nature, even if it emerges out of necessity in the space of subjection. The viewer more readily able to identify with others, both "subject and object, human and nonhuman," learns the ethical practice of responding to and being responsible for alterity. Karin Barber suggests we might think of the personal, individual experiences of intimacy with otherness that occur in the movie theater as experiences that move from the self outward to others beyond the self. She writes: "Since

personal morality is a more immediate concern to most people than political morality, it is through the personal that the political is understood."[101]
"In popular arts political discourse is often indirect, conducted through the
medium of a personal moral discourse, and . . . this may not be a deliberate
concealment . . . so much as a way of thinking about politics."[102] As we saw
earlier, affective-ethical experiences can serve an important substitute function in the place of political ineffectualness, where a subject population is all
but barred from political engagement.

    While South Africa's cultural landscape was dominated by discourses that
conceived of films as having far-reaching and largely negative influences on
black South African audiences, identification practices, as ethical theorists
continue to intone, elicit a process akin to transubstantiation in which the self
becomes, at least temporarily, other to itself, in its reaching out toward the
interiority and subject position of one quite unlike the self. When Northern
Rhodesian councilman Harrison Chungu worried that "'these [Jack] films
are leaving a very bad impression on the children and it is easy for them to
imitate' . . . argu[ing] further that 'the showing of "Jacks" and people fighting
should entirely go off because even for the adults *they are infectious*; they
affect their minds,'" he inadvertently underscores the way that identification
brings into the self foreign bodies that carry with them a very palpable threat
of danger.[103] While the next chapter leaves behind the affect of fear and danger epitomized here in the councilman's concern about cowboy movies, it
remains with the subgenre of the Western. From its popularity in the cinema
to its adaptation into other media forms, the cowboy and Western genre, as
it reappeared in the 1960s and 1970s in the form of the photocomic or pho-
tonovela, allows for a situated examination of the ethical stakes of interracial
reading practices.

CHAPTER 3

Race, Reading, and the Photocomic

In 1976, residents of Soweto burned down a newsstand because it was selling the propagandist comic *Mighty Man*, the eponymous hero of which was a black caped crusader modeled on the Marvel superheroes from U.S. comics.[1] In it, Mighty Man "leaps across rooftops in a single bound, dodges bullets with lightning speed and smashes one pot-smoking gang of bad guys after another."[2] Bill Mantlo, a commentator in *Comics Journal*, explains that the comic attempts to persuade its black readers to conform to apartheid's ideology: "*Mighty Man*," he writes, "preaches against the owning of firearms—to blacks. He propounds a message of nonviolence—to blacks. He sermonizes subservience to the white man and the police—to blacks."[3] The comic even extols apartheid police: "Bless that fearless crimefighter called *Mighty Man!* And bless all those *gallant police officers* who protect us from the evil forces that would *destroy* us all!"[4] The comic understandably outraged its targeted black readers since its message propounded subservience to whites and policemen. Yet their incendiary act did more than just destroy the comics.[5] The fire, set by black readers who took the situation into their own hands, links reading to the development and expression of political agency. Though only a minor precursor to the tragic events of the Soweto uprising, this act of dissension highlights how textual production and consumption are frequently implicated in everyday material relations. This chapter looks at another popular genre that many blacks read during apartheid—the photocomic—to consider particularly the roles that readings in mass culture played in the formation of black ethical consciousness.

Since photocomics are unfamiliar to most contemporary readers and no longer circulate except among collectors of apartheid-era memorabilia, this chapter introduces them before turning to readers' responses to, and memories of, photocomics. Focusing particularly on Western, or "cowboy" photocomics, the chapter explores how the apparent visual apartheid of South African photocomics was circumvented via ethical reading practices. These ways of reading destabilized the supremacist fantasies that photocomics' formal organization seemed to propagate. Thus the photocomic represents an iteration of popular culture in which the productive ambiguity occasioned through reading that is often deemed a work's *literary* quality, emerges through engagements with genres entirely overlooked by ethical criticism.[6] This chapter continues, therefore, to expand theories of literature and ethics to include mass-produced and popular genres.

THE PHOTOCOMIC[7] WAS a popular form of mass entertainment in the mid-twentieth century, consumed widely in Europe, Latin America, and Africa.[8] Yet despite its international reach, this now almost defunct genre has received scant critical notice within literary and cultural studies—an omission that has been attributed to the photocomic's status as the "most degraded form of mass 'literature.'"[9] In their survey of the black press in South Africa prior to 1979, Les Switzer and Donna Switzer characteristically exclude "the large number of photo-novella or photo-story magazines in comic-book format for blacks that have appeared in the past 25 years or so. Although these publications have undoubtedly filled a need," they continue, "*their value as potential source material for researchers remains questionable* and, in any event, it would take another book to describe the publications in this field."[10] Singular exceptions to this scholarly lacuna exist, such as Jan Baetens and Ana González's *Le Roman Photo*, yet the analyses in their collection are largely Eurocentric and rarely engage with the considerable theoretical contributions of postcolonial studies. When photocomics are studied in colonial and postcolonial contexts, critics attend mostly to their recent reincarnation as pedagogic tools[11] and do not consider them as aesthetic forms interpellating their own specific reading practices.[12]

This chapter locates the photocomic in the historical context of apartheid South Africa and within the theoretical framework of postcolonial studies. While certain universal characteristics of the photocomic may explain its global success, the South African examples took particular forms, shaped as they were by the political, cultural, and racial stipulations of a censorship board with quite different aims from those of similar regulatory bodies elsewhere.[13] Of course, censorship extended far beyond institutional and administrative boundaries; under apartheid, white supremacist ideology inevitably shaped cultural production through consent as well as coercion.

MIRRORING TRENDS IN popular genre fiction, photocomics tend to follow narrative conventions of romances, mysteries, Westerns, and crime thrillers popularized in pulp fiction and film. Familiar characters and plot conventions from these were modulated (usually by anonymous authors) to fit the photocomic form, which consisted of sequences of photos overlaid with text (fig. 2).

Much like comic books, they were often serialized, and many of the popular titles in South Africa, such as *Great, Kid Colt, Tessa, Dr. Conrad Brand,* and *Grensvegter,* ran for upward of twenty years.[14] An especially popular photocomic, *See: Romantic Adventures in Photos,* ran for over thirty years between 1963 and 1995.

Though studies of photocomics have largely overlooked the African continent, we can assume from their long publication history as well as the abundant references to them in published and online memoirs and in novels that theirs was an extensive and multiracial readership.[15] Precisely quantifying the numbers of readers is difficult as photocomics circulated mainly in a secondary economy of informal distribution through trading, swapping, and lending. We do know, however, that in Spain, for instance,

> following analysts' estimates from that time, and keeping in mind that photonovels were swapped, left in public places, hair salons and so on, and that there was also an important lending market, this kind of publication had more than five million readers every fifteen days, more than a third of the country's female population.[16]

Such analyses are hard to locate in the South African context. Indeed, with such undervalued,[17] disposable forms of mass entertainment, it is impossible to establish a trustworthy account of how many people read the photocomics in South Africa, though we may assume their success in the marketplace only hints at the level of readership they actually acquired. Zakes Mda's novel, *The Madonna of Excelsior,* describes these magazines' appeal to a range of readers. The narrator writes of the local Greek café owner who

> introduced to our town *Kyk,* a picture-story magazine whose pictures took the citizens of Excelsior to great flights of fanciful romance. And *See,* which was the English version of *Kyk.* He also introduced *Mark Condor,* a picture-story magazine of adventure, spies and crime-busters. Issues of this used to circulate among our boys, who would hide them in their exercise books and read them in class. Then there was *Scope,* a magazine whose pages were full

Fig. 2. A page from "The Key to Murder" story in *Flash* (1965). Image courtesy of Special Collections, MSU Libraries, Michigan State University, East Lansing, MI.

of white women with stars on their tits. If the Afrikaner women of Excelsior caught a black man reading *Scope*, they would beat him to pieces. Black men had no business ogling topless white women. But the brave men of Mahlatswetsa Location had no qualms about risking broken limbs by smuggling the magazine under their shirts. To this day, many of us believe that white women have black stars on their breasts instead of nipples.[18]

Mda's narrator provides a snapshot of the kind of interracial demographic reach these books had. But he also conveys the fervency of the desire they enabled—to go on "great flights of fanciful romance"—often directly contravening the injunctions of authority figures (embodied here by teachers and Afrikaner women) who attempted to limit black readership. Plentiful references to the "bookies" can also be found online, where readers of the photocomics reminisce at length about these childhood staples. In a 2009 radio report, one former reader asks:

Who does not remember the row of "bookies" hanging from a string at your corner café shop or sneaking a copy and reading it surreptitiously under the bed—because "there were people kissing in it, for heaven's sake!" If you were ever caught with these "haraam (forbidden) bookies" as a youngster, no way would you be spared a hiding, because naturally you would have been "ougat" (precocious).[19]

In lieu of any systematic or quantifiable evidence about the readership of these photocomics, this chapter assembles an alternate archive out of evidence found, at times serendipitously, in novels, memoirs, and online forums to put together a sense of who read these photocomics, in what contexts, and what reactions they produced. For instance, in James Matthews's novel *The Party Is Over*, set during apartheid, the main character bemoans the fact that his wife is addicted to photocomics. He "had tried to get her interested in the books from the library."

At first she had dutifully read them all, but she had soon given up. Faulkner was too heavy to absorb. Picture love-stories and the *Golden City Post* with its weekly close-ups of rapes and robberies, were easier to assimilate.

She showed the same lack of interest in his writing. She was bored when he spoke of his ambition. A writer with their background was a foreign idea to her. The more his writing drove him into moods, ranging from elation to despair, the further she retreated behind the covers of her picture magazines.[20]

For her, photocomics enable a retreat from domesticity, like Janice Radway's readers of romance novels. Additionally, however, they provide her a universe of fantasy to counteract the "despair" she wishes to avoid in her husband, a despair he feels because apartheid made it nearly impossible for someone like him, despite literary talent and aspiration, to succeed as a writer.

ORIGINS AND AESTHETICS OF THE PHOTOCOMIC

The photocomic is generally thought to have emerged in postwar Italy, but its beginning is difficult to pinpoint.[21] Sylvette Giet argues that it emerged via the "fumetti" (Italian cartoons) or "romans dessinés" (cartoon novels), which were already mixed genres, combining literature, theater, and film.[22] Benoît Peeters situates the photocomic within a larger history of sequential photography and cinema stretching all the way back to the early works of Edward Muybridge and Etienne-Jules Maray.[23] Roland Barthes enigmatically locates the genre's birth "in the lower depths of high culture."[24] Other critics suggest that the primary precursor to the photocomic was the comic, with its obvious combination of images and text. Indeed, the term *photocomic* is itself unstable since it attempts to splice two very separate genres—the photograph and the comic—into one unified cultural product.[25]

For Peeters the dearth of critical responses to the photocomic is due, precisely, to this generic instability: "Its deadlock stems from the fact that it has never existed as a genre in of itself, but simply as a sub-product, derived from another medium. . . . In this sense, the photoroman would have no history. It would be immediately associated with borrowing, adaptation, copying."[26] Scholars have compared the photocomic to the telenovela, to soap operas, to cinema, to photo-essays, to the "Nouveau roman," even to the dream[27]— indeed, few know how to discuss the genre without resorting to a comparison. Perhaps the predominance of comparative analyses has contributed most to the photocomic's belittlement. Critical focus on its generic instability contributes to its denigration and obsolescence rather than rehabilitating it as a worthy object of study.

Yet its generic inscrutability is hard to avoid, and the processes of photocomic production further contribute to this.[28] South African photocomic producers followed European examples both by revamping Italian ones for South African consumption—by translating and reprinting them—and by producing their own series of photocomics.

Dianne, a white actress in several popular serial photocomics published by South Africa's Republican Press—the firm largely responsible for producing and distributing the popular titles of the period—describes the relatively simple process of shooting a photocomic:

> On the whole, it only took a morning to shoot the entire book. We used to get there by 08h30 and were finished between 12h00 and 14h00 depending on your part in the book. Dennis Griffiths was the co-ordinator and he would phone and tell us (for example) to bring 3 day outfits, 1 evening outfit and a bikini. Obviously in the "period" books like "Ruiter in Swart" or "Kid Colt" we would wear the outfits from that era in which case we had to take off our watches and were not allowed to wear nail polish.
>
> We used to shoot all the scenes in location: all the scenes in the doctor's office, then all the scenes in the restaurant etc. A note was made of what outfit was worn so that there was continuity and we used to have to change clothes countless times during the shooting of a book. All of us were quite adept at changing in the back of the Combi! Even then, it was a good laugh to go through the books when they were published and see all the mistakes that were made![29]

In addition to being cheap to make—a car functioned adequately as a changing room—photocomics were sold alongside other cheap magazines and were thus associated with other denigrated genres such as pornography.[30] In 1963, under the Publications and Entertainments Act in South Africa, "the import of all publications costing less than 50¢ was prohibited, in a move claimed by the authorities to be targeted against pornography."[31] This subsumption of the cheaply produced and cheaply acquired photocomic under the umbrella of the pornographic (the average price in 1971 was around twenty cents) could only have augmented its position as a devalued, "trashy" genre. Yet the prohibition of photocomic imports also strengthened the domestic industry.

Previously, the production process was highly transnational. Take a Latin American example:

> The stills for *Corín Tellado* were shot in Spain. It was published in Miami, and sold throughout Spanish-speaking North and South America. The central distributor in the Americas was headquartered in Miami. In mid-1975, the company decided to shift filming away from Spain and instead produce the stories in Mexico where they were cheaper and sold better. The negatives were sent to American magazine distributors in Miami, where they were printed.

North and Central America and the Andean countries were the areas of distribution.[32]

This patchwork production process helped confirm the photocomic's status as popular culture's banished Frankensteinian monster. Implicated within an increasingly common global mode of post-Fordist capitalist production, the photocomic was made up of parts brought together from around the world that were then combined to produce a semblance of formal unity. In addition to this bricolage of a production process,

> the romantic photoroman's cheapness (in both price and presentation), that it was not sold in reputable bookstores, and also the protocols by which it was read collectively, all apparently contributed to the traditional photoroman's reduction to nothing more than a degraded object, less read than consumed.[33]

The production process certainly mirrors the genre's contradictory aesthetic properties. Photocomics' reliance on photographs seems to emphasize realism and mimesis, differentiating their thematic concerns from comics obsessed with outer space, the supernatural, and the superhuman. Altarriba suggests that in the "photoroman" "everything is done to make readers believe that life is a photoroman."[34] But it is precisely this semblance of realism that best facilitates the articulation of ideological fantasy while seeming to portray reality as it is. In their very function as carriers of positivist images—the photo that "never lies"—photocomics mask a complex subterranean reality of fantasy and social control.

On the surface, the racial segregation of the South African photocomics— those for whites only featured white actors, and those targeting blacks only starred blacks—reflects the fantasy of apartheid's "apart-hood." However, these photocomics, unwittingly or not, employ polyvocal, extra-literary discourses even when they attempt, particularly in their reliance on hyper-stylized genres, to reify narrative monolingualism. Indeed, these works persistently remind us how difficult it was for apartheid to erase the mixture that was not only a part of everyday life in South Africa but even a part of Afrikaner heritage—and all forms of whiteness—itself.[35]

What follows is an attempt to contextualize the photocomic's commodity status within the larger social dictates of apartheid culture. Thereafter, I turn to the content of photocomics and, in particular, to the popular Western photocomic. Other popular forms (depicting the border wars of *Grensvegter* or *Kaptein Duiwel*; the black detectives in *Flash* and *Drum*; romances in *True Love* and *Sister Louise*; the jungle stories in *Takoeza* and *Great*; and the sexualized escapades of provocative *Tessa*) deserve individual attention—indeed, the photocomic genre as a whole requires a much longer treatment. While the Western has its own racial and historical contexts, this foray into its specifics also sheds light on the other photocomics and, in particular, on the relation between readings in popular culture and the emergence of ethical being.

READING PHOTOCOMICS IN SOUTH AFRICA

To be interested in reading practices in the Global South often means to look beyond the strict confines of the literary to understand how it is that other forms of textual production are used in the inscription and devolution of ideology, hegemony, subjectivity, and sociality.[36] As work in cultural studies shows, attention to popular culture reveals alternative insights about the structural formations of the society in question to those garnered from works of "high culture," such as novels and paintings. A few artists interested in crossing the boundaries between popular and "high" art have incorporated the photocomic in their work, yet these expropriations did not have the popularity of the photocomics under consideration here.[37] For scholars interested in the intersection between reading and the development of ideologically suffused subjectivities in colonial and postcolonial places, the photocomic provides rich material.

Lin Sampson recalls that in South Africa photocomics "were commonly known as books, so someone saying he or she loved books might well have been referring to a literary knowledge consisting of every edition of *Sister Louise*."[38] For many readers these photocomics were *the* books people read. Nonetheless, the photocomic is maligned, I suspect, because of its popularity—to invoke Benjamin's famous essay on art and mechanical reproduction, the photocomic has neither author nor "aura." This has led some critics to mistakenly assume that it merely reflects hegemonic capitalist ideology and is thus unworthy of any examination that might assign it more substance.[39] Even if it is true that in contrast to "protest literature" the form promises no overt political agency or engagement, it is, at least in terms of its consumption, one of the most "democratic" of genres.[40] Studying it may reveal more than studying novels can about the role culture played in the production, for most people living under apartheid, of everyday ethical life.

Photocomics certainly traveled more freely than humans across the racial divides cemented and policed by the apartheid state. The covert tales they tell about race in their plots, their aesthetics, and the networks of consumption they precipitated forged interracial relations (at least at the imaginative level), even while their segregated format seemed to foreclose this. Indeed, direct engagements with South African race relations were absent from most forms of popular fiction. One reader explains:

> If you were a person of colour, like most other reading material of the time, the photo stories had very little to represent you. There was hardly ever any person of colour included in these stories. If one had to be depicted, than [sic] a white person was painted black and basta![41]

This minstrelsy, as I explore, although superficially a way to maintain racial separation, actually collapsed the differences between black and white as the actors' bodies became symbolic sites of racial ambiguity.

Another reader, T. Job Mzamo, learned English and perfected his Afrikaans by reading the photocomics: "I started reading and writing from an early age," he explains,

> before I even started attending school. I was fascinated with letters and numbers. In the 60s we used to read comics like *True Africa* where we read about Samson the Lionheart, Chunky Charlie and Battler Ben; that's when I started learning English. My Afrikaans was also perfected through reading comics such as *Takoeza, Die Ruiter in Swart, Kyk* and others.[42]

People thus frequently read photocomics not directly targeting them: readership repeatedly crossed racial lines, despite the state's intention to have readers "imagine communities" of fellow readers as segregated as the photocomics themselves. This was also facilitated by the format of the stories since, unlike other "books," photocomics do not require a high degree of literacy. Socioeconomic circumstances also contributed to photocomics' success among black and coloured children. One reader recalls:

> It was the late 1970's and in my home town of the Strand, the only way you could gain access to a library for so-called Coloured people was if you trekked all the way to the City Centre and used a relative in Cape Town's address to gain membership. Within this void, photo stories like *Ruiter in Swart, Arend,*

Takoeza, Condor, Chunky Charlie, Sister Louise, Saal 10, Tessa and weekly inserts in magazines like *Look, See* and *Keur* became popular weekly reading material.[43]

The photocomics mentioned here mostly featured all-white casts. Yet due to sheer availability, blacks may have read these more frequently than the ones meant for them. There also were *more* made for white audiences. One white woman recalls: "We weren't allowed to read them but our maid had them and we would spend our lives in her room pouring [*sic*] over them."[44] Yet white people were also exposed to photocomics made for black readers. One online forum reader, "Junta," waxes nostalgic about the photocomics and magazines for black readers:

> Chunky Charlie was my girlhood hero. Our gardener, then at the ripe old age of 72 when we first met, read three magazines; *Drum, True Africa* and *Bona*. They were always dog-eared copies, so they obviously did the rounds. Chunky Charlie was read to me every Friday afternoon at tea by our erstwhile gardener, inappropriately named "Boy" Mthembu, whilst we sat on the garage floor on two empty 25L oil drums. It was a ritual that lasted 3 or so very short years. The other story I loved dearly was Satana, also serialised in the mag.[45]

She continues:

> When we moved up to Jhb I missed those fortnightly mags, but have to admit developing a secret fetish for *Ruiter in Swart*. . . . I collected them and hid them in the chicken coop from my English language pedant father. . . . Ah . . . poesboekies. . . . They were a cultural assassination, but strangely comforting back then. But . . . vastly inferior in all ways to the guile and chudspa [*sic*] of [Chunky Charlie].[46]

In a different comment forum, another anonymous nostalgic writer enthuses: "Oh Man! I remember Chunkie Charlie. I used to buy them and share them with our houseboy, Amos, at the time. I was about 11 living in Durban. That would have been around 1966."[47]

In South Africa, then, despite the vision of racial purity promulgated by apartheid photocomics, reading practices defied segregation policies and led ironically to the formation of black and white subjectivities more open, at least via imaginative identification, to racial otherness and heterogeneity than normally assumed. Yet blacks were far more likely to read the photocomics made for whites. The example of "Junta," the white reader who identified with black characters, is an important anomaly in the substantial nostalgia mill available online. Thus blacks' experiences as readers provide the most convincing instruction when thinking about relationships between receptivity and alterity. As Homi Bhabha suggests, "It is from those who have suffered the sentence of history—subjugation, domination, diaspora, displacement—that we learn our most enduring lessons for living and thinking."[48] As this book argues, reading practices that encourage encounters with alterity are essential for the production of subjectivities open to the uncomfortable and the unknown, resistant to colonial tendencies that violently and symbolically erase otherness. When Breyten Breytenbach asks, "Is imagination not the first expression of identification and therefore of generosity?" he enjoins us to think of the imagination provoked by reading as well as writing.[49] In what follows, the chapter turns to an examination of such ethical identifications as they emerged through readings in a particular sub-genre of the photocomic—the Western.

WESTERNS AND SERIALIZED TIME

The photocomic's etymological, etiological, and generic instability tests the limits of any strictly disciplinary theoretical model. And given the heterogeneity of the Western photocomic, particularly, efforts to contextualize its formal and thematic qualities benefit from engaging with a considerable range of theoretical sources, including genre and reader-response theories, as well as scholarship in postcolonial studies, art and comic history, narrative theory, and studies in popular culture. Understandably, the formal, thematic and material character of the photocomic necessarily requires an equally flexible, interdisciplinary theoretical approach.

Kid Colt, Skrikruiter, and *Ruiter in Swart* were among the most popular of the Western-style South African photocomics in the 1970s. Originally, Kid Colt was a successful American comic book character featured in an eponymous set of comics between 1948 and 1979; the South African photocomic was a spin-off of these. It follows the adventures of Kid Colt, a lone cowboy-like figure who spends his time "defending the law" in Mexico and the Wild West through the power of his gun. His enemies include Native Americans, "no-good" outlaw whites (in contrast to himself, the "good" outlaw), Mexican bandits, and the occasional female trickster. *Skrikruiter* and *Ruiter in Swart*, Afrikaans equivalents, follow the main characters—the Fearsome Rider and the Rider in Black, respectively—through similar tales of gun-wielding adventure (*Kid Colt* was also published in Afrikaans as *Kid die Swerwer*—Kid the Drifter). All three follow standardized formats and have highly predictable narrative arcs.

In the opening pages, the hero kills or catches a "baddie," thus establishing his physical preeminence. After the hero performs this inaugural feat, the central story of the photocomic commences, usually beginning when the hero apprehends a misdeed he then sets out to rectify for the duration of the rest of the story. Whether or not a woman is the person wronged, at least one female character is always introduced as the hero's (temporary) love interest. She falls for the hero, he saves her from danger—by killing a series of other men—and then, after a brief romantic interlude, the hero leaves on another journey of solitary, violent "law-keeping." And thus ends a typical issue.

These photocomics emulating the popular American Western also acutely resemble the epic, a nostalgic form that locates value in a past presumed superior to the present. "The world of the epic," Mikhail Bakhtin writes, "is the national heroic past: it is a world of 'beginnings' and 'peak times' in the national history, a world of fathers and of founders of families, a world of 'firsts' and 'bests,'" and "one can only accept the epic world with reverence."[50] Narratives of the American West have almost always possessed this epic quality, recalling a golden preindustrialized era peopled by strong, brave men, "noble savages," and an expanding frontier promising great wealth. As Amy Kaplan explains, this United States-in-formation, with its iconic, beckoning horizon, resurfaces in other non-Western genres, such as the Romance novel of the late 1890s. Much work has been done to explain how anxieties about industrialization, modernization, and anomie manifested themselves in nostalgic forms like the Western.[51] André Bazin confirms this link between the epic and the Western when he writes that "the migration to the West is our Odyssey."[52] Jorge Luis Borges similarly claims that "while literary men seem to have neglected their epic duties, the epic has been saved for us, strangely enough, by the Westerns."[53]

Yet despite the epic's position as "a genre cut off from the present, a textual museum of antiquated speech, and a simulacrum of official values," *epicness* is not only a mode of the past since it also inhabits the present, weaving itself consistently in and out of contemporary discourse.[54] Michael Holquist explains:

The epic is . . . not a genre confined to a moment in the distant past. It is historical precisely in the sense that it represents an always-still-available possibility. *It is the genre typical of societies in which diversity and change either go
unrecognized or are actively suppressed.*[55]

In this way, in apartheid South Africa, the epic narrative of the Westerns
expresses the utopian fantasies of a ruling class with aspirations for a future
always and forever enclosed within the parameters of white supremacy. As
the genre of censure and fascistic control, it should come as no surprise that
the epic Western should see its efflorescence in 1970s South Africa, a particularly draconian period in apartheid history. Despite the inconsistencies,
inaccuracies, and anachronisms in the ostensibly "historical" photocomics,
the story lines' circularity suggests a world in which relations and behaviors
are predictable, "natural," and permanent.[56]

Yet the Western photocomic contains contradictory depictions of time.
On the one hand, time and space collapse, as in an image meant to depict the
American West, which is actually a photograph of a house in the Cape Dutch
architectural style (fig. 3). How receptive to this nuance readers may have
been is unclear, but we do learn from this that *Kid Colt*'s creators were not
particularly concerned with historical accuracy. That a South African setting
might adequately serve as an overlay for an American one suggests that the
two countries could be seen as cognates or mirror images of one another. This
substitution occurs both at the level of the nation and at the level of depictions of national subjects.

But another representation of time in the photocomic might be described
as "tangle[d] up."[57] The relationships between a series of frames and the "gut-
ters" between images, the shapes of the frames, not to mention the appearance or absence of text, can create a variety of experiences of time for the
reader. Scott McCloud's observations for comics are applicable to the photocomics since they borrow essential formal elements from comics. Of particular importance is the way that readers "perceive time *spatially*," since for
McCloud, "in the world of comics, *time and space* are *one and the same*. . . . As
readers, we're left with only a vague sense that as our eyes are moving through
space, they're also moving through time."[58] In this sense, reading spatially,
readers experience process, yet they can see peripherally the future and past
(in other frames) even as they experience the present frame. This perception
of time suggests the possibility of change, in addition to that of history. Yet
while each photocomic ends with an invitation to read the next one in the

Fig. 3. From *Kid Colt*. The house is in the Cape Dutch architectural style, not that of the American West. Image courtesy of Special Collections, MSU Libraries, Michigan State University, East Lansing, MI.

series, the overriding tenor of time in these photocomics is static rather than revolutionary, as the plot repeats itself with slight variations only in the order and nature of the action and the actors.

This cyclical representation of time conveys the ideological message that the time of white, patriarchal hegemony is permanent, closed off from the possibility of change, inevitable, and perduring. As Bazin insists, "The western does not age."[59] Clark and Holquist confirm this in their interpretation of epic time and space, where "the represented world stands on an utterly different and inaccessible time and value plane, separated by epic distance. It is impossible to change, to rethink, or to reevaluate anything in epic time, for it is finished, conclusive, and immutable," just as are the plotlines of the photocomics.[60] While time repeats itself—the hero never ages, never has children, and the world in which he lives never changes—place also remains fixed, so much so that certain background images recur in *Kid Colt* issue after issue. This is a world in which the paradoxical law-keeper/outlaw is a figure for the apartheid state and its representatives. As a permanent fixture, he is mobile only from frame to frame of the photocomic, which, through serialization, implicates him in a vicious circle of violent "heroic" acts.

But the moment that is fixed in these narratives matters for its symbolic resonance. The epic is a time, as Bakhtin says, of "fathers and founders," and we see in the Western photocomics a nostalgia for a certain moment in Afrikaner history.[61] Shula Marks notes that the collective historical memory for most South African whites during apartheid was selectively "the history of South Africa [as] the history of the triumphant progress of their pioneering ancestors who overcame both nature and black savagery in the interests of 'Christian civilization.'"[62] The Western photocomics celebrated precisely such a vision of the "wild" Voortrekker frontier in their stories of racial, sexual, and territorial conquest. One reader with the online moniker "Boerseun" confirms the persistence, even today, of such a vision—linking the photocomics to the articulation of white supremacy. In response to another poster's comment in a forum about photocomics—"who could resist 'Tessa' or 'Louise' . . . those were the days," writes "Proffie"—"Boerseun" bluntly adds, "Ja, bring back all the good, WHITE, heroes." The nostalgia for a long gone historical moment thus even extends to the photocomic itself and to a form of "nation narration" now obsolete.[63]

Indeed, although the Western photocomics flourished in South Africa, they were not popular everywhere.[64] Similarities in the histories of white South Africa and the American West may account for the Western's particular resonance in South Africa. Such parallels have been explored in a number of studies comparing these two historical frontier cultures.[65] Yet while these works focus on the material and social processes at these shifting zones of contact, few examine the ideological and imaginative similarities condensing in the concept, or myth, of the frontier.[66]

Frederick Jackson Turner's isolation of the frontier as *the* defining spatial symbol of American identity referred in fact to *a series of frontiers* that moved farther west as the country expanded. This expansion encouraged prevailing attitudes toward frontiers—each new acquisition of territory created new frontiers, providing the necessary justification for further territorial incursions. Similarly, although there was a spate of material and conceptual frontiers in South Africa prior to the well-known Voortrekker movements northward and eastward, it is the nineteenth-century movements north that most obviously parallel the U.S. shifts westward. The famous "Go West, young man" is parodied in South African writer Marlene van Niekerk's 1994 novel,

Triomf, in the oft-repeated quip made by the character Treppie: "Look north, fuck forth!"[67] Indeed, despite the ample differences between the actual, material conditions of the frontiers and the social relationships they produced, in both of these expanding nations the myth of the frontier (and its loss or reconstruction) was a determinant in the production of national identities.

Fictional and nonfictional narratives about this time describe a world inhabited by "lawless" whites scrambling and squabbling over vast expanses of land; travelers dotting the landscape with their snaking wagon trails; and families with gun-toting men and tough but domestic (and domesticated) women. It also meant, as "Look North, fuck forth" suggests, racial mixing through acts of rape and consensual sex. This, in broad strokes, is the vision of many versions of the histories of this period on both continents.

White South African conceptions of indigeneity also bore certain similarities to those described in American narratives. Encounters with members of the indigenous populations are described in corresponding ways by the invading whites in both countries. Again there are further historical parallels.[68] In both instances the white settlers were mostly Calvinist, bringing with them the belief that God *selectively* designated the saved—an idea conveniently used to justify claims to racial, as well as spiritual, superiority. Both countries also relocated large numbers of the indigenous population: into reservations in the United States and later into Bantustans in South Africa. And the United States and South Africa were both settler states that chose to extend racist legislation into the postwar era, a time largely characterized elsewhere by liberation movements. These commonalities link the two white governments, at least through the religious, geographic, and legal discourses that served to justify the mistreatment of others.[69]

Alterity in its colonial Manichean expression certainly underwrote many of the stories in the photocomics, including the Westerns. As one reader notes, the themes of the photocomics "were simple—the Power of Good—the Power of Evil—the constant battle between the two—and the Triumph of Good over Evil. Not bad messages for a young mind."[70] Yet the Western, although seeming to reify such Manichaeism, simultaneously undercuts it with heroes as brutal and violent as its villains. An illogical tension underwrites the Western since, much like the state, its hero inhabits a zone of exception in which he may kill without punishment.[71] Indeed, just like Bakhtin's favored genre, the novel, the photocomic is characterized by coterminous and contradictory discursive registers—high and low, ancient and mod-

Fig. 4. From *Kid Colt*. Image courtesy of Special Collections, MSU Libraries, Michigan State University, East Lansing, MI.

ern, familiar and strange. Therefore, while the Western photocomic possesses characteristics symptomatic of the epic (mirroring the apartheid society in which it circulated), its hybrid origin coupled with its formal heterogeneity suggest we should think of it as a sometimes conservative genre simultaneously undergoing processes of "novelization," occasionally revealing the fractures within apartheid's fantasy of total control.[72]

Within the photocomics there is ample evidence of such heteroglossic dialogism. Afrikaans itself, as Breytenbach puts it, is a "bastard" language (Afrikaners are *"bastervolk"*), a fact willfully ignored by the National Party government, which tried, in declaring Afrikaans along with English the country's "standard and official language," to solidify an incontrovertible image of Afrikaans cultural, racial, and linguistic purity.[73] Afrikaans and English mixed in these photocomics much as they must have mixed in day-to-day speech. In one example conflating Afrikaans, English, and a U.S. Southern drawl, characters use an Afrikaans orthography—"waal"—to mimic the English word "well" as it would have sounded if said by an American cowboy (fig. 4). Western-themed photocomics also include snippets of Spanish in addition to language culled from many other sectors of society. Heroism, farming, romance, sex, legality and illegality, slang and propriety, third-person narration and orality, irony and honesty, narratorial moralizing, parody, deception, witchcraft, medicine, and capitalism are all dialogic registers of the photocomic.

DISPLACING RACE

If the language of the South African photocomic undoes strict divisions between dominant and emergent discourses, on the form's surface the photocomic denies interracial intersubjectivity by avoiding all depictions of cross-racial interaction. In the world represented in these "bookies," it appears that apartheid was so successfully realized as to preclude *all* interracial contact. It is as though blacks do not encounter whites in public spaces—at work, on the street, or in the form of a policeman demanding to see a person's passbook—or in the private spaces of the home, the bedroom, and the prison interrogation chamber. Despite the interracial reading practices that often characterized photocomics' reception during this period, their visual substance constitute a segregationist fantasy in which there are two worlds so unequivocally separated from one another that the existence of the racial other disappears entirely.

How, then, is it possible to talk about the ethical encounter between subjected groups and those who exploit them when there is never a depiction of such an encounter? How are modes of subjectivity formed through contact with the everyday oppressing other when there is no evidence in these works of such instances? We might begin by remarking that the glaring absence of this type of relation—so much a part of apartheid existence, particularly in the urban areas, where many of the photocomics are set—is the first important marker that something is being covered up by this radical erasure of everyday life. Depicting such encounters, from both sides of the creative zone, was so fraught to begin with that, for purely practical reasons, those involved in the production of photocomics often chose to leave out this aspect of existence altogether. Unlike the literary output of the time, which often portrayed interracial encounters, photocomics' production process required actual people, not just imagined ones, to interact and work together to make photographs, presenting, perhaps, the threat of uncontrollable contact between members of different racial groups working as equals toward the same end.

How could a genre like the photocomic, an art form so dependent on synopsis, describe the dangerous friction of everyday interracial encounters? And why should they have? Photocomics, we have been led to believe, are fun, whimsical distractions from the more challenging or mundane requirements of daily existence. Why deal, in photocomics, with exploring the more difficult and politically fractious themes of racism and apartheid?

It couldn't really be avoided. Though these works failed to directly address apartheid, they were in fact doing so in all kinds of alternate ways. Some but not all of these works present subversive discussions of apartheid; others are subversion's opposite—namely, ideological representations of apartheid thought and practice. No matter the political bent, it is possible to see apartheid's long shadow haunting the pages of even the most seemingly innocuous of photocomics, such as *See* or *Great*.[74]

Yet that segregationist fantasy that many of these photocomics worked to assert was never fully realized beyond the pages of the photocomics. Different races mingled frequently, most often because of the labor demands South African society placed on its black populace. In urban spaces, especially, interaction was the rule, not the exception. Black and white men worked in the mines together (in rigid hierarchies of power); black farm laborers worked alongside white landowners; black women in domestic work lived in specially designated servant's quarters on the property of their white employers; black police worked with white police; and despite the ban, black and white men and women engaged in sexual intimacies ranging the gamut from consensual to forced.[75]

There were also cultural connections between blacks and whites, particularly in urban areas. Katie Mooney draws attention to the subculture of the white "Ducktail" gangs, who were known to sell alcohol to blacks "*almost* openly," as one worried woman commented in *The Star* in 1954.[76] (Her qualifying "almost" suggests that the interaction between blacks and whites often hovered just beneath the surface of acceptance.) "Interactions with blacks," Mooney writes, "could be peaceful if business was being transacted or if an activity was consensual."[77] Though the apartheid state fantasized about instituting total racial segregation—apart-hood—the day-to-day reality of capitalist accumulation and socialization required constant interaction between the races.

In addition to a shared hatred of the police,[78] another commonality, often underexplored in histories of black and white youth culture of the early apartheid period, is the obsession and imitation of all things American, as discussed in chapter 2. Studies of Americanization in South Africa tend to limit themselves to exploring the United States' influence on one racial group, thus unintentionally reinforcing the historiographic record of apartheid as making good on its own segregationist fantasy.[79] Mooney points to the inherent irony in a culture that "despite rock-'n-roll's roots in black rhythm and blues . . . propelled youth subcultures in the 1950s with young white rebellious males being the aesthetic role models."[80] Not only were blacks and whites interacting on levels ranging from the intimate to the highly disciplined, but they were also often listening to the same music, watching the same films, and wearing the same clothes. A 1963 fearmongering screed titled *Crime in South Africa* deplores the fact that

> White Ducktails in jeans and colourful shirts have been known to take their "quacktail" tarts to brothels in African areas. Here they meet the African tsotsis dressed in zoot suits, and their black molls dressed in "Suzie Wong" skirts. They are sometimes joined by Indian boys and girls from Fordsburg. Kwela music or rock-'n-roll records are played, to liven up the party, and when brandy is taken and "giggleweed" smoked, *the colour line in sex is speedily forgotten.*[81]

Racial mixing *was* occurring, both culturally and sexually, in contradistinction to the historiographic narrative often passed on that emphasizes apartheid's segregation at the expense of acknowledging the many and various ways this separation broke down.[82] In this respect, despite its surface-level segregation, the photocomic was perhaps *the* prototypical apartheid genre, promoting at one and the same time a conservative segregationist platform and a hybrid, cross-genre, heteroglot admixture of people, places, times, and spaces.

In addition to the photocomics' discursive heterogeneity, the repeated appearance of white actors masquerading as Native Americans produced an unexpected form of visual hybridity in the white-targeted Westerns (figs. 5 and 6). In some instances this involved men and women wearing face and body paint, and in all cases it involved actors donning what they believed audiences would receive as accurate, authentic, and/or convincing "Indian" dress and accessories. Practically speaking, these disguises (Barthes writes that the photocomic "has something to do with disguise") were necessitated by the segregationist policies of the country that made it difficult for non-white actors to work alongside white actors.[83] But the very racist act of applying "brownface" can have unintentional consequences, as performance studies scholars have shown. Disguising the body as the "other" blurs the boundaries between self and other, thereby undoing (in the case of the racialist policies of apartheid South Africa) the "naturalist" racial theories that were the cornerstone of the justification for segregation itself.[84] The ambivalence expressed in portraits of Native Americans that alternated between depictions of violent uncivilized savages and idealized denizens of a premodern natural world sug-

Fig. 5. The cover of *Apache* no. 38 depicting Cha, "the last Apache warrior." Image courtesy of Special Collections, MSU Libraries, Michigan State University, East Lansing, MI.

Fig. 6. A *Kid Colt* cover. Image courtesy of Special Collections, MSU Libraries, Michigan State University, East Lansing, MI.

Fig. 7. From *Apache* no. 38. Image courtesy of Special Collections, MSU Libraries, Michigan State University, East Lansing, MI.

gests an inherent instability within the notion of whiteness too (fig. 7). The need in these photocomics to consistently define whiteness in contrast to the mythologized "noble savage" (by having characters engage in endless battles to defend the markers of their identity) reveals deep anxieties underpinning definitions of whiteness.[85]

In her study of representations of Native Americans in the United States, Shari Huhndorf remarks: "Often, these representations and events . . . reflect upon other power relations within the broader society, including the advent of overseas imperialism, changing gender ideals, and the devastating histories of African Americans in the United States."[86] For Huhndorf and others, depictions of the Native American were often used as doubles for African Americans as a way for white Americans to explore black-white race relations without directly referring to them.[87] Similarly, Native Americans provided the perfect foil through which South African whites could explore their attitudes toward South African blacks while seeming to adhere to segregationist ideals by excluding actual black figures and actors from the photocomics themselves. White South Africans could explore race relations through the figure of the Indian, who was further distanced from black South Africans by not being an antecedent of South African history. This twice-deferred substitution—the Native American is neither black *nor* a part of South African history—attests simultaneously to the lack of representational devices at hand for discussions of race under apartheid as well as to the volatility that such a direct confrontation in the form of mass-consumed entertainment could provoke. Thus references to intersubjective relations between blacks and whites in South African society had to be doubly masked in shrouds of racial and temporal equivalency.

We can understand this substitution as a collective repression, the obsession with the Indian as a symptom of an obsession with black South Africans. Sigmund Freud posits that such displacements are "a product of compromise, correct as regards affect and category but false owing to chronological displacement and substitution by analogy."[88] Collective forms of displacement were, of course, also famously described in Freud's account of totemism. If we temporarily bracket off the racism of his association of totemism with "primitives" and children, we might accept his more basic premise that such forms of symbolic substitution are symptoms of all social groups. Totemism also involves disguising the self *as* the totem. "The clansmen are there," Freud writes, "dressed in the likeness of the totem and imitating it in sound and movement, as though they are seeking to stress their identity with it."[89] One photocomic instance of such an identification through substitution is *Apache*, featuring Cha, "the last Apache warrior," who is played by a white man dressed in generic "Indian" clothing. Examined closely, he cuts an incongruous patchwork figure as a cross-dressing white man/Apache/Spanish speaker imitating a nineteenth-century stereotype of the "Old West" in a South African landscape (figs. 5, 7, and 8).

When Cha thinks (in thought bubbles), he is ascribed stereotypically "Indian" aphoristic thoughts that express themselves in slightly awkward English and refer to ancestors, nature, and the spirit world (see fig. 7). Issue 38, for instance, tells a story of revenge. Cha is after the man who has killed three of his tribesmen. He confronts the priest Gaston, son of the Mexican bandit who has killed these men, who "disrobes" to fight in order to avenge the death of his father. In a series of frames, the sexual positioning of Cha's seminude body in a range of postures suggests a violent sublimated confrontation with homosexual desire, adding a further level of complexity to the South African Westerns. Cha tells Gaston, "Go back from where you came.

Fig. 8. From *Apache* no. 38. Image courtesy of Special Collections, MSU Libraries, Michigan State University, East Lansing, MI.

This is not your land . . . not your life," yet he refuses to kill a man of the cloth.[90] A nun, Maria, sides with Cha and is chastised by the other men. Ultimately, Cha befriends Maria and Gaston but leaves them for his "warpath."[91] The narrative invokes the stereotyped "noble savage" who is at once brave, honorable, and good and simultaneously savage, ferocious, and evil.[92] In the Western photocomic, this physical embodiment of the repressed black other returns virtually unrecognizably in the guise of the Indian. Only by imitating this totemic figure could whites fulfill their desire for a confrontation with the original inhabitants of their own country.

The Western photocomic also provided an excellent forum for treatments of Afrikaner identity; as a form it was disguised enough to allow for the erasure of black bodies but familiar enough to strengthen particular notions of white masculinity, femininity, and power. White masculinity is the primary preoccupation of *Kid Colt, Swart Ruiter*, and *Skrikruiter*; however, it must always be asserted in contrast to encounters with nonwhite or non-male others.[93] As conflict with Native Americans in the United States provided a foil for the production of white American masculinities, so too was Afrikaner masculinity formed at the point of contact with black and white female South Africans.[94]

POPULAR CULTURE AS POLITICS

Critics of popular culture on both sides of the political spectrum often charge it with creating escapist utopias that sidetrack people from attending to everyday structural inequalities and injustices.[95] Some commentators follow this line of thought in suggesting that photocomics do not depict worlds mirroring reality but instead portray lives that readers aspire to having.[96] But Amy Kaplan argues that dismissing popular genres as distracting, "light" entertainment ignores how they function politically precisely *because* they invoke escapist fantasies. "Critics," she writes, "have long dismissed the popular . . . as a collective form of blowing off steam. . . . this approach ignores how nostalgia can abet modern imperial force, and *how an outworn genre can be refurbished to represent a new political context.*"[97] In his study of the popular U.S. dime novels, Michael Denning points to the direct link between the escapism of individual daydreams and culturally determined forms of collective unconscious: "In the case of a daydream which is mediated by the collective and historically specific processes of narrative production and reception, that unconscious is social and political."[98] For Kaplan, then, "to call these [works] escapist . . . is to show not their avoidance of contemporary political discourse, but their reproduction of it."[99]

The Western's revival in photocomic form reflects desire for a racially segregated utopia through its nostalgic vision of a time and place in which powerful white men dominate and conquer land, indigenous inhabitants, and women. Even if the photocomics provide avenues for escaping the present, we must consider why and how these forms are the ones chosen by consumers to effect their escapes. Indeed, nostalgia for the past permits fantasies of the present while simultaneously avoiding direct confrontation with the obstacles of the present that hinder these fantastic visions from becoming realities.[100]

Kaplan argues that the "modern Western, initiated with Owen Wister's *The Virginian*, finds its immediate genealogy in [the historical romance], which reclaims the American West through the course of overseas empire."[101] This link between the invention of the Western and external colonialism also helps to explain the resurgence of Western narratives in the context of apartheid South Africa's own colonial ambitions. Events in Lesotho, Namibia, Angola, Mozambique, and Zimbabwe—the edge, so to speak, of South Africa's frontier—remind us what a pivotal epoch of decolonization this was for those countries bordering (and surrounded by) South Africa.

The apartheid government strove to retain regional power financially and militarily by supporting anti-independence movements. Despite the United Nations' 1967 declared protectorate status in Namibia (known until then as South-West Africa), South Africa remained illegally in control of the region until 1990. The government was also closely involved in monitoring the first elections in newly independent Lesotho in 1970 and maintained an antagonistic relation with that country throughout the apartheid years since it welcomed so-called ANC and PAC terrorists. The successful Angolan and Mozambican independence movements culminated in 1975 despite South African collaborations with the Portuguese to sabotage them, and Zimbabwe similarly gained its independence from the National Party–supported Ian Smith government in 1979–80.

Despite the government's best efforts, South Africa's frontiers were rigidifying into national borders that thwarted white Afrikaner identity's association with expansion and adventure.[102] The country was also, in a sense, becoming smaller as Bantustans were declared "independent" states by the government. What would happen to national identity if there were no more frontiers to extend? The cultural symptom of this crisis returns in the form of nostalgic genres like the Western. White South Africans returned to the cowboy because it provided an ersatz expression of their nostalgia for the Voortrekker days, coterminously permitting a series of indirect confrontations with South Africa's contemporary racial dynamics. The nostalgia of the Western could impede change that comes about via historical reckoning and understanding. Nostalgia, Christopher Lasch warns, "undermines the ability to make intelligent use of the past."[103] For Lasch, nostalgia abets the misuse and abuse of history, though as we will see in the next chapter, Jacob Dlamini's 2010 memoir of black life under apartheid, *Native Nostalgia*, complicates any understanding of nostalgia as a purely conservative discourse.

And the cowboy figure *was* also appropriated by black readers, transformed and reworked as a figure of resistance to hegemonic racial discourse.[104] Bloke Modisane describes how resonant the Western was for black children in Sophiatown:

Like America, South Africa has a frontier or voortrekker mentality, a primitive throw-back to the pioneering era, the trail-blazing days, when the law dangled in the holster and justice was swift, informal and prejudiced. Instant justice, lynching and horse-whippings are deep in the traditions of these countries; both are compulsive addicts of horse operas, we are always playing cowboys and Indians. The mud pool was the Wild West of America or the dark interior of Africa; and to us, out there in the pool, the white boys were the Red Indians, and we were the cowboys. The symbols were undoubtedly reversed in the white camp.[105]

Thus, even in the Western's nostalgic conservatism, there were breaches in the form that allowed for alternative interpretations of the grand narratives, for what James Scott calls the "hidden transcripts" of resistance.[106] Despite their apparent allegiances to white supremacist thinking, Western photocomics provided more heterogeneous modes through which to read race, poking holes in the apartheid screen of vision by fostering practices of interracial readership that crossed legal, imaginative, and narrative boundaries.

READING PLAYS A vital role in the development of the capacity for projective identification during childhood, particularly explaining how, as Fanon notes, "the black schoolboy . . . identifies himself with the explorer, the bringer of civilization, the white man who carried truth to savages—an all-white truth."[107] By studying how colonized children read these photocomics, we observe how cross-racial identifications were cultivated to produce docile subjects but also how the modes of identification created by reading destabilized the very rigid binaristic relations that certain texts aimed to reproduce.

Ideology, following Louis Althusser, is importantly reproduced at the discursive as well as the material level. German Nazi propaganda comic books such as *Der Giftpilz* (*The Poison Mushroom*) were used in this way to inculcate anti-Semitic ideas in children. The belief that children's reading practices fundamentally effect their political consciousness is well documented in Julia L. Mickenberg's *Learning from the Left*, which explores how communist and left-wing writers in the United States aimed to create a generation of antifascist leftists through the development of certain kinds of narratives for children. Children's reading materials (just like all textual documents) are always implicated in the production and reproduction of ideology.[108]

In "African Literature as Restoration of Celebration," Chinua Achebe writes, "I did not see myself as an African to begin with. . . . The white man was good and reasonable and intelligent and courageous. The savages arrayed against him were sinister and stupid or, at the most, cunning. I hated their guts."[109] Thus, the story of Achebe's coming to literature is equally a story of the transformation of the child Achebe, who identifies with the white hero, into the adult Achebe, whose novels condemn white colonialists and their legacies. Many colonized children, however, were not able to shrug off the harmful consequences of idolatry and identification that were simultaneously encouraged and denied by the colonial world. Ironically, it is often only in the literary descriptions of the awareness of this process, that is, in the *loss* of such an identification and in the gain of a new black or colonized subject position, that we know of the existence of such children and adults.

For Freud, this kind of reverse identification was not an infrequent part of childhood development. In "Group Psychology and the Analysis of the Ego," Freud identifies the process whereby a child identifies with the object he loses, *becoming* that object in his own mind: "A child who was unhappy over the loss of a kitten declared straight out that now he himself was the kitten, and accordingly crawled about on all fours, would not eat at table, etc."[110] This identification, it must be noted, is not the type of identification Freud considers "healthy"; indeed, it is an incorrect identification brought about in response to the trauma of loss. If we apply this to the context of textual identification during apartheid, it is almost as though the loss (of power, of land, of education, etc.) is the constitutive experience in black children's literary identity formation. Lack, perhaps more than loss, was a driving force in black children's identification practices, such that their close identification with white figures like Kid Colt and other cowboys is an expression or imaginary fulfillment of their wish to possess agency and to mold the course of their own lives.

WITH ITS EUROCENTRIC FOCUS, most criticism on the photocomic fails to consider the very different effects of reading practices on colonized subjects, though they constitute one of the largest groups of their readers. Consider Baetens's optimistic statement that, in addition to being a reader, the photocomic's purchaser

> can also feel himself to be a consumer (incited to buy products advertised in the pages of the photocomic), a citizen (judging the moral attitudes of the

heroes, capable of imitating or refusing their behavior), an actor (thanks to the beauty competitions organized by the magazines), a writer (because he is invited to correspond with the actors in the photocomics) or a scriptwriter (if he decides to answer the questionnaires published at the end of each issue of the "open" feuilletons).[111]

All of these subject positions were denied to black readers of photocomics. Particularly in the white-targeted photocomics, when blacks are invited to be neither consumer, citizen, actor, writer, scriptwriter, nor even reader, what is left for them to engage with beyond a basic readerly response of identification and/or alienation? Even within the photocomics for blacks, which do allow for greater definitions of subjectivity for black readers than the photocomics targeting whites, blacks were not permitted to see themselves as citizens, the most politically necessary subjectivity of which they were unjustly deprived.[112] For Baetens's European subject, the reader's subjectivity and possibilities for alternate subjectivities are multiplied, which explains, for him, the "success of the genre."[113]

For black South African children, reverse identification compensates for this overdetermined lack, but in the reparative process a new wound is created, namely, an awareness that this identification can only be permitted in the fictional space of fantasy. No black child is permitted under apartheid to behave like, let alone *be*, the powerful figure of masculine agency represented by the white heroes of the photocomic.[114] The black child therefore simultaneously experiences identification with and alienation from the white "hero" of the photocomics.

Bloke Modisane's autobiography provides a description of this double trauma and conscientization. First, there is the misidentification with the fantasy of the good white man; it is followed by the disintegration of this identification, a further loss, which leaves Modisane without a substitute for this loss, in his Fanonian words with "a demolition of personality":

> My father wanted me to grow up to be a good man. . . . I was educated into an acceptance that the white man is noble in reason and just, the impression was burned into my mind, until whiteness was invested with the symbol of purity and justice; but this reality was disorganized, the foundations of my faith broken up, when the lie exploded in my face, and in that moment I suffered a disorientation of values, a demolition of personality. The relevation [*sic*] was a traumatic experience, both shocking and cruel.[115]

As this passage reminds us, it is important to recognize the detrimental side effects of over-identification, particularly when such identifications seem only limited to the sphere of fantasy. But, as I have argued, processes of cross-racial imagining and identification permit simultaneously for the construction of alternative narratives of individual lives and for imagining new social formations. That black children might imagine themselves as powerful agents of their own destiny, even when apartheid most crudely denied them agency, may have contributed to the strength of South Africa's considerably vocal youth organizations and thus to the formation and imagining of such powerful, if infamous, protests as the 1976 Soweto uprising. By placing themselves "in the shoes" of powerful, if fantastical, fictional figures, black students engaged in reading practices that allowed them to imagine that a national sphere might exist beyond the material confines of apartheid.

In the process, reading practices that involved the photocomic clearly elicited identifications that refused to respect the color line so often adhered to in the photocomics themselves. These imaginative forays into the being of alterity, as argued previously, may not have themselves been enough to provoke subjects to corresponding ethical acts. But they laid the groundwork, through everyday practice, for establishing imaginative connections between racial groups, destabilizing the identities the state was so intent to uphold. With the close of apartheid, as the subsequent chapter shows, these cross-racial identifications that occurred at passchecks, in reading practices, and in the movie houses were finally given room for their full expression—in writing produced after the transition of power. In what follows, I argue particularly that the transition not only permitted for the articulation of this cross-racial attunement but enabled such identifications to transform into ethical events, most often through the acknowledgment of shared responsibilities and complicities.

CHAPTER 4

Writing Ethics After Apartheid

When voters in the democratic elections of 1994 placed Nelson Mandela and the ANC at the country's helm, many black writers lost their reason for writing. For black South Africans, the abolition of apartheid was the driving catalyst behind their creative work. And while such explicit instrumentalism caused considerable debate both at home and abroad about the aesthetic merits of writing geared to effect social change and about culture's relation to revolutionary political platforms, it is undeniably true that with the demise of the National Party's system of legislated racism, the central motivation undergirding much black writing disintegrated, introducing an unprecedented paralytic crisis into post-apartheid black writing.[1]

To make matters worse, it quickly became evident that the political promises that were thought to be coextensive with apartheid's demise were not to be so easily realized, if at all. Describing the post-apartheid moment, Rob Nixon explains that "for artists steeped in the resistance mode . . . this has proven to be not just a bewildering period, but a vexing one. They have . . . maintained that, whatever the political gains, this half-baked situation was not the revolution they had been creating for."[2] While many debates about black writing in apartheid South Africa revolve around whether writing ought to try to directly influence politics, less scrutiny has been given to considerations of whether such effects are even possible. Writing's instrumental capacity is largely assumed in these debates, even when it is considered to represent a sacrifice of artistic merit. On the other hand, writing's inherent *failure* to bring about new social structures is less commonly addressed. After apartheid's demise, however, it became increasingly apparent that the "half-baked" political situation emerging was not what "[artists] had been creating for." Nixon identifies a crisis for black South African writers in the post-apartheid period, pitting anti-apartheid artists' belief in their works' ability to produce a more just society (what Timothy Bewes calls "the natural tendency of the prerevolutionary work . . . to insist . . . on the meaningful, truth-telling capacity of literature and the exceptional status of the writer") against a sudden consciousness that their creative output had failed to do just that.[3] In other words, the post-apartheid moment drew sudden and painful attention to art's ineffectualness in the realm of political transformation and placed the writer's function under serious scrutiny as well. In this chapter I turn to black South African writers' negotiation of this fraught relationship between writing and politics, moving from the book's earlier focus on black readers and spectators to recent post-apartheid writers. I contend, furthermore, that a considerable number of black writers have moved to engagements with the more overtly *ethical* dilemmas of the post-apartheid period as they confront the impasse of writing in the face of the moment's *political* failures.

These writers' awareness that writing failed to adequately effect political change has expressed itself most obviously in an affective response of disappointment.[4] Literature and writing are newly made to signify modes of production that fail to adequately transform the political sphere. In Zoë Wicomb's 2014 *October*, the protagonist repeatedly acknowledges that her attempts at memoir writing are unnecessary, ineffectual, and unhelpful. Toward the close of the novel, "she finds the file . . . still on her desktop, and without opening it, drags it into the trash bin."[5] And in Wicomb's earlier, also post-apartheid, novel, *David's Story* (2002), its titular character castigates writing as a profession for being too intimately linked with privilege and thus too distant from the material "struggle."

Yet black writers have continued to write, and new writers and "born frees" have honed their craft in the post-apartheid moment. This chapter argues that ethics becomes a new terrain of politico-philosophical engagement for writers keen to continue to feel that their work has wider social relevance in South Africa and abroad. But the politics that emerges most successfully through the turn to ethics—though at times still instrumentalist in ambition—is also frequently undergirded by a non-teleological structure of relation that resists the desire for an end goal (the liberation of Mandela, the fall of apartheid, etc.) in order to work within rather than beyond the disappointments of the "post-anti-apartheid" period.[6] Black writers who continue to write or who begin to write after apartheid accept that writing is a deeply compromised occupation vis-à-vis political commitment and that it can no longer be convincingly thought to possess solely morally righteous intentions. There is therefore a certain modesty characterizing the tenor and scope of writing's ambitions after apartheid, owing much to the disappointments of the South African present and to the shame incumbent in the recognition of writing's failure.

For Primo Levi, who survived the Holocaust when many others did not, "a person's life, his or her very existence, is a cause of shame."[7] Timothy Bewes's *The Event of Postcolonial Shame* links postwar authorship to this experience of shame, arguing that Levi's shame of survival manifests itself in his writing. Bewes's understanding of the affective links between the act of writing and shame is crucial for this chapter's consideration of post-apartheid black South African writing, though after apartheid, the shame of continuing to write or of taking up writing as a métier is less a shame of survival than a shame of failure, particularly, writing's failure to adequately counteract ongoing political and social injustices. To write after apartheid is, however, also shameful, because to choose to continue to write, given its acknowledged inefficacy, is to admit to and live on in one's own privilege. To put this in starkly binarist terms, to continue to write in South Africa in the face of writing's impotence might mean relinquishing a messy populist struggle at the front lines in exchange for a private desk in the peaceful interiority of a library, all the while knowing that the library can no longer be envisioned so neatly as a space of liberation. The engagement of black South African writers with writing's own ethical complicities constitutes this chapter's principal attentions. The shift in the focus of post-apartheid writing from political concerns to ethical ones is in part a response to this exposure of writerly work as ethically compromised in the post-apartheid period, and much of the writing that has emerged during this time grapples precisely with these questions about writing's political relevance.[8]

As the previous chapters sought to establish, there is a long history of black engagement with ethical crisis that gave black writers in the post-apartheid period a nuanced appreciation of the stakes and structures of ethical relation after the end of apartheid. Black apartheid experiences, as I have shown, were riven through and through with ethical thinking and ethical being. Only in the post-apartheid period, however, are black writers able to *choose or refuse* ethical engagements with whiteness, as interracial ethical relation becomes transformed from a survival strategy or a state mandate (under the TRC) to becoming one possibility among several for rebuilding an affective South African or African landscape that eschews repeating the divisive and unjust social logic of apartheid.[9]

Which is not to say that the post-apartheid turn toward themes of ethics and responsibility was only, or always, an examination of interracial ethics. As this chapter shows in discussions of the works of Pumla Gobodo-Madikizela, Sindiwe Magona, and Jacob Dlamini, black ethics after apartheid are often concerned with how best to extend ethical feeling into an interracial world. Yet there is also a turn in post-apartheid black writing toward an exploration of intrablack modes of responsibility, which hearkens back to and makes contemporary again some of the ideas central in Steve Biko's Black Consciousness thought.

What all these writers share is a turn away from the grand sweep of political and historical narratives to a focus on the local, the immediate, and the intimately interpersonal. While politics is a notoriously capacious signifier, I use it here to mean the social and legal structures, organizations, laws, and individuals that regulate life, emphasizing the public realm of politics that operates on a grand scale as opposed to the smaller, more intimate gestures that concern me in ethical relation. Recently, Megan Jones and Jacob Dlamini have insisted that "what we have denied about our history and what we continue to deny is a very strong tradition, using the word 'tradition' loosely, of social intimacies."[10] Njabulo Ndebele takes this observation into the realm of philosophy to consider the implications of these intimacies for the experience of selfhood in South Africa. During a roundtable discussion in 2011 he asks:

> Is there any . . . South African born here, or who has come from somewhere or other, who actually can claim not to have something in you of the other?
>
> It suddenly struck me that there will be very few such people. That what we do actually share is a sense of having in each one of us what the other is; it's the most common thing that all of us have across the country. But in a sense we have been rejecting the implications of this, because it seems that each of us, to various degrees, wants to hold onto some notion of purity that has not been tainted by the other. But in fact, it's impossible to find such purity.[11]

An admission like this would have been difficult during the anti-apartheid era, when more exclusionary solidarities were required in order to form strong oppositional stances to apartheid ideology and practice. For strategic purposes, these alliances had to ignore the implications of interracial intimacies for individual psychic and emotional life. Increasingly, however, black writers refuse binaristic apartheid logic, despite the country's continued reliance on racially determined structures of economic inequity. In the post-apartheid moment writing has become detached from its formerly political agendas and now seeks alternative ways to imagine the futures of social relation.

An obvious forum foregrounding ethical relation in South Africa occurred at the TRC hearings. These were public staging grounds for the explicit mobilization of black ethics in the post-apartheid interregnum. Relying on a theory and practice of inclusion, the TRC sought to incorporate all South Africans into the process of national reconciliation through the re-narration of the country's violent past. *Ubuntu* explained its ethico-philosophical underpinnings,[12] emphasizing a shared universal humanity across racial and ethnic groups. This was reflected in the TRC's hope that participants would register their interconnectedness and intimacy over and above any social, racial, or economic differences. In a series of written reflections, Pumla Gobodo-Madikizela, a commissioner on the Human Rights Violation Committee of the TRC, endorsed this strand of "African humanism," made known internationally through the public statements of the commission's chair, Archbishop Desmond Tutu. This chapter returns to the ethical imperatives of the TRC a little later to consider more recent events in South Africa, including attacks on African migrants and the Lonmin tragedy—both lynchpins in recent South African political consciousness that deeply compromise the reconciliatory aims of the TRC's final report.

Gobodo-Madikizela's work on the TRC led her to an encounter with Eugene de Kock, the white apartheid-era state assassin known as "Prime Evil," that was the first of many subsequent meetings she held with him. In 1997 she began a series of interviews with him while he was imprisoned in Pretoria's maximum-security prison serving a 212-year sentence for crimes against humanity. As leader of Vlakplass, the state's secret "counterinsurgency" paramilitary hit squad during apartheid, de Kock had been responsible for horrifically violent acts of torture and murder aimed at destroying anti-apartheid activism. At the commission hearings he made a series of admissions about the crimes that he had either participated in or arranged.[13] Gobodo-Madikizela records her responses to her meetings with de Kock in her 2003 memoir, *A Human Being Died That Night: A South African Woman Confronts the Legacy of Apartheid*.[14] Unlike Hannah Arendt's accounts of Adolf Eichmann at the trials in Jerusalem in 1961–62, *A Human Being Died That Night* describes Gobodo-Madikizela's meetings with de Kock far more intimately. This leaves her invested in de Kock's well-being yet simultaneously disturbed by this investment.

At the time of her first interview with de Kock, and after her initial shock at being in the same room as Prime Evil (his "bright orange prison over-alls" remind her of *Silence of the Lambs*), Gobodo-Madikizela soon develops responses to him she describes interchangeably as "sympathy," "empathy," or "pity." Even her first description of de Kock suggests he is more than a stock figure of brutality: "This was the closest I had ever been to Eugene de Kock. As he smiled shyly, perhaps politely, rising to greet me, I saw a flicker of boy-ishness, of uncertainty."[15] She finds it difficult to see the "banality of evil"[16] in this lackey of the apartheid government, despite his extensive and well-documented acts of premeditated and sadistic violence. Almost from the start, Gobodo-Madikizela affirms that sympathizing with de Kock is essential to ensuring the creation of a South Africa that is not another one of the "countless examples in history of government by people who have risen out of oppressive rule to become oppressors themselves."[17] For Gobodo-Madikizela, ethical relation will help to differentiate past regimes of injustice from that which she wishes to construct in South Africa. "If showing compassion to our enemies," she writes, "is something that our bodies recoil from, what should our attitude be to their cries for mercy, the cries that tell us their hearts are breaking, and that they are willing to renounce the past and their role in it?"[18] For Gobodo-Madikizela, the intimacies between blacks and whites fomented during apartheid created structures of feeling that can be reworked toward ethical ends as the imbalance of power reorients. What she calls "empathetic repair" is made possible because apartheid has been abolished and the ANC and the TRC, for all of their imperfections, have repositioned political power in the hands of some of apartheid's victims.

For Gobodo-Madikizela, forging the space to forgive the atrocities committed by whites during apartheid is an ethical mode of relation that is also agential—it allows those who have previously thought of themselves as unwitting victims of white supremacist ideology and violence to choose their own involvement in the restructuring of post-apartheid South African society. She writes,

> The victim in a sense *needs* forgiveness as part of the process of becoming rehumanized. The victim needs it in order to complete himself or herself and to wrest away from the perpetrator the fiat power to destroy or to spare. It is part of the process of reclaiming self-efficacy. Reciprocating with empathy and forgiveness in the face of a perpetrator's remorse restores to many victims the sense that they are once again capable of effecting a profound difference in the moral community.[19]

For Gobodo-Madikizela ethical relation can subvert entrapment in positions of victimhood, offering a methodology for appropriating agency. While acknowledging that agency requires first and foremost a redistribution of access to economic, legal, and political structures, she suggests that it is also constituted by people's ability to conceive of their oppressors as complexly structured themselves. This recognizes the formative role played by everyday affect in the production of agential ethical relations.

Gobodo-Madikizela's investment in social interconnectedness as a way to repair South African society is echoed in her decision to position her dialogues with de Kock as the fulcrum for the development of her text. Dialogic forms of narration subtend much black post-apartheid writing, a formal organization that embeds ethical concerns about ambivalence, uncertainty, and relation into the very fabric of the texts being produced. There is a considerable history of the use of dialogic form in black South African narratives, and despite their myriad differences and their different uses, they all emphasize the imbricated experience of existence over and above thinking that places the individual at the narrative and theoretical center of being. Writings by Gobodo-Madikizela and other authors touched on in this chapter draw from this long history of dialogic forms to make new use of its implicit ethical charge. Other formal notes repeating with intensity in post-apartheid black writing include metonymic, hypothetical, and interrogative structures. Throughout this chapter I examine how these formal devices contributed to proposing a post-apartheid ethical stance that veers away from the teleological emphases of the anti-apartheid movement toward more nebulous terrains of intimacy, ambivalence, and ethical refusal.

AN ETHICS OF REFUSAL: STEVE BIKO'S LEGACY

While Gobodo-Madikizela's work elaborates the methodology for reparation endorsed at the TRC, as others have pointed out, the TRC's testimonial organization placed the onus for reconciliation almost entirely on South Africa's black citizens. In its function as a conduit enabling the transition from apartheid to democracy, the TRC also institutionally entrenched that same reliance on black sympathy for whites that was a mainstay of apartheid. That public narratives of black and coloured political agency moved so quickly from condemning white acts to including language that "forgave" and "forgot" the wrongs of the past indicates not so much a sudden change in attitude as a politico-historical shift that made possible the public articulation of these modes of interracial relation characterized by recognition as well as opposition.

Despite the various forms of confession, self-abasement, and shame exhibited by the perpetrators of apartheid who took the stand at the amnesty hearings, the envisioned transition leaned most heavily upon blacks' abilities to imagine white consciousness and to forgive it. While whites did also listen to blacks' testimonies on the stands, and were thus forced necessarily to engage in unprecedented acts of cross-racial identification and even empathy, they were rarely asked to forgive blacks. The bestowal of forgiveness tended to be unidirectional, placing the burden for the reparation of the nation's wounds in the hands of those who had already suffered for many decades as its victims. One writer asks: "Why should it always be the indigenous people who have to reconcile and teach whites about the pain that apartheid inflicted on us?"[20] Thus it was that the hardest labors of apartheid *and* the hardest labors of transition were undertaken by the same people. South African philosopher Mabogo P. More goes so far as to say that "Black South Africans have been . . . humiliated by the TRC."[21] While the perpetrators were asked to disclose the full details of their political crimes during amnesty hearings, no affective or moral requirement was exacted from them. Because perpetrators were not required to express remorse, and once an individual was granted amnesty he could no longer be liable in a civil trial—and thus the victims or the victims' family members could not be financially compensated beyond the pittance they received as financial reparation from the state[22]—the entire responsibility for effecting a successful transition at the level of collective national sentiment lay with those who were persistently ignored by apartheid structures of moral responsibility.

Nonetheless, they were expected to accept the commission's reliance on their sympathy as essential to the establishment of New South Africa's moral order. While black South Africans were finally given a forum in which to tell their own stories, the absence of any kind of material reparation meant that the TRC reinscribed moral hierarchies, putting blacks once again in the position of having to identify with (and forgive) white guilt.[23]

Bhekizizwe Peterson describes the TRC as a moment in which

> the difficulties and imperatives of forgiveness are recast and turned into yet another trial of the compassion and humanity of those who have been offended and hurt. As far as reconciliation is concerned, there seems to be little

appreciation that its pertinence exceeds the boundaries of black and white relations. Individuals . . . need to come to terms with themselves and their experiences, relatives need to reconcile with families, relations between neighbors and communities need to be restored where they have been broken.[24]

Because some people were aware that relations between blacks were just as important to think about and that reconfigurations of *that* moral order were as essential as the interracial one the TRC emphasized, certain victims of apartheid refused to take part in the hearings. Most famous among these was the family of Steve Bantu Biko, which refused to forgive the perpetrators responsible for Biko's death.[25] Jann Turner, a journalist covering the TRC whose own father was shot and killed in front of her, sees the desire to hurt the killers of your loved one as a healthy reaction to the trauma of his or her absence. The response encouraged by the TRC—to just sit and ask perpetrators carefully why they committed the crimes they did—seems outlandish to her, for whom a desire for retribution is "more normal . . . than wanting to sit down and face [the perpetrators] in this extraordinary Kafkaesque Truth Commission, where we sit and listen and go in the breaks and have cups of tea."[26]

We can link Biko's family's response to Biko's own writings, because their refusal to extend sympathy to or forgive whites resembles a crucial political move in Biko's Black Consciousness philosophy. Following a detour through Biko's writings we uncover, retroactively, a current of black ethical thinking in circulation during apartheid that represents an ethics of refusal. This ethics opposes being conscripted into imagining whiteness empathetically and is one that endures in present-day black South African thought and creative practice, providing an alternative way to think about the restructuring of the country's relations on the heels of apartheid.

Biko's Black Consciousness movement called for liberation from the material and psychological effects of apartheid through a platform and practice of black solidarity.[27] Crucially, for Biko, freedom could only come about through a politically conscious period of separatism. He believed blacks needed to achieve economic and psychological independence apart from the so-called help of white liberals. The condescension Biko observed in whites' benevolence or "sympathy" often belied their hidden racism, so he called for blacks to throw off the effects of apartheid through the cultivation and promotion of black cultural, historical, and economic achievement.

This focus on the restitution and reconstitution of black life and its eschewal of white liberalist benevolence echoes both preceding and coeval philosophies espoused across transatlantic space, including those of Jamaican political leader Marcus Garvey, Francophone Négritrude thinkers Aimé Césaire and Léopold Senghor, and American political thinkers Malcolm X and Stokely Carmichael. Yet Biko's philosophies are also distinctly linked to the South Africa of the 1970s and to the imagining of a future there that would be, in his words, a distinctly "non-racial, just, and egalitarian society in which colour, creed and race shall form no point of reference."[28] This call for a disengagement from whites in order to reconstitute or build anew a political future for all South Africans recognizes what philosopher Lewis R. Gordon calls "the paradox offered by blackness as the limit."[29] For the black separatism, or "limit," Biko espoused was meant, ultimately, to produce its opposite—an "egalitarian society"—in which the "black" of Black Consciousness would cease to be a "point of reference." Biko's writings increasingly suggest that the psychological liberation he intended Black Consciousness to bring about, with its attendant material and social improvements, should be conceived of as a stage in a teleological process culminating in "National Consciousness."[30]

His most compelling ethical idea lies less in this "non-racial" vision than in his understanding of how a localized ethics of the immediate (black separatism) can prepare the way for a more universal ethics that could eventually include the denizens of entire nations in its compass. Biko's ideas recognize the power that comes with the *refusal* to sympathize, a refusal of relation, a move, in other words, to separate in order to strengthen and build political unity through isolationism. Gayatri Spivak's "strategic essentialism" echoes the thinking behind Biko's understanding of "black solidarity [as] an essential instrument to counter white domination."[31] This utilitarian language used by the authors of the introduction to *I Write What I Like* suggests a dual recognition: first, that Black Consciousness is conceived of as a tool to liberate blacks; but, second, that after a certain period the realization of this liberation would allow for the reintegration of blacks with whites in entirely new configurations of relation. For Biko, such integration does "not need to [be] plan[ned] for." He writes:

> Once the various groups within a given community have asserted themselves to the point that mutual respect has to be shown then you have the ingredients for a true and meaningful integration. At the heart of true integration is the provision for each man, each group to rise and attain the envisioned self. Each group must be able to attain its style of existence without encroaching on or being thwarted by another. Out of this mutual respect for each other

and complete freedom of self-determination there will obviously arise a genuine fusion of the life-styles of the various groups. This is true integration.[32]

This Fanonian teleology, involving the reconstruction of the black self out of the horrors of slavery, colonialism, and apartheid, leading eventually to the creation of a larger, more just, and more "free" "community," expresses the desire for a nation characterized by an ethics of racial interrelation and integration, presupposed, importantly, however, on an initial period of ethical refusal.

Ultimately, then, Biko does not refuse to include whites in his vision of a more ethically motivated world, though his push for black solidarity and its exclusion of whites (liberal and conservative, Afrikaner and English alike) importantly draws attention to the way that the withholding of ethics, or its confinement to a limited range of recipients, can be the occasion for the reclamation of power for those largely divested of it. His thinking reveals how intrinsically linked ethical feeling is to the dynamics of power that undergird our world. Who feels sympathy or empathy for whom and who is expected to feel this way is mandated by the political and cultural structures of our time. When anti-apartheid writer and activist Breyten Breytenbach bemoans the lack of sympathy he receives at the hands of his black jailers in the employ of the apartheid government—"How stupid I was, Mr. Investigator! I thought these blokes at least must have some sympathy left in them somewhere. Aren't they *black* after all, members of the oppressed majority"—we note how black sympathetic feeling for anti-apartheid white activists is *expected*, notable only in its absence.[33] To withhold ethics, Biko's thinking reminds us, can be politically and ethically generative.

It is in the context of Biko's call to refuse an empathy with whiteness that we might consider Biko's own family's refusal at the TRC to extend forgiveness to Biko's murderers. Biko's family's unwillingness to cooperate with the newly elected ANC government's plans for interracial reconciliation suggests an awareness that some black people were not ready, *yet*, to again spend time caring for or about whites. While apartheid demanded this of them in order to survive, the post-apartheid moment provided an opportunity to break with this social structure that placed the onus for feeling ethical on blacks. The shift after apartheid in black ethics lies, then, in the emergence of the possibility for blacks to refuse an ethical response to whiteness. Interracial or, to use Biko's terminology, "non-racial" National Consciousness is a work in progress, particularly for black South Africans, who are more stymied by the economic and psychological legacies of apartheid than Biko would have wished. The withholding of forgiveness by the Biko family exists in the limbo or "transition" state that continues to be the truth of the post-apartheid moment. Like Biko's thought itself, it calls for a consciousness of the politics of ethical relation, suggesting also that, though withheld today, it could possibly reemerge in a world divested of the inequalities structured by white supremacy—an ethical relation in abeyance, then.

It is within this ambivalent space that is neither the egalitarian dream of anti-apartheid activism nor the ethical abyss of apartheid itself that today's black writers engage. Now that the imperative to write against apartheid has been removed, there is less of an impediment to those black writers keen to focus on more intimate topics of interpersonal relations. Writers are finally free to directly address interracial intersubjectivity and are well positioned to use their finely honed attunement to whiteness to produce stories that touch as much upon whites' experience as upon blacks'. Zakes Mda's novel *The Madonna of Excelsior*, for instance, hones in on various forms of intimate relations between black and white South Africans, including those sexual relations that persisted despite the Immorality Act of 1950 forbidding sexual relations between whites and "non-whites." In addition, the novel spends considerable time tracing friendships between black and Afrikaans South Africans. These intimacies were not uniform or easy to stereotype, since whiteness itself has always been an unstable category in South Africa, despite the supremacist claims of the National Party government. The differences between Afrikaners and English-speaking South Africans are as important to observe as their similarities.

Writing of various friendships in the novel between Afrikaners and blacks, the narrator of *The Madonna of Excelsior* asserts:

> We . . . were not bothered by these friendships. We put them down to the old love affair between black people and Afrikaners that the English found so irritating. Even at the height of apartheid, blacks preferred dealing with Afrikaners to the English-speaking South Africans. The English, common wisdom stated, were hypocrites. They laughed with you, but immediately you turned, they stabbed you in the back. The Afrikaner, on the other hand, was honest. When he hated you, he showed you at once. He did not pretend to like you. If he hated blacks, he said so publicly. So when you dealt with him, you knew who you were dealing with. When he smiled, you knew he was genuine. One could never trust the smile of an Englishman.
>
> We never questioned what informed these generalisations.[34]

That the novel, set largely during apartheid, was published in 2002 attests to writers' newfound ability to discuss the interracial intimacies and inter-dependencies of the past and the present—a kind of frank address made possible by apartheid's demise. As Derek Attridge writes, new works are "a response to a cultural situation in which the pressures and fractures inherited from the past make possible the emergence of what has been suppressed or disguised."[35] The ethical attunement to white interiority that apartheid mandated becomes, in the post-apartheid moment, less a psychological strategy for survival than one conduit among many through which writers can imaginatively access themes of otherness and difference. Buried during apartheid, since most admissions of compassion for whites were seen as political and literary suicide, interracial relation is now able to exist as a topic of literary exploration in a space with notably more room to breathe in.

Contemporary writers oscillate between wanting to extend ethics beyond Biko's philosophy of black separatism and remaining conscious that this is now a choice rather than a requirement of the post-apartheid moment and that such a choice is neither always possible nor desirable. It is into this space of ambivalence that a novel such as Sindiwe Magona's 1998 *Mother to Mother* appears, recognizing both the need to include whiteness within a black redefinition of ethical relation in South Africa and the limits of such inclusion.

Structured as an address by a black South African mother to a white American mother, Magona's novel relies upon affective affinities that transcend the national space, suggesting that an interracial dialogue between empathetic mothers may be more possible from a certain geographic distance.[36] The international range of the novel's conceit intimates that the skewered racial structures of relation fomented by apartheid may only be remediable via an ethical circuit that first extends beyond the national space into the transnational one as a model, or lesson, for the more difficult negotiations that remain at home. All the same, though *Mother to Mother* joins these titular figures from the Global South to the Global North, the novel remains alert, simultaneously, to the material and aesthetic contingencies limiting the possibilities for global, interracial, ethical relation. Writing, *Mother to Mother* suggests, attempts reparation through the articulation of open-ended dialogue and interrogation, but it is also insufficient to the task of social repair that it faces.

The novel opens in the transition of 1993, though the transformations of the period have hardly affected the protagonist, Mandisa. Mandisa lives in Gugulethu township outside of Cape Town, and she works as a domestic for a white family. She is the mother of three children, including Mxolisi, who in this retelling is the sole murderer of American Fulbright scholar Amy Biehl. The novel fictionalizes a real event that occurred when Biehl was working on black voter registration efforts in South Africa before the first democratic elections of 1994. She was murdered by a group of boys the day before she was due to return home. The book presents Mandisa's address to Amy's mother, Linda, back in the United States.

In an interview, Magona explains that she wrote the novel after learning that one of Biehl's actual murderers was the son of a childhood friend.

> Well, we grew up together! As we say in the township, "I know her saliva!" because I have eaten candy from her mouth. I was horrified that someone I knew . . . I thought of the little Mandisa—how was she handling this? . . . I had a vague kind of sympathy for the Biehls, whom I do not know; I did not know them. But now I thought of Mandisa and I thought, my God, how is she? I wonder what has happened? How is she feeling? How has she dealt with it? I didn't go to see her. I came back [to New York], and for two years I was in grief for her. For two years I had this urge to go to the Biehls, especially the mother, to explain how this woman Mandisa was as a child. . . . And I imagined the rest of her life. The horror, the poverty.[37]

Magona's focus of connection is between women, particularly between herself and her childhood friend, Mandisa, and between herself and Amy Biehl's mother—"especially the mother," she states—suggesting that shared history and gender offer the opportunity for forging connections.[38] This kind of intersubjective relation, fictional though it may be given the distance that imaginative work entails, refuses the apartheid ideology that offered race as the only identitarian framework across which solidarities might be formed.

While Magona's earlier works also focus on black women's lives during apartheid, *Mother to Mother* is the first of her works to examine black female subjectivity *after* apartheid.[39] Nonetheless, it continues her oeuvre's previous emphasis on the relational structure underlying acts of storytelling, as all her works deploy first-person narrators directly addressing explicit audiences. In *Mother to Mother*, Magona similarly mobilizes a dialogic structure, although the narrative alternates between three forms of storytelling. First, there is Mandisa's direct address to Linda Biehl. This frames the novel and sporadically interrupts the other two strands of narrative. Second is a series of sections narrated by Mandisa that describe events that occurred on the day of Amy Biehl's death (August 25, 1993) and on the day after. The majority of the narrative, however, is constituted by Mandisa's first-person account of her own life as a fifteen- and sixteen-year-old girl in 1972 and 1973. Asynchronously, Magona accomplishes the goals she describes in the interview: to tell Mandisa's story and to tell it all to "especially the mother," Linda Biehl.

A major difference between *Mother to Mother* and Magona's earlier autobiographical works with their implied or explicit dialogic forms is that a shift has taken place in terms of the addressee, as the dialogue is now explicitly interracial. In *Mother to Mother*, Magona intentionally makes a black woman's address to a white woman the structural fulcrum of the book. "My Sister-Mother," Mandisa tells Amy Biehl's mother, "we are bound in this sorrow."[40] This link suggests that what unites people across blood, race, and space, creating a sort of global family, is a shared experience of suffering.

"MY SON KILLED YOUR DAUGHTER."[41] Thus begins Magona's novel, making explicit through one independent clause the fundamental interdependency of the four main personae of the book: Mandisa, the narrator; Mxolisi, her son; Linda Biehl, the woman to whom the novel is addressed; and her daughter, Amy. The simple grammatical union of all four that Magona brings about in one sentence highlights the centrality of themes of commonality and togetherness that dominate the rest of the work.[42] But the central verb, the pivotal word that cleaves the sentence—"killed"—also introduces the reader to less conciliatory themes of perpetratorship and victimhood, of crime and punishment. In addition to the act's undeniable violence, a violence mirrored in the sentence's own terrible precision, Magona's beginning neither explains nor excuses the fact of the murder. It is a factual claim about the past devoid of judgment.

Its simultaneous expression of togetherness and division insists from the start on the ambiguity of Magona's experience of the post-apartheid period. This thus differentiates Magona's writing from the "protest lit" of apartheid. That Magona now articulates this ambiguity, and in fact marks it as the starting point for her entire story, suggests an imaginative shift that refuses both the simplistic thinking of apartheid as well as that of someone like Amy Biehl herself, whose "naiveté" "tricked her into believing in the blanket, uniform guiltlessness of those whom she came to help."[43] Magona's entire novel hovers in between these poles of guilt and guiltlessness and refuses to come down on either side with any resolution. It is in this nebulous zone of shared, if uneven, responsibility, her book suggests, that the most productive work can be done in order to both process and repair the past and imagine and confront the present and future of South Africa.[44]

Some critics have pointed out that Magona's deployment of dialogical narration also dovetails with traditional forms of oral storytelling. But Meg Samuelson suggests that Magona's use of the oral tradition reveals her disconnection rather than her attachment to a community of oral storytellers since she is writing, after all, in print.[45] For Samuelson, Magona's narrative choice evinces her desire to assert her authenticity as a South African township dweller while actually being a writer abroad among the urban middle-classes as a UN employee. Samuelson's comments propose that Magona is anxious about the validity of her position as a writer in the United States and that she seeks to subsume this anxiety in the authenticity of traditional storytelling. Yet as Caroline Levine points out about forms more generally, dialogism is applied across time and space to different ends. To accuse Magona of overcompensating for her exilic guilt is to ignore the way dialogic forms of storytelling permeate Magona's works written *before* she left for the United States. And while the text's conceit is that it is structured as one international dialogue, it really works as a series of dialogues and modes of narratorial address.

Recounting a childhood memory, for instance, Mandisa recalls being told the history of South Africa by her grandfather—a very different history than that taught in schools. She lovingly remembers his narration as "soft and far-away, as though he were talking to many people, whose ears were filled with nothing else except the sound of his voice."[46] The lessons he teaches her about the history of the resistance of the Xhosa people are heteroglossic, as Mandisa, the child, interrupts his narrative with questions, and they frequently stop to "wet [their] mouths at the gourd," and her grandfather "[says] his voice would go unless he kissed his pipe."[47] Embedded within the larger dialogue between Mandisa and Amy Biehl's mother are other dialogues such as these between young Mandisa and her grandfather. Indeed, Magona's reliance on dialogical forms suggests that the conversational, relational approach is a way of writing herself into a conversation with the world in lieu of a narratological articulation of a unified, non-dialogic "pure" apartheid or post-apartheid subject. The only certain ethical approach Magona promotes is that of conversation as the narrative form least conducive to closure. Her stories are explicitly contrapuntal, admitting ambiguity and incommensurability to eschew the linguistic absolutism of apartheid's approach to discourse (what Bakhtin calls a "unitary language").[48] For Magona, dialogue is the *only* ethically viable mode of expression and representation. By insisting on open dialogue, Magona "compel[s] us to reflect on the costs of moral absolutism, the violence latent in trying to construct fully realized ethical forms of life."[49] Dialogic forms do ethical work for both participants. For Magona via Mandisa (as Wenzel and Samuelson note, the two often merge more than we might wish), writing *to* someone is a way of writing herself into the world that long refused her participation in any process of communal, political, or national discourse. The presence of an explicit (rather than implied) reader ensures, via her own creation, the recognition so long denied her. In psychoanalytic terms, Mandisa's dialogues reproduce the intersubjective encounter essential to the establishment of mutual co-recognition, which is itself a precursor for an emergent ethics.

Apartheid dogma institutionalized a psychic imbalance in which the white other (and the black other) was most frequently understood as an object, an imagined fantasy version of the real outside subject—as mere intrapsychic irreality. The "'outside' other," to use Jessica Benjamin's terminology, was so often "cancelled" by the "'inside' other" to produce distorted versions of that other, not to mention of the self as well. Magona's novel insists on revisiting her own distortions of those "outside" others, and by repeatedly identifying audiences, she constructs an ethics of readership that resuscitates the importance of mutual co-recognition in the post-apartheid moment.

Mandisa can be seen to enact reparation through narrative; indeed, she explains that she aims to "ease the other mother's pain . . . if a little."[50] By intentionally making a black woman's address to a white woman the central organizing axis of the book, the writer operates as a mediator in a literary kind of reparative work—her function is to bring these different experiences together, to draw the lines of similarity and difference in order to foster an awareness of the complexity and complicity of being. The act of imagining Amy Biehl's final hours, which is one of the opening sequences of the novel, performs this ethics of reparation through Mandisa's willed attempt to think herself into the mind and body of a white woman, indicating the facility with which Magona (and Mandisa) can do this. This shows, again, that imagining the interiority of the representative of oppression is a skill in which the disempowered are well versed.

This is not to say that Magona is unaware of the difficulties inherent in such a conjectural move, and here we witness an articulation of the post-apartheid writer's consciousness of the impotence of her own imaginative work, coterminous with her desire to write, though it produces only failure. A series of questions informs us that Mandisa is not entirely certain of Biehl's final hours, not certain that her efforts to imagine them result in anything accurate at all. Mandisa asks, "Does your daughter drive with others to school or is she by herself? Is the car radio on or does she put in a cassette, play a song that brings to mind her young man so far away? What plans does she have for the evening?"[51] Pearl Amelia McHaney suggests that the novel "arise[s] out of questions," questions like the ones listed here.[52] If Mandisa's series of interrogatives express uncertainty, her creativity also emerges from not knowing; the questions are what provoke her to write.

The question is a rhetorical mode equal to both expressing the ambiguity of meaning and, simultaneously, allowing meaning to emerge, arranging and alleviating the ongoing human urge to narrativize and make sense of the world. This linguistic preference for the interrogative suggests a writerly ethics of imagining alterity in which curiosity coexists with the potential for error, replacing the certainty and erasure of difference inherent in the declarative discourse of colonial and apartheid discourses. As we can see in the interview, when Magona recalls the thought process leading her to write *Mother to Mother*—"I thought of Mandisa and I thought, my God, how is she? I wonder what has happened? How is she feeling? How has she dealt with it?"—she shows how creative acts are born from acts of imaginative interrogation. Clearly, Magona values this stylistics of ambiguity since she makes it Mandisa's as well as her own.[53]

What does it mean for a black woman raised under the apartheid regime to say to white interviewers: "For having allowed such a climate to thrive in South Africa, we are all culpable. We are all culpable"?[54] In an interview Magona explains her task: "It is not in loving our neighbor that we become better human beings: the challenge before us is in learning to understand and perhaps one day love our enemy."[55] Or as she puts it again in another context: "It is not enough to love one's neighbor—we have to love our enemies."[56]

This appeal gestures toward a mode of intersectional familial global relation based upon neither blood, race, nor nation, but on the shared experience of human suffering, loss, and melancholy. Such a conceptualization of global connection via shared suffering echoes the concerns of international solidarity movements, yet its emphasis on shared affective modes of knowing rather than on shared economic alienation suggests that connections between the structures of feeling that govern the everyday realm of intimate or "imagined" connections are just as necessary for social transformation.

The work represents ethics in all its overwhelming, multidirectional, and cross-scale complexity since Mandisa not only demands an ethical response from others but also enacts an ethics in directing her narrative to the mother of Amy Biehl. In choosing such an auditor, Mandisa—and Magona—refuses the simplicity of legal definitions of justice that hold her son accountable as the sole bearer of responsibility and instead embeds herself and us within overlapping circles of complicity, looking inward and outward for gestures to recalibrate social coexistence.

In the opening pages of *Native Nostalgia* (2009), Jacob Dlamini narrates a story that, to him, delineates "a fine line between resistance and collaboration. Sometimes collaborators would become resisters and vice versa. It was never simply a case of resister on this side and collaborators on the other."[57] Dlamini's book, in tandem with his more recent 2014 *Askari*, directly challenges a number of "master narratives" about black apartheid experience, seeking, like Magona, to complicate the historical narrative of apartheid's ethical (dis)order. He writes:

> [*Native Nostalgia*] should be considered a modest contribution to ongoing attempts to rescue South African history and the telling of it from what Cherryl Walker has correctly identified as the distorting master narrative of black dispossession that dominates the historiography of the struggle. The master narrative would have us believe that black South Africans, who populate struggle jargon mostly as faceless "masses of our people," experienced apartheid the same way, suffered the same way and fought the same way against apartheid. That is untrue. Black South African life is as shot through with gender, class, ethnic, age and regional differences (to name only the most obvious distinctions) as life anywhere else in the world.
>
> The master narrative blinds us to a richness, a complexity of life among black South Africans. . . . I challenge facile accounts of black life under apartheid that paint the forty-six years in which the system existed as one vast moral desert, with no social orders, as if blacks produced no art, literature or music, bore no morally upstanding children or, at the very least, children who knew the difference between right and wrong—even if those children did not grow up to make the "right" moral choices in their lives.[58]

Dlamini's point is underscored by Magona's novel, which complicates understandings of responsibility by positioning the "child-murderer," Mxolisi, near the center of *Mother to Mother*. While the novel operates as a testimonial about black life under apartheid, complicating, much as Dlamini's works demand, any monological narrative of that experience, during a pivotal

moment in the text, Magona also uses writing to stage the dangers attendant to witnessing in language, or, in other words, the pitfalls of writing as a
medium for accessing justice.

When Mxolisi is four, Mandisa often leaves him in the company of some
older boys in a house nearby so she can work. These boys play with Mxolisi
and befriend him, but as they become increasingly involved in the struggle
politics of apartheid education, they leave Mxolisi more and more to his own
devices. One day, during a school boycott and in pursuit by the police, the
boys hide in a wardrobe inside their house. They toss a jacket into the back-
yard to make it appear to the police as though they had escaped through the
back and jumped the fence. The police are angry and take out their frustration by "viciously kick[ing] at the lifeless jacket on the ground . . . viciously
stamp[ing] on it. . . . battering it although it offered no fight."[59] As they are
leaving,

> "*Naba!*" clear as spring water high up the mountains, rang the voice, once
> more raised in excitement.
> "*Nab'ewodrophini!*" Here they are! Here they are, in the wardrobe!" screamed
> Mxolisi, pointing to the wardrobe. A clever little smile all over his chubby face.
> He said those terrible words, and swift as a wink, witnessed their outcome. The
> boys jumped out and made for the window. But when they hit the back garden the
> police were waiting and shot them then and there. He was struck mute by what he
> saw the police do to the two boys.[60]

Mxolisi's silence lasts for two full years, his response to having "witnessed
the children of the words his mouth had uttered."[61] While Mxolisi obediently
desires to help the police locate the boys, their abrupt violent murder teaches
him that having intentions for words is no guarantee that they will bring
about the desired result. Indeed, more troubling than this is the recognition
that words are not merely ineffective, but lead instead to a string of horrors
in which the speaker is unwillingly, but nonetheless, complicit. The potential
for danger that inheres in speaking or writing—the way in which words, once
unleashed into the world, can be used and misused for purposes sometimes
antagonistic to their speakers' and authors' intentions—might reaffirm, for
some writers, a commitment to more muted, or silent, engagements with the
world. And, indeed, this is the path Mxolisi takes, until years later when his
unspoken self emerges to make, as Dlamini puts it, the wrong "moral choice,"
even after knowing what was the "right" one. Mxolisi serves as a figure for

writerly ethics, and as such his silence stands as an acknowledgement of the failure—even the shocking violence—that speaking might bring about; his life becomes the traumatic reminder of how discourse, during apartheid but afterward, too, not only can fail to bring about ethical improvements but bears the potential to do precisely its opposite.

THE POST-APARTHEID LITERARY turn toward ethical relation is thus intrinsic to the form as well as the theme of black post-apartheid writing. Yet what are the implications of a turn toward ethical relation that is also a move away from overt political engagements of the most obvious kind? And how does the admission in the post-apartheid period of an apartheid-era ethics of interracial relation transform the historiography of protest? Does it negate the "spectacularity" of political writing or, worse, hold its polarized aesthetics responsible for its failure to produce a more liberatory politics after apartheid?[62] In his recent study of Askaris, black South Africans who were coerced into working for the apartheid state as assassins, Dlamini emphasizes the ways in which collaboration entailed "fatal intimacies" between Askari and their "bosses," like de Kock. The book focuses on Glory Lefoshie Sedibe (known as Comrade September during his guerilla days in uMkhonto we Siswe, the ANC's military wing) and hones in on his relationship with de Kock, who at one crucial moment, for Dlamini, gave Sedibe his own medicine, thereby saving his life. Dlamini asks: "What could be more personal than De Kock sharing his anxiety meds to prevent Sedibe from dying of a heart attack, or using his bare hands to beat Sedibe to within an inch of his life, almost precipitating the very heart attack he did not want to claim Sedibe?"[63]

In this final section of the book, I suggest that the turn away from politics on a grand scale is really a reorientation of the political toward the inclusion of more minute everyday acts and interactions between human beings. This does not entail a relinquishing of the necessity for policy and its implementation across national scales but asserts a commitment to reassessing and reinvesting in the types of political effects that aesthetic forms might influence and model.

FIGURING CONNECTIONS

Black writing after apartheid coheres, crucially, in a reevaluation of temporality as an organizational structure for narrative and politics. A turn toward ethics can be construed as a turn away from dreams of the future, a reorientation to a temporary structuring of everyday relations unimpinged upon by teleological ambitions. Because the momentum of black apartheid writing was largely driven by desires to produce and effect the future, that future was imagined, narratively, in various ways, but always as a future without apartheid. Rob Nixon presciently asks in 1996, "What is the future of that stalwart of South African literature, the future itself?"[64] Now that this future is here, and yet not here, writers, disappointed with such teleological, instrumentalist forms of imaginative creativity, have turned against this kind of temporal organization in their work to construct, instead, "an uncovered, permeable, unknown, undisclosed, future" expressed through forms and themes of relation.[65]

Ethics has fewer teleological aims than politics, and its ambit, though frequently ambitious and wide reaching, as in the case of Mandisa's attempt to connect in suffering to Linda Biehl across transatlantic space, is nonetheless restricted to instances, acts, or events of relation. Ethical theory and ethical practice are less concerned with grandiose, earth-shattering revolution than with the interpersonal, day-to-day ways that people can be open, receptive, and responsible to one another. Being with otherness involves a willed suspension of time and an openness to seeing what occurs. It eschews the heroism associated with epic and revolt, and seeks more modest, everyday intimacies.

Friendship may be a particularly useful way of thinking about such forms of relation, since it is conducive to mutual, equal, ethical exchange. As both Leela Gandhi and Jacques Derrida explore, friendship can serve as a model for social exchange that might be replicated beyond the precise parameters of particular friendships. Elsewhere, Dlamini reminds us, for Theodor Adorno friendship is quintessentially ethical because it is non-teleological. Adorno writes that "tenderness between people is nothing other than awareness of the possibility of relations without purpose."[66] Dlamini goes on: "To treat people, including strangers, with kindness is to treat people as ends in themselves."[67] This anti-instrumentalism of friendship obliterates *telos*, as friends act responsibly toward one another merely out of friendship and for no other future purpose. As we have seen in Gobodo-Madikizela's and Magona's contemplations of interracial relation after apartheid,

> when some of the selves who make up a culture loosen themselves from the security and comfort of old affiliations and identifications to make an

unexpected "gesture" of friendship toward all those on the other side of the fence . . . There is no finality in this action, no easily discernable teleological satisfaction.[68]

This is not to say that adherents of friendship as a model for ethical relation entirely forgo political engagement or the hope for a future that is an improvement upon today. But as Derrida has written of the belief system underlying friendship, the hope is for a future "yet 'to come,' 'indefinitely perceptible,' 'always insufficient and future.'"[69] The radical insufficiency of the future as it was imagined by black writers during apartheid, and its exposure as insufficient, can now be embraced and understood as *part* of a political program rather than as evidence of its unviability.

While friendship operates temporally, in a zone of immediacy that denies it any instrumentality, it also epitomizes ethical relation in its non-prescriptive, non-tyrannical forms. Carol Jacobs proposes we detach ethical thought from its association with systems of morality. "What if ethics were neither prescription nor action?" she asks:

> How could one conceive an ethics . . . in which language does not simply tell us what to do? . . . What if such disruptions were not the failure of the ethical but rather the beginnings of a redefinition of it as responsibility, another display of it, a nontyrannical ethical no longer irrevocably bound to a must?[70]

> What kind of ethics could this be that doesn't go by the rules but rather goes by them and goes on to upset the ruling, that offers us no definitive shape, no pure idea, no absolute good, no access to heaven after all, no promise of spoils, no reassurance of source, no final judgment? And which, all that notwithstanding, is certainly no call to anarchy?[71]

What it might look like, if we understand friendship via the circuits explored in Gandhi's work, is a rendering vulnerable of the self to alterity, a willingness to live in discomfort or precarity, along with Jacob's refusal of moral imperatives and social absolutes. But what role can writers play in envisioning such a cloudy form of futurity? Recall that Wayne Booth saw the novel as being exemplarily ethical because of its ability to recreate the experience of being with a friend in each readerly encounter. If friendship is the relational structure most conducive to a reciprocal ethics, then art forms like the novel, Booth implies, reproduce such ethical encounters mimetically. And does the recognition of ethics as the core concern of the contemporary period absolve post-apartheid writers of the pressure to be politically *engagé*? What more modestly reconfigured avenues for social change are available to writers? As postcolonial theorist and poet Edouard Glissant suggests, writing, even when not instrumentalist or even when explicitly anti-instrumentalist, may nonetheless affect the world. He asks: "Let us not stop with this commonplace; that a poetics cannot guarantee us a concrete means of action. But a poetics, perhaps, does allow us to understand better our action in the world."[72] Black writing in the wake of apartheid seeks to understand what relation might look like after apartheid both in terms of relation across the races and also as relation transforms through other social prisms like gender, class, ethnicity, and language. In their 2013 collection *Categories of Persons: Rethinking Ourselves and Others*, Dlamini and Megan Jones suggest that the task of each writer (and citizen) in the post-apartheid period "is to place ourselves in the shoes of another":

> Try to understand, for example, what it means to live in a shack along the N2 on the Cape Flats. If there is a moral failure [in the present], it is this inability to put ourselves in the shoes of another—but how do we help engender a new sense of empathy?[73]

The collection of essays they gather suggests, provisionally, that writing may help to form such empathetic links. This, of course, is nothing, if not a reiteration of ethical theory's claims that art produces ethical feeling. Furthermore, Dlamini and Jones use language for imagining oneself as other that harkens back to eighteenth-century Enlightenment philosophy.

Often theorists, philosophers, and writers seeking to explain how imagination produces ethical feeling rely on this same metonymic formulation asking humans to place themselves in the shoes of another. Consider a much earlier example of this from novelist Sol Plaatje's 1916 plea protesting the Natives Land Bill of 1913, which foreshadowed apartheid land dispossession laws:

> Some readers may perhaps think that I have taken the Colonial Parliament rather severely to task. But to any reader who holds with Bacon, that "the pencil hath laboured more in describing the afflictions of Job than the felicities of Solomon," I would say: "Do, if we dare make the request, and place yourself in our shoes."[74]

Citing Bacon becomes a way for Plaatje to forge a link with his white European and South African readers, but for explicitly instrumental ends, namely, to convince government officials to implement fairer land distribution practices.[75] Thus, for Plaatje, author of *Native Life in South Africa*, writing has an express purpose and is the correct medium through which to accomplish that purpose. But the language he relies on to beget empathetic response is a phrase so often evoked that it becomes a kind of uninspired cliché for how one might imagine oneself as other. Indeed Gobodo-Madikizela also writes of "stepping into the shoes of the aggressor."[76] Mostly, this phrase is tossed off without analysis. Yet to imaginatively put oneself in someone else's shoes is not necessarily a call to change the self in any drastic way.

But to imagine the dissolution of a self, or the self held apart or in abeyance, when confronted with the other is to cede the Hegelian demand for recognition, creating an opening up of the self to alterity that produces a state of extreme vulnerability or precarity. For Leela Gandhi, friendship is a site for the production of such vulnerability:

> The ethical agency of the host-friend relies precisely on her capacity to leave herself open, in Blanchot's terms, to the risk of radical insufficiency. Poised in a relation where an irreducible and asymmetrical other always calls her being into question, she is ever willing to risk becoming strange or guestlike in her own domain, whether this be home, nation, community, race, gender, sex, skin, or species.[77]

This "self-estrangement" or "self-othering" (Nancy), or what Gandhi calls a "minor (insignificant?) gesture of self-endangerment," represents an alternative response to otherness than that figured by the mere exchange of corporal or geographic perspective.[78]

Though the figure of the other's shoes is an unsatisfactory model for imagining an ethics after apartheid, understood historically, it is a trope with very particular colonial, anti-colonial, and postcolonial resonances. Indeed, in such contexts, feet, shoes, boots, and bootstraps have local, political, and socioeconomic symbolic purchase that restores value to a phrase easy to dismiss because of overuse.

Early in the *Wretched of the Earth*, Frantz Fanon notes that "the colonist's feet can never be glimpsed, except perhaps in the sea, but then you can never get close enough. They are protected by solid shoes in a sector where the streets are clean and smooth, without a pothole, without a stone."[79] Fanon's implication is that the covered feet of the colonists are axiomatic representations of colonial power; the nude or unshod foot marks a vulnerability or a poverty, a subject position that colonists refuse to inhabit. In "The Big Toe," Georges Bataille argues that bare feet are traditionally maligned in Western thought.

> Since by its physical attitude [of erectness] the human race distances itself *as much as it can* from the terrestrial mud . . . one can imagine that a toe, always more or less damaged and humiliating, is psychologically analogous to the fall of a man—in other words, to death.[80]

For this reason, for Bataille, the foot becomes the target of the "rage" humans feel, as it reminds them of their own fallibility and of their link to that which is "base," "refuse," and mortal.[81] For Fanon's colonists, hiding such a synecdochic symbol of human weakness is essential to the continued propagation of imperial rule and to the concomitant perpetuation of colonialists' assertions of their own moral probity.

In Emmanuel Levinas's ethical thought, however, it is the face, famously, that signifies the humanity of the other, demanding a responsibility toward that other that precedes any conscious, cultural awareness. "The nudity of the face," writes Levinas, "is a stripping with no cultural ornament," which "by its nakedness, by its destitution . . . is [a] summons to respond."[82] This "summons" announces the entrance of ethics into human relations. Levinas's first philosophy includes an ethical responsiveness to the other's face that if stripped of "cultural ornament" must precede consciousness of cultural markers, such as race, for instance. Since for Levinas, "before cultural expression, before the said, lies the universal but deformalized humanism of the other," there is no need for discussions of race since the appraisal of race or racialization occurs subsequent to the ethical imperative called forth by the face of the other.[83] But given the extensive evidence we have that many colonial, postcolonial, and, indeed, contemporary apprehensions of alterity rely inordinately on racial distinctions, Levinas's severing of preconscious reflex from cultural effects disregards the way that culture often shapes the very formation of preconscious affect and response. To put this otherwise, if Levinas is correct to assume that the apprehension of alterity is preconscious, his assessment that our preconsciousness is not itself a product of external, cultural, epistemological structures seems less convincing. Racism is not only a conscious ideological position but a felt, affective, and often preconscious response to external prompts, and as Gary Taylor puts it in his history of responses to skin color, "skin is a signed façade."[84] The actual face of the other that we encounter every day is always and already marked by culture in such a way as to be indistinguishable from it. This does not negate, necessarily, the ethical claim that the other makes upon us; indeed, a recognition of such semiotic marking may in fact increase our responsibilities to others.

Interestingly, and perhaps because Levinas himself might have sensed the limits of his ethical figure, he uses a different bodily symbol to describe the sensation one experiences when this full humanism, provoked by the encounter with the face, emerges. "To be human," for Levinas,

> is to care for the other above oneself, to overcome the natural indifference and countercurrent of being in nonindifference and compassion toward the other—the "wisdom of love." It is a painful wisdom, *a skin turned inside out* . . . providing for the other the food one would enjoy eating, the clothing one would enjoy wearing, the money one would enjoy spending.[85]

With "a skin turned inside out," the cultural markers that we use to identify difference disappear, and only the flesh and blood of the subcutaneous insides (the *prima facie*) remain. While Levinas disregards the importance of culture in determining ethical response, this may be because in its fullest expression—"a skin turned inside out"—what unites us is a vulnerability lying beneath the skin, our blood and bone, our mortality. As Levinas puts it, "The self, from head to toe, all the way to the marrow of the bones, is vulnerability."[86] Such a physical, mortal shared vulnerability always precedes social constructions.

If the face and the feet present certain difficulties as figures for ethical response in South Africa, hands in both Gobodo-Madikizela's and Magona's works present an alternative set of figurations. In a pivotal scene in Gobodo-Madikizela's book, de Kock becomes emotionally distraught by the conversation they are having together, so Gobodo-Madikizela reaches her hand across the table to comfort him. She explains:

> I asked de Kock to talk about the meeting with Pearl Faku and Doreen Mgoduka. His face immediately fell, and he became visibly distressed. I could hear the clatter of his leg chains as he shuffled his feet. Sitting directly across from me in the small prison consulting room, his heavy glasses on the table

that separated us, he started to speak. There were tears in his eyes. In a breaking voice he said: "I wish I could do much more than [say] I'm sorry. I wish
there was a way of bringing their bodies back alive. I wish I could say, 'Here
are your husbands,'" he said, stretching out his arms as if bearing an invisible
body, his hands trembling, his mouth quivering, "but unfortunately . . . I have
to live with it."

    Relating to him in the only way one does in such human circumstances, I
touched his shaking hand, surprising myself. But it was clenched, cold, and rigid.[87]

After touching what she realizes is his "trigger hand," she recoils, yet the
intimate act provokes a series of reflections upon responsibility and victimhood, suggesting in true Levinasian form that physical and affective ethical
responses precede cognitive ones. In one way, she writes, "I was angry that
the same society that had created de Kock, that had accepted his murderous
protection of their privilege, had ostracized him and was now standing in
judgment of him."[88] Yet,

> in touching de Kock's hand I had touched his leprosy, and he seemed to be
> telling me that, even though I did not realize it at the time, I was from now
> on infected with the memory of having embraced into my heart the hand that
> had killed, maimed, and blown up lives. . . . My act of empathy had drawn me
> into *intimate complicity* with him.[89]

While Levinas's "humanism of the other" is figured in the other's face, for
Gobodo-Madikizela it is contact with and through the hand that crystalizes
her recognition of de Kock's human otherness. Though his face—described
in her initial encounter with de Kock—marks his otherness as a call to ethics, it is her hand reaching out that instantiates ethical action. In spite of, or
rather *because* of, touch's collaborative, contaminated, and complicitous pact,
Gobodo-Madikizela's intimate gesture transforms the moment's potential
into an ethical act of complicit relationality.[90]

    Hands, Bataille points out, "have come to signify useful action and firm
character," and in Magona's and Gobodo-Madikizela's works they function as
agents of social connection.[91] In her autobiographical *Forced to Grow*, Magona
recalls that neighbors would often look after her children when she went to
work. She explains: "There was no charge made for this neighborly act. However, as we say, '*Isandla sihlamba esisihlambayo*. A hand washes that which

washes it.'"[92] The interdependency of the hands in this Xhosa expression presents a figure of neighborly social organization that stresses the absolute necessity of community for the health and well-being of its society's youngest members. Two hands are necessarily required for the washing of each hand; thus, the task is both collaborative and intimate, while each member of that collaboration remains discreet and distinct. As a metaphor for dialogue and relation that Magona's books promote in their link between storytelling and relationality, the proverb elaborates a social configuration based on mutuality, dependence, and shared responsibilities—with hands again made the figure for a practice of living together and also for making clean that which has been sullied.

During another charged symbolic moment at the TRC that received significant media attention due to its highly demonstrative presentation, erstwhile apartheid minister of law and order Adriaan Vlok washed the feet of a man he had formerly attempted to poison: Frank Chikane, secretary-general for the South African Council of Churches. While considerable scholarly and journalistic analysis of this moment has appeared, the episode of restitution returns us full circle to Fanon's observations about colonizers' feet. Because the bare foot exposes vulnerabilities and, following Bataille, is also the synecdochic locus of all that is base and messy in human existence, Vlok's act of stooping to clean Chikane's feet was a highly charged, possibly overdetermined, act of repentance reminding us once again how limbs or parts of the human body serve—mimetically—as conduits for making others known and for acting upon and in the world.

We might conceive of this metonymical reflex undergirding representations of intersubjective relation in the cases elaborated here as evidence of some kind of amputation of relation, but there are also more ethically productive ways to cast this discursive and material isolation of body parts. By breaking relation into discussions of feet, hands, and faces, wholeness, or the fantasy of a discrete subject, is replaced by bits of bodies that touch, infect, and repulse, simultaneously affirming and undermining notions of absolutism, thus emphasizing relation as *the* mode of being over and above individuation. In Lacanian terms, these fragments of a body both stand as the temporary objects that fill the gaps in symbolic reality and simultaneously mark the gap or void in that reality (the *objet petit a*). This paradoxical affirmation of meaning that appears along with its absence operates much as a question does, allowing us to recognize all attempts to know, imagine, and experience otherness as always temporary, always contingent processes that emphasize exchange between parts rather than between discrete, isolate, or fixed individuals.

AS THIS CHAPTER means to suggest, ethics is neither anathema to politics nor its opposite. The (re)turn to ethics reveals, in part, the failures of organized politics on a grand scale in the wake of the demise of apartheid, and it seeks to restructure modes of envisioning, understanding, and implementing relation (through friendship, particularly, perhaps) in order to instantiate a different kind of political intervention. This politics is less heroic and is conscious of its own limits, of the dangers of teleologically inclined visions of hope, as well as of the dangers of capitulation and inertia. Black writers after apartheid give ethics political charge by relying on the unstable and ambiguous literary figures of dialogue, metonym, and interrogation.

Gandhi reminds us that Vladimir Lenin believed that thinkers who were concerned with ethics were immature, and he cast their "utopianism" as wrongheaded idealism in contrast to the pragmatism he linked with politics. Lenin saw politics as epistemologically linked to rationality, whereas ethics he denigrated as a site of messiness, irrationality, and affect. For Gandhi, these qualities are ethics' most promising strengths. Like Biko before her, Ghandi sees ethical utopianism as characterized by "qualities of disorganization, provisionality, coincidence, and conjuncture . . . [qualities that] make up the fabric of a utopian politics of inventiveness, bearing within itself the mutually complementary gestures of refusal and relationality."[93] Along with Gandhi, then, I have sought to ascribe a kind of instrumentalism to ethics that is a non-instrumentalism—a poetics that accepts its power to change mentalities, albeit unquantifiably and intangibly, an ethics that produces imprecise and momentary transformations in epistemological and political schema. Echoing Édouard Glissant, Gandhi asks:

> Does a politics of relationality . . . ever change the world? Does it successfully dispatch imperial governments and occupying armies from native soil? Lead a disenfranchised people into the promise of self-determination? Mitigate in any way the burdens of colonial inheritance? Certainly not with anything like the speed and efficiency of those better organized and better focused (and more mature) revolutionary movements less inclined to found social change upon the painstaking labor of personal transformation. *Yet precisely because of its inability to work its effects at industrial speed and scale*, the[se] poli-

tics . . . often *alter the genetic structure of the societies in which they eventuate, subtly varying for future use their ethical, epistemic, and political composition.*[94]

Unlike other revolutionary movements, ethical change involves gradualist transformations of the intimate, personal, interpersonal, and everyday and does not require the total overhaul of a political system or "civil society" at one fell swoop. Ethical approaches, suggest the writers considered here, cannot provide clear answers to post-apartheid relation and its shapes to come, and instead lay relation open to question, time and time again, in defiance of both the categories and the absolutisms of apartheid. Their work promotes partial visions, contact, contamination, and discomfort, laying the groundwork for such radical, episodic moments of openness to alterity that makes just relation possible.

ETHICS TODAY: A CONCLUSION

Since the demise of apartheid, palpable symbolic gains have been made in both political and ethical realms. This is perhaps most fully articulated in South Africa's democratic constitution, which is based on the premises of "non-racialism" and "non-sexism," laudably forbidding the state to "discriminate directly or indirectly against anyone on one or any more grounds, including race, gender, sex, pregnancy, marital status, ethnic or social origin, colour, sexual orientation, age, disability, religion, conscience, belief, culture, language and birth."[95] The post-apartheid moment has allowed for the emergence of debates around questions of gender, class, language, and queerness that were never possible in the public political spheres of apartheid rule.[96] Such discussions find voice in mainstream, academic, and popular forms and inevitably touch as much on questions of ethical as of political relation, as they seek to navigate and define vexed categories such as community, responsibility, and reparation in the post-apartheid order.

Yet it is, of course, quite commonplace nowadays to note that the post-apartheid moment has not lived up to expectations. The reasons for this are not hard to miss, but certain moments in recent South African history particularly explain the increased tendency within South Africa, and internationally, to view the democratically elected ANC government as having grossly disappointed the democratic visions of all those who fought—and longed—for the end of apartheid. Two moments in particular stand out as exemplary of the failure of the new order, though there are unfortunately many others one could name.

When thirty-four miners were brutally gunned down by South African police at the Lonmin platinum mines in 2012, what was already obvious to many became unavoidably apparent, namely, that capitalism had supplanted justice as the government's primary modus operandi dictating affairs of state. By exercising its right to kill—what Giorgio Agamben calls the government's "state of exception"—the post-apartheid ANC-led government exposed an operative logic that deemed certain lives—poor ones, laboring ones, black ones—to be expendable. Indeed, the logic of capital at work that day depends upon a model for understanding human life that continues to subscribe to hierarchical valuations along a scale from human to subhuman, a way of thinking violently in contradiction with all that is enshrined in the country's new constitution. The miners gunned down at the Lonmin mine were thought superfluous, by this logic, and thus less human and less deserving of the life that the politicians and mine owners, concerned that the strike disrupted the flow of profits, deemed their own inalienable right. The Lonmin massacre exemplified how acute the crisis of ethical relation remains within macro-political spheres. Furthermore, it highlights how flimsy the constitution's written commitments to the equality of all are and how insufficient a prophylactic they represent against the priorities of capitalist accumulation and its violent and murderous methodologies.

The other great failure of ethics of particular relevance for my focus on black ethics after apartheid appeared as a failure of hospitality, that ethical injunction to welcome all, to treat all as one would wish to be treated, despite, or even because of, difference. This burgeoning inhospitableness culminated in 2008 when African migrants mainly from neighboring Zimbabwe and Mozambique were subject to a spate of violent attacks by black South Africans who deemed these extranationals *amakwerekwere*, "the undesirable foreigners," resulting in more than sixty deaths.[97] These non-South African Africans were scapegoats for the economic dissatisfaction many black South Africans felt and continue to feel after it became apparent that the transition to democratic rule was failing to significantly improve most black lives. For Grant Farred, there was great betrayal at the heart of this violence because these attacks targeted "those whose language, ethnicity, and culture make them alien to South Africa; yet they are precisely those who historically supported the anti-apartheid struggle."[98] The solidarity with black South Africans that many other African nationals expressed during apartheid was forgotten during this post-apartheid moment and was replaced, instead, by a vengeful and deeply inhospitable series of violent acts. The attacks of 2008 were the worst in terms of sheer numbers, but xenophobic violence directed against other Africans continues to plague South Africa, foregrounding the emergence of new social rifts. These violent acts may appear more structured along economic and national lines than along the racial ones of apartheid, yet they still participate in and draw upon those racist practices associated with the long history of segregation in South Africa.

These crises and failures of ethical relation (and there are others) inevitably found their way into contemporary South African writing. Arguably, crisis and disappointment has become the central subject of much recent scholarship in South African literary studies in South Africa, on the continent, and abroad as well. Several important studies have appeared recently to assess the fictional works that have emerged since apartheid's demise. As early as 2004, the *South Atlantic Quarterly* published a special issue on South African fiction, aptly titled "After the Thrill is Gone." Andrew van der Vlies's *Present Imperfect: Contemporary South African Writing* similarly conceives of contemporary South African literature through frameworks of disappointment, disaffection, and stagnation. Leon de Kock's *Losing the Plot: Crime, Reality, and Fiction in Postapartheid Writing* suggests that the failure to achieve the democratic telos envisioned by anti-apartheid adherents has resulted in fictions that depose the primacy of plots, foregrounding, instead, alternative approaches to temporal, historical, and future times in South Africa. In a forthcoming collection, *States of Transition: The Temporalities of South African Writing*, coeditor Rita Barnard describes the affect or mood of the "post-anti-apartheid" moment as "autumnal."[99]

In contrast, then, to recent studies of contemporary South African literature that emphasize the disappointment and frustration of the post-apartheid "transition" period, this chapter's purpose has been to identify a shift in black post-apartheid writing away from the political sphere and toward the ethical. The book, overall, has sought to show that this shift is part of a longer historical engagement with ethical concerns in black writing that stretches all the way back to the thinking and writing of Sol Plaatje[100] and Tiyo Soga,[101] concerns that necessitated suppression, however, during the apartheid years, when the political situation required more overt political engagements to command literary and thematic attention.

For Farred, writing in 2004, the immediate post-apartheid moment is a time of the "not-yet counterpartisan," when responses to the failures of the

ANC have failed to materialize. But in more recent years, particularly in mobilizations centered around the #FeesMustFall and the #RhodesMustFall student protesters, a certain amount of resistance to the post-apartheid ANC-led government has emerged, in evidence with the recent demise of Jacob Zuma's presidency. Achille Mbembe's important speech "Decolonizing Knowledge and the Question of the Archive," addressed particularly to these student activists, calls any "counter-partisan" approach a return to *ethical* philosophies of relation. He argues that "we need to connect in entirely new ways the project of non-racialism to that of human mutuality," extending his injunction, as well, into the realm of the nonhuman and the planetary. He enjoins people to strive for a "humankind ruling in common for a common which includes the non-humans, which is the proper name for democracy."[102] As we have seen, the ethical and the political often interpenetrate in ways exemplified here by Mbembe. But my point has been throughout the book to argue that the ethical forms of response to injustice were underplayed during apartheid and only reemerge now in the wake of apartheid's official close. As Leela Gandhi has suggested, the everyday ethical realm may, after all, be the only practical option for many to engage with and resist injustice as daily praxis.

Despite the many gains accrued as apartheid rule was replaced by universal suffrage, politics still remains a sphere that is largely impenetrable to most black South Africans. And writers, too, have felt with considerable severity how akin they turn out to be, at least in this regard, to other South Africans, increasingly acknowledging the impotence of writing, at least in terms of its ability to directly influence the political sphere.[103] But ethics and engagement with various forms of intimate relationality provide an alternative and valuable source for agential engagement as a counterpart(isan) approach to the anomie or despair "after the thrill [of 1994] is gone."

While the focus on disappointment has only had purchase in South African writing quite recently, there is a long history of this affective state in postcolonial writing from the wider African continent. Earlier works such as Ayi Kwei Armah's *The Beautyful Ones Are Not Yet Born*, Ngũgĩ wa Thiong'o's *Weep Not, Child*, and Chinua Achebe's *No Longer at Ease* bemoan in different ways the failures of the newly independent postcolonial states of Ghana, Kenya, and Nigeria, respectively, to live up to and provide for the visions of the anti-colonial fighters and philosophers of the first half of the twentieth century. These canonical novels represent the tip of the iceberg in terms of what Gaurav Desai calls "novels of disillusionment," a subgenre in African literary production that dwells on the deeply complex responses Africans have had across the continent to their state's various degrees of abandoning their democratic and egalitarian visions.[104] David Scott has shown, most recently, how disappointment has an even longer history throughout the postcolonial and now postsocialist world.[105] Thus, a turn toward the smaller, intimate, affective modes of engagement may seem a capitulation of sorts to the dominant world order represented by global capital's relentless efforts to accumulate wealth no matter the cost to human life or indeed to the earth's longevity. But if an ethical focus is certainly in some ways such a relinquishing of engagement, and a turn away from an emphasis on overt political agency, it also provides a mode for ongoing sustained life that is not only a form of survival but also an avenue for finding love among the ruins.

NOTES

INTRODUCTION

1. A recent surge in cognitive science studies links reading novels to changes in the neurological pathways that promote ethical forms of behavior. See Belluck, "For Better Social Skills, Scientists Recommend a Little Chekhov," and Knapton, "Great Novels Can Change Your Life . . . And Your Brain." Scholars working in "cognitive cultural studies" include Blakey Vermeule, Lisa Zunshine, Murray Smith, Carl Plantinga, Raymond Mar, and Keith Oatley.

2. "I had always disappeared when I was reading—that was almost the whole point of reading for me, to be no one for a few hours. Now it happened while I was writing. To disappear in that way, to enter a state of selflessness, is something I believe every musician, painter, actor, director and writer knows. It lies at the very base of creation." Knausgaard, "I Am Someone, Look at Me," 97.

3. "The house was quiet and the world was calm. / The reader became the book." Stevens, "The House Was Quiet and the World Was Calm," 358.

4. "There is no art except for and by others." Sartre, *"What Is Literature?" and Other Essays*, 52.

5. The term comes from Hale, "Aesthetics and the New Ethics: Theorizing the Novel in the Twenty-First Century." Other prominent twentieth- and twenty-first-century ethical theorists include Martha Nussbaum, Wayne Booth, and J. Hillis Miller.

6. Brooks and Jewett, *The Humanities and Public Life*, 3. What is meant by "the ethical," or how these thinkers conceive that literature produces ethicality, varies significantly. Some attend to the way specific literary works treat or disregard ethical themes (Nussbaum, *Poetic Justice*; Palumbo-Liu, *The Deliverance of Others*; Blumenthal-Barby, *Inconceivable Effects*). Others expound on the ethics intrinsic to creative acts such as writing or performing (Attridge, *The Singularity of Literature*; Miller, *The Ethics of Reading*). Still others examine ethics that emerge through practices of reading or reception (Attridge, *The Singularity of Literature*; Booth, *The Company We Keep*; Iser, *The Act of Reading*; Miller, *The Ethics of Reading*; Palumbo-Liu, *The Deliverance of Others*).

7. Fanon, *Black Skin, White Masks*, 146.

8. Adichie, "The Danger of a Single Story."

9. "A disidentifying subject is unable to fully identify or to form what Sigmund Freud called that 'just-as-if' relationship. . . . [Wh]at stops identification from happening is always the ideological restrictions implicit in an identificatory site. . . . For the critic, disidentification is the hermeneutical performance of decoding mass/high or any other cultural field from the perspective of a minority subject who is disempowered in such a representational hierarchy." Muñoz, *Disidentifications*, 7, 25.

10. Glissant, *Poetics of Relation*, 183.

11. Two excellent exceptions to this include Joshi, *In Another Country: Colonialism, Culture, and the English Novel in India*, and Ten Kortenaar's *Postcolonial Literature and the Impact of Literacy: Reading and Writing in African and Caribbean Fiction. Book History* has begun publishing more articles on print culture and book history in the Global South, but as Elizabeth Le Roux writes, "Reception studies [in Africa] have a shorter history still [than literary studies], and there is a great deal of work to be done in this field." For a look at what she claims is "the first attempt to organize book historical studies set in an African context," see Le Roux, "Book History in the African World" 261, 250. See also McDonald, "Semper Aliquid Novi: Reclaiming the Future of Book History from an African Perspective."

12. Anderson, *Imagined Communities*; Chartier, *The Order of Books*; Moretti, *Atlas of the European Novel*.

13. Hoggart, *The Uses of Literacy*; Febvre and Martin, *The Coming of the Book*.

14. When ethical critics occasionally look beyond literature, they restrict themselves to discussions of works that would likely be considered "highbrow" in film, dance, and the visual arts.

15. This has ideological consequences since it unwittingly implies that ethical development through cultural consumption is not available to those who do not, or cannot, read literary works. Furthermore, recent work from the humanities' "ethical turn" focuses mostly on a few canonical writers; works outside the Western canon are almost entirely absent from the discussion. Thus, inadvertently, most ethical criticism rests upon several exclusions. By ignoring the avenues for ethical development that occur through engagements with non-Western literary and popular forms, it produces, despite itself, an unethical or anti-ethics, since the ethical being in such criticism emerges only through contact with rarified literary works from the Global North and usually from within that same space.

16. For important considerations of popular audiences in African contexts, see Ambler, "Popular Films and Colonial Audiences"; Barber, "Preliminary Notes on Audiences in Africa"; and Jaji, *Africa in Stereo*. For work on underexamined readers and reading practices in South Africa, see Dick, *The Hidden History of South Africa's Book and Reading Cultures*; Couzens, "Moralizing Leisure Time." In the United States, see McHenry, *Forgotten Readers*. For work on black film audiences in the United States, see Stewart, *Migrating to the Movies*.

17. Malcolm Bradbury, quoted in Booth, *The Company We Keep*, 73.

18. Iser describes it similarly: "The literary text enables its readers to transcend the limitations of their own real-life situation; it is not a reflection of any given reality, but it is an extension or broadening of their own reality." Iser, *The Act of Reading*, 79.

19. Booth, *The Company We Keep*, 60–61.

20. Booth, *The Company We Keep*, 189.

21. Booth, *The Company We Keep*, 64.

22. Jameson, *The Political Unconscious*, 38. Similarly, Wolfgang Iser suggests that while "the novel deals with social and historical norms, this does not mean that it simply reproduces contemporary values. The mere fact that not all norms can possibly be included in the novel shows that there must have been a process of selection, and this in turn . . . is liable to be less in accordance with contemporary values than in opposition to them." Iser, *The Act of Reading*, xii.

23. Miller, *The Ethics of Reading*, 3. Carol Jacobs is adamant that we distinguish between a work's ethical theme or intention and its production of ethics through form. Miller, Attridge, and Jacobs are interested in locating the ethical force of a work *outside* its thematic preoccupation with ethics.

24. Miller acknowledges that the "act of reading" is "extraordinarily hard work. It does not occur that often. Clearheaded reflection on what really happens in an act of reading is even more difficult and rare. It is an event, traces of which are found here and there in written form, like those tracks left in a bubble-chamber by the passage of a particle from outer space." Miller, *The Ethics of Reading*, 3–4.

25. Attridge, *The Singularity of Literature*, 64.

26. Attridge, *The Singularity of Literature*, 3.

27. Attridge, *The Singularity of Literature*, 3, 10.

28. Attridge, *The Singularity of Literature*, 61. Miller widens the generic scope of his argument somewhat, suggesting that "in principle the ethics of reading could be explored by way of examples chosen from poetry, from philosophy, even from political texts or essays in literary criticism." Miller, *The Ethics of Reading*, 2.

29. In 1978 Wolfgang Iser argues that substance inheres neither in a text nor in its reader but is instead produced at the *intersection* between a text and its consumer. Meaning arises between "the poles of text and reader," so that a reader "assembles" the text, creating value through "a re-creative dialectics." Iser, *The Act of Reading*, ix–x. This processual understanding of how readers make meaning from texts allows us to see mainstream works of popular and mass culture as equally capable of producing ethical response as literary works. Attridge also emphasizes this process of meaning's *becoming* in his discussion: "I have been talking as if the work were a preexisting object to which the reader, wholly independent of it, responds, whereas it is in fact a set of coded signals which become a poem or a novel only in a specific reading, and within which the reader too comes into being. . . . Reading a work therefore makes it happen." Attridge, *The Singularity of Literature*, 87. Likewise, Iser insists that "the meaning of a literary text

is not a definable entity, but, if anything, a dynamic happening," and Miller, too, relies on this language of process or movement, writing of these "acts" that occur over time to produce literature's effects. Iser, *The Act of Reading*, 22.

30. Barber, "Popular Arts in Africa," 55.

31. "Textualterity" is Attridge's coinage denoting a text's ability to bring about encounters with difference.

32. Attridge, "Ethical Modernism," 669.

33. Iser, *The Act of Reading*, 37.

34. Hall, "Encoding, Decoding."

35. Butler, *Giving an Account of Oneself*, 8.

36. Butler, *Giving an Account of Oneself*, 102; my emphasis.

37. My use of the designation "black" in this book follows Steve Biko, who used the term to denote all racial and ethnic groups subject to apartheid's legalized white supremacy.

38. Important exceptions include Mokoena, *Magema Fuze*; Dick, *The Hidden History of South Africa's Book and Reading Cultures*; Hofmeyr, *Gandhi's Printing Press*; Hofmeyr, *The Portable Bunyan*; Fouché, "Reading and Libraries in the Socio-Cultural Life of an Urban Black Community"; and Sandwith, *World of Letters*.

39. Because television in South Africa has a somewhat belated history (its introduction was delayed until 1976), it does not meet the criteria I set in this book—to trace sustained histories of black ethical engagement with cultural forms from the earliest days of apartheid until the recent era. There are important studies of South Africa's television history, however, including but not limited to Krabill, *Starring Mandela and Cosby*; Horwitz, *Communication and Democratic Reform in South Africa*; Wasserman and Jacobs, *Shifting Selves*.

40. Gunner, Ligaga, and Moyo, *Radio in Africa*; Krog, *Conditional Tense*.

41. Coplan, *In Township Tonight!*

42. Peterson, *Monarchs, Missionaries & African Intellectuals*; Kruger, *The Drama of South Africa*.

43. In Tsitsi Jaji's forthcoming afterword to *South African Writing in Transition*, edited by Barnard and Van der Vlies, she reminds us that Sol Plaatje's 1930 *Mhudi* articulated a transnational ethical project. Such engagements with relationality constitute a thematic concern throughout the history of black writing in South Africa.

44. Gandhi, *Common Cause*, 16.

45. Apartheid-era censuses did not record literacy rates for black South Africans, but even in South Africa's third post-apartheid census in 2011, the discrepancy between black literacy rates and those of the other groups tallied shows the direct inheritance of apartheid's unjust and unequal education system. "For black African males illiteracy levels decreased from 40% in 1996 to 20.9% in 2011, whilst amongst coloured men the decrease was from 27.5% in 1996 to 16.5% in 2011. In both groups women have a higher likelihood than men to be illiterate, but women have also significantly increased their literacy rates since 1996." "Census 2011, Statistical Release (Revised)," 39–40.

46. Phillips, *The Bantu in the City*, 215; my emphasis.

47. Mda, *The Maddona of Excelsior*, 98.

48. Edward Said makes this point but takes it further, not only noting how social marginality generates a difference in outlook but also arguing that this outsider status to the dominant status quo is precisely what makes for successful intellectual work. The exile "exists in a median state, neither completely at one with the new setting nor fully disencumbered of the old, beset with half-involvements and half-detachments, nostalgic and sentimental on one level, *an adept mimic or a secret outcast* on another." Said, *Representations of the Intellectual*, 49; my emphasis. See also Bhabha, *The Location of Culture*. While most black South Africans were not officially exiled (though a fair number of members of the African National Congress's military wing, Umkhonto we Sizwe, were indeed that), they were subject to unofficial exile within the nation both physically, through the state's internal "homelands" policies, and psychologically, because the state refused to accord them full rights of citizenship.

49. Sandoval, *Methodology of the Oppressed*, 104.

50. Sandoval, *Methodology of the Oppressed*, 105.

51. Iser also understands the discombobulated state a reader feels immediately after having read a "literary work" as exemplarily conducive to critiquing reality: "The fact that we have been temporarily isolated from our real world does not mean that we now return to it with new directives. What it does mean is that, for a brief period at least, *the real world appears observable*. The significance of this process lies in the fact that *image-building eliminates the subject-object division essential for all perception, so that when we 'awaken' to the real world, this division seems all the more accentuated*. Suddenly we find ourselves detached from our world, to which we are inextricably tied, and able to perceive it as an object. And *even if this detachment is only momentary*, it may enable us to apply the knowledge we have gained by figuring out the multiple references of the linguistic signs, *so that we can view our own world as a thing 'freshly understood.'*" Iser, *The Act of Reading*, 140; my emphasis.

52. In addition to the work by Bhabha and Said discussed here, central texts on the subject of colonized methodologies include Chatterjee, *Nationalist Thought and the Colonial World*; Fanon, *Black Skin, White Masks*; Lott, *Love & Debt*; and Taussig, *Mimesis and Alterity*. For an important study of mimesis as an ambivalent subjective mode in an African context, see Ranger, *Dance and Society in Eastern Africa, 1890–1970*.

53. Auerbach, *Mimesis*; Lukács, *The Theory of the Novel*.

54. Miller, *The Ethics of Reading*, 62.

55. Peter J. Rabinowitz refers to reading as another form of imitation. Rabinowitz, *Before Reading*.

56. *Oxford English Dictionary*, s.v. "ethos."

57. Du Bois, "The Souls of Black Folk," 364.

58. Du Bois, "The Souls of Black Folk," 364–65.

59. Achebe, "The Truth of Fiction," 112.

60. Biko, *I Write What I Like*, 22.

61. Nandy, *The Intimate Enemy*, xvi; my emphasis.

62. Attridge, *The Singularity of Literature*, 126.

63. Debates over the decision by families of Ethel Lance and Myra Thompson to "forgive" Dylann Roof, the white supremacist who shot and killed Lance, Thompson, and seven other black churchgoers in South Carolina in June 2015, suggest continued parallels between the United States and South Africa.

64. Teitel, *Transitional Justice*.

65. Quoted in Dlamini, *Askari*, 45.

66. Boltanski, *Distant Suffering*, 11.

67. Martin Weiner, "The Political Unconscious of Postcolonial History," unpublished talk, History Department, the Graduate Center, City University New York, March 4, 2011.

68. See Sanders, *Complicities*; Dlamini, *Askari*; Dlamini, *Native Nostalgia*; Scott, *Conscripts of Modernity*; Scott, *Omens of Adversity*; and Gandhi, *Affective Communities*.

69. As Gandhi points out, early anticolonial thinkers such as Frantz Fanon and Aimé Césaire already refused merely Manichean critiques. Gandhi, *Common Cause*, 4.

70. Sanders, *Complicities*.

71. Nandy, *The Intimate Enemy*, xvi. Many scholars have criticized rigid models of guilt and victimhood. Jessica Benjamin problematizes the polarizing infantocentric model of traditional psychology that figures the child *as an innocent victim*—"the self was always the recipient, not the giver of empathy." Benjamin, *Like Subjects, Love Objects*, 32. Robert Reid-Pharr also questions these attributions of guilt, responsibility, and victimhood, particularly in relation to understandings of racial violence in the United States. He enjoins us to remember that "even as we must memorialize and seek to undo the grave human tragedies enacted by our countrymen, and perhaps ourselves . . . it is nonetheless true that the people most caught up in these ugliest of human dramas (the blacks, the Negroes, the coloreds) were never passive victims." Reid-Pharr, *Once You Go Black*, 2–3. None of this thinking is particularly new, nor is it foreign to South Africa: "We had kept saying in the dark days of apartheid's oppression that white South Africans would never be truly free until we blacks were free as well," Desmond Tutu writes. He quotes Judge Ismail Mahomed, who reiterates the point: "The wicked and the innocent have often both been victims." Tutu, *No Future Without Forgiveness*, 25.

72. Dlamini and Jones, *Categories of Persons*, 10.

73. Dlamini and Jones, *Categories of Persons*, 22.

74. The meaning of the word *sympathy* has since shifted, but these moral philosophers generally used it to mean something akin to our modern understanding of empathy—imagining oneself as other.

75. Michael Meranze reminds us that Adam Smith's *The Theory of Moral Sentiment* was published in 1759, smack in the middle of the Seven Years' War, a struggle for colonial power between France and Britain. See also Hume, "An Enquiry Concerning the Principles of Morals"; Hume, *A Treatise of Human Nature*; Rousseau, *A Discourse on*

Inequality; Rousseau, "On the Origin of Language"; Locke, *An Essay Concerning Human Understanding*; and Smith, *The Theory of Moral Sentiments*.

76. Hume, *A Treatise of Human Nature*, 180.

77. There are echoes of Levinasian approaches to alterity in Leela Gandhi's concept of the anti-colonial practice of "counter-*askesis*, or spiritual regimen of imperfectionism." "This comprised aberrant practices of self-ruination, or an anti-care of the self, aimed at making common cause both with the victims and abettors of unjust sociality (by defending the former and reforming the latter)." Gandhi, *Common Cause*, 2.

78. Ahmed, *The Stillbirth of Capital.*

79. Hume, *A Treatise of Human Nature*, 319.

80. Rousseau, "On the Origin of Language," 32.

81. Spivak, "Ethics and Politics in Tagore, Coetzee, and Certain Scenes of Teaching," 23. A similar sentiment appears in recent comments made by Ishamel Reed. He asks, "What would have happened if those citizens who greeted President Obama with the waving of the Confederate flag had stayed home and read some slave narratives?" Reed, "Cure the Canon of Literary Agoraphobia."

82. Fanon, *The Wretched of the Earth*, 6.

83. Fanon, *The Wretched of the Earth*, 9.

84. Khalip, *Anonymous Life*, 24. Thus, while *Black Cultural Life in South Africa* draws on the thinking of the "New Ethicists," for whom, pace Northrop Frye and F. R. Leavis, reading is ethical because it *destabilizes* the idea of the Enlightenment subject, such studies' concentration on Euro-American reading publics and texts requires examination. While poststructural scholars challenge theories that reify Enlightenment notions of the individual subject and commend the way that "reading" binds readers and texts together in irresolvable encounters with alterity, the hypothetical readers they conjure up are still largely imagined as inhabiting legally constituted spaces of citizenship and privilege.

85. Yancy and West, "Cornel West: The Fire of a New Generation."

86. Mogale, "Crime for Sale: Another Escapade," 29.

87. Kruger, "Rev. of *Media and Identity in Africa*, and *Cinema in a Democratic South Africa*," 192.

88. Particularly vital scholarship concerned with nonliterary forms of African cultural production include Barber, *Africa's Hidden Histories*; Cole and Thomas, *Love in Africa*; Jaji, *Africa in Stereo*; Larkin, *Signal and Noise*; Mbembe, *On the Postcolony*; Newell, *Readings in African Popular Fiction*; Newell, *The Power to Name*; and Fair, *Pastimes and Politics.*

89. Many theorists of ethics and literature draw on James's oeuvre as an exemplary site of literary ethical production. See, particularly, Booth, *The Company We Keep*; Iser, *The Act of Reading*; Nussbaum, *Love's Knowledge*; and Miller, *The Ethics of Reading.*

90. Docker, *Postmodernism and Popular Culture*, 253.

91. Hitchcock, "The Genre of Postcoloniality."

92. Levine, *Forms*, 8.
93. Dlamini, *Native Nostalgia*, 22.
94. Levine, *Forms*, 6.
95. Dlamini, *Native Nostalgia*, 32–33; my emphasis.
96. Coetzee, *Elizabeth Costello*, 41; my emphasis.
97. This term, originally the name of a specific kind of projector that was easy to transport and thus popular among people with traveling movie theaters, was often applied to later models of projection in cinemas and is now the name of an art house cinema in downtown Johannesburg.
98. Jameson, *The Political Unconscious*, 20.
99. These numbers are from Marinovich, *Murder at Small Koppie*.

CHAPTER 1

1. Paton, "To a Small Boy Who Died at Diepkloof Reformatory," 71–72.
2. Among these photos etched into popular memory are those featuring Nelson Mandela and Walter Sisulu setting their passbooks on fire.
3. "Pass Laws," 1957.
4. Weld, *Paper Cadavers*, 6.
5. Weheliye, *Habeas Viscus*, 12.
6. Spivak, *Critique of Postcolonial Reason*, 30.
7. Breckenridge, "Verwoerd's Bureau of Proof"; Giliomee and Schlemmer, *Up against the Fences*; Hindson, *Pass Controls and the Urban African Proletariat in South Africa*; Marks, "Southern and Central Africa, 1886–1910."
8. Mbembe, "African Modes of Self-Writing."
9. Sole, "Authority, Authenticity and the Black Writer," 2. I follow Njabulo Ndebele in seeing continuity between the literary productions of the 1950s and 1960s and those influenced by the Black Consciousness movement of the later period. Though certain obvious shifts in philosophical orientation can be noted—most noticeably in the overt declaration by Black Consciousness writers that they were writing explicitly for black audiences—the two generations of writers are strongly united by the fact that their writing was, almost uniformly, a form of political engagement with the world.
10. Attridge, *The Singularity of Literature*, 97.
11. Darwish, "Identity Card."
12. Breckenridge, "The Biometric State," 105. Nor were the pass laws specific to *apartheid* South Africa. A prototype of the "internal passports" system was set up as early as the eighteenth century in the Cape Colony to control the movement of slave laborers on Dutch farms. This practice continued and spread inland under Afrikaner control, particularly after the Great Trek (1830s), and also under the British Union government established at the turn of the century as the Anglo-Boer War concluded. Hindson, *Pass Controls and the Urban African Proletariat in South Africa*.
13. The Natives (Abolition of Passes and Co-ordination of Documents) Act No. 67

of 1952 amended the Population Registration Act No. 30 of 1950, mandating passes for all black South African men. Women were also required to carry passes in urban areas and were particularly visible in the anti-pass campaigns of the 1950s and 1960s.

14. Breckenridge, "Verwoerd's Bureau of Proof," 85.

15. Quoted in Breckenridge, "Verwoerd's Bureau of Proof," 97.

16. Breckenridge, "The Biometric State," 271.

17. Recent deaths of black Americans either in custody or stopped by U.S. police suggest we are far from finished examining what occurs when black people encounter the state through the figure of the (armed) policeman or policewoman.

18. In particular, the response to the WikiLeaks reports released by Julien Assange and to the arrest and imprisonment of Chelsea Manning registers the degree of public outrage when learning of the scale and expense of Western governments' espionage networks.

19. See Klein, "Enough. It's Time for a Boycott," *Guardian*, January 9, 2009. Apartheid has now come to have a fairly wide semantic application, as evidenced by Edwidge Danticat's recent use of the term to describe the racist laws passed in the Dominican Republic to exclude those of Haitian descent from their rights as citizens ("Urgent Action Requested: Boycott the DR for Making Apartheid and Racism Legal," http://www.ezili danto.com/zili/wp-content/uploads/2013/11/EdwideDRboycott.mp3; accessed January 4, 2018). Two recent books look at the use of the term to describe Israeli policies: Soske and Jacobs, *Apartheid Israel*; and Pappe, *Israel and South Africa*.

20. Quoted in Phillips, *The Bantu in the City*, 204.

21. La Guma, *In the Fog of the Seasons' End*, 80.

22. La Guma, *In the Fog of the Seasons' End*, 80.

23. La Guma, *In the Fog of the Seasons' End*, 81–82.

24. Abrahams, *Mine Boy*, 62; my emphasis.

25. Foucault, *Discipline and Punish*, 137. The encounter on a city street has often been used by writers and philosophers to trope the emergence of subjectivity, selfhood, and citizenship. This scene recalls Louis Althusser's description of interpellation as a mechanism instantiating subjectivity in everyday encounters on city streets: "*Interpellation*, or hailing . . . which can be imagined along the lines of the most commonplace everyday police (or other) hailing 'Hey you there!' . . . [and] in the street, the hailed individual will turn round. By this mere one-hundred-and-eighty degree physical conversion, he becomes a *subject*." Althusser, "Excerpts from 'Ideology and Ideological State Apparatuses' (1968)." https://www.marxists.org/reference/archive/althusser/1970/ideol ogy.htm

26. La Guma, *In the Fog of the Seasons' End*, 65.

27. As Mahmood Mamdani explains, the pass system also strengthened the gendered divisions between the rural and urban limiting access to urban areas to men mostly, thus keeping women in their traditional or "customary" roles as mothers and wives in the "homelands." Marks, "Southern and Central Africa, 1886–1910."

28. Barnes, "'Am I a Man?'" 6.

29. Themba, "Ten-to-Ten," 47.

30. Dhlomo, *An African Tragedy*, 21.

31. Themba, *The Will to Die*, 78.

32. Themba, *The Will to Die*, 79.

33. La Guma, *In the Fog of the Seasons' End*, 128.

34. Foucault, *Discipline and Punish*, 137.

35. Ndebele, "Rediscovery of the Ordinary"; Nkosi, "Postmodernism and Black Writing."

36. Ndebele, "Rediscovery of the Ordinary," 64, 20.

37. Rogosin and Davis, *Come Back, Africa*, 28.

38. In Williamson's "A Few South Africans" series, she includes an homage to Annie Silinga, a resident of Langa, Cape Town, who "all her life . . . refused to carry a pass." Williamson, *Resistance Art in South Africa*, 76.

39. Another version of this image is available. A key choice Goldblatt made in producing this final image was to crop out three other men also flanking the two central figures.

40. Goldblatt, "Audio Transcript."

41. Caplan and Torpey, *Documenting Individual Identity*, 6. Caplan and Torpey's reluctance to totalize state practices overcompensates somewhat, however, by reading the "new identities and relationships" that emerge in response to the state as always ontologically positive, thus ignoring the more ambiguous "identities and relationships" (such as "passing" subjects who defended apartheid dogma) these practices engendered. It is not remiss for Caplan and Torpey to want to open up a place within the practices of state surveillance systems for citizen-subjects to subvert juridico-political attempts at total spatial domination; however, when new identities that are moral and material improvements on previous ones emerge out of such a system, it is important these be understood as anomalies rather than commonalities.

42. Nxumalo, "The Birth of a Tsotsi," 20.

43. La Guma, *In the Fog of the Seasons' End*, 123.

44. For a study of the relationship between agency and writerly anonymity in an African context, see Newell, *The Power to Name*.

45. Timothy Longman shows that this flexibility did not always work to the advantage of those seeking to resist the violence of subjection. During the Rwandan genocide, he notes, the inherent *instability* of official documents and the easiness with which they could be forged sometimes paradoxically reinforced rather than undid essentialist racial categories: "During the genocide, the realization that official documents could be forged created an uncertainty about individual identities. This suggests that in Rwanda today *ethnic identity is understood as an essential characteristic of individuals, not an official designation*. Placing the onus of *in*authenticity on official identity cards led the ethnic, ironically, to become understood as an essential biological trait, verifiable through the body if not on paper. Longman, "Identity Cards, Ethnic Self-Perception, and Genocide in Rwanda," 347.

46. La Guma, *A Walk in the Night*, 30.
47. La Guma, *A Walk in the Night*, 31.
48. La Guma, *A Walk in the Night*, 31.
49. Modisane, *Blame Me on History*, 56.
50. Modisane, "The Dignity of Begging," 10–11.
51. Attridge, *The Singularity of Literature*, 82.
52. Booth, *The Company We Keep*, 70.
53. Sandoval, *Methodology of the Oppressed*, 104–5.
54. Sandoval, *Methodology of the Oppressed*, 86.
55. Sandoval, *Methodology of the Oppressed*, 29; my emphasis.
56. Sandoval, *Methodology of the Oppressed*, 86.
57. Sandoval, *Methodology of the Oppressed*, 129.
58. Abrahams, *Mine Boy*, 62; my emphasis.
59. Abrahams's main character, Xuma, is the focalizer for a surprising number of portraits of characters that defy Ndebele's suggestion that protest literature necessarily relies on representations that involve flat, Manichean structures. While he comes to Johannesburg firmly wedded to the notion of whites and blacks as intrinsically unalike, Xuma willingly changes his opinion of them and of other policemen and figures of authority at the mine, regularly referring to them as "a kind one" or "a good one." Abrahams, *Mine Boy*, 66.
60. Consider Abrahams's narrator's statement: "One could understand a white person as well as a black person. And be sorry for white as well as black." Abrahams, *Mine Boy*, 174.

CHAPTER 2

1. Abrahams, *Tell Freedom*, 127.
2. For Miriam Hansen, film is a quintessentially vernacular or popular genre that relies less on the spectator's mastery of a set of codes and languages to decipher its meaning and more on visual literacies. Hansen, "Tracking Cinema on a Global Scale."
3. Abrahams, *Tell Freedom*, 127.
4. Abrahams, *Tell Freedom*, 127.
5. Tomaselli, *The Cinema of Apartheid*.
6. See, particularly, Balseiro and Masilela, *To Change Reels*; Botha, *South African Cinema 1896–2010*; Gavshon, "Levels of Intervention in Films Made for African Audiences in South Africa"; Gutsche, *The History and Social Significance of Motion Pictures in South Africa, 1895–1940*; and Tomaselli, *The Cinema of Apartheid*.
7. Notable exceptions include Maingard's chapter "Black Audiences: 1920s–1950s" in *South African National Cinema* and Jaji's chapter "What Women Want: Selling Hi-Fi Consumer Magazines and Film" in *Africa in Stereo*.
8. Dovey, *African Film and Literature*, 15.
9. Barber, "Popular Arts in Africa," 55.

10. Morris, "Vernacular Modernism and South African Cinema," 650.

11. This distinction was complicated in the 1970s by the introduction of the "B scheme" films that were made in South Africa, featured black actors speaking indigenous languages, and were paid for by the apartheid state. These were a phenomenal success and have been subject to recent post-apartheid reassessments of them as films and as vehicles for black creative and ideological agency. See Paleker, "The B-Scheme Subsidy and the 'Black Film Industry' in Apartheid South Africa, 1972–1990"; and Onishi, "Honoring a Filmmaker in the Shadow of Apartheid."

12. In her groundbreaking work on television viewers' responses to *Dallas*, Ien Ang asserts that "the search for a total and definitive explanation for the way in which different groups of viewers experience the programme would seem to be particularly frustrating because at a certain moment we have to acknowledge that we are chasing an illusion: such an all-embracing explanation is a rationalistic fiction. . . . What [viewers] say about *Dallas* is no more than a snapshot of their reception of the programme. . . . there are always things which remain unexpressed and implicit." Ang, *Watching Dallas*, 14.

13. Nonetheless, it is important to note that people involved in the production of propaganda also often had "their own game within the game," as one actor in the apartheid state–funded B scheme movies has noted. Onishi, "Honoring a Filmmaker in the Shadow of Apartheid."

14. Quoted in Dovey, *African Film and Literature*, 13–14.

15. Powdermaker, *Copper Town*, 271.

16. Powdermaker, *Copper Town*, 258.

17. Powdermaker, *Copper Town*, 258.

18. Quoted in Maingard, *South African National Cinema*, 69.

19. Classical cinema dominated filmmaking aesthetics from approximately 1920 to 1960.

20. Stewart, *Migrating to the Movies*, 109.

21. Stewart, *Migrating to the Movies*, 110.

22. Stewart, *Migrating to the Movies*, 113.

23. "Gang leaders often controlled local cinemas and concert halls, where they sponsored [musical] shows." Coplan, *In Township Tonight!* 163. In a James Matthews's novel set during apartheid, the cinema is the locus apart where personal relationships can flourish, as it becomes both the site for an adulterous affair and the place where newlyweds spend their honeymoon. Matthews, *The Party Is Over*.

24. The Odin was said to be the largest cinema in the whole of Africa, with a seating capacity of about 1,100. Mattera, *Coming of Age in South Africa*, 74.

25. Mattera, *Memory Is the Weapon*, 83.

26. Hansen, *Babel and Babylon*, 106.

27. Barber, "Popular Arts in Africa," 47.

28. Abrahams, *Tell Freedom*, 15.

29. Hall, "Encoding, Decoding," 509.

30. Miller, *The Ethics of Reading*, 8–9.

31. Whiteness in South Africa has never been straightforward, of course, with Afrikaner identity operating in a tense dialectic with the seemingly more modern and more urban English white South African identity.

32. Quoted in Chapman, *The "Drum" Decade*, 187.

33. Davis, *In Darkest Hollywood*, 49.

34. Mattera, *Memory Is the Weapon*, 75.

35. Quoted in Davis, *In Darkest Hollywood*, 49; my emphasis.

36. Hansen, *Babel and Babylon*, 86.

37. Hall, "Encoding, Decoding," 510.

38. Hall, "Encoding, Decoding," 511–13.

39. Hall, "Encoding, Decoding," 510.

40. It is not surprising that such viewers have largely escaped the purview of cinema studies. Most scholarly work on cinema remains anchored in the West, and when this is not the case, it concerns itself, much as in literary studies, with *auteurs* rather than with audiences. Attempts to address the content of more popular films have grown, yet these continue to be the exception rather than the norm, probably because scholars gravitate toward what they enjoy, which often means films with "serious" or "artistic" intentions (or pretensions). In the African context, scholarly interest in Nollywood films is a notable exception.

41. For a useful critique of the application of Adorno and Horkheimer's critique of capitalism to African spaces, see Higginson, "What Is and Where Is Francophone African Popular Fiction?"

42. Adorno, *The Culture Industry*; Kracauer, "Boredom." "According to Adorno and Horkheimer . . . the experience of pleasure in mass culture is a false kind of pleasure, even part of the trick of manipulating the masses more effectively in order to lock them in the eternal status quo of exploitation and oppression. 'Marxists, in particular, have interpreted the fact that people *enjoy* mass culture as a reason for gloom.' . . . Stuart Hall even talks of the stubborn refusal of the left to consider pleasure." Ang, *Watching Dallas*, 14, 18.

43. Jaji's work on black South African women's consumption of popular magazines around this same time is an essential reminder that gender is as likely to determine responses to cultural artifacts as is race. Furthermore, urban and rural film-going experiences modulated cinematic responses in considerably different ways.

44. Hansen, *Babel and Babylon*, 108.

45. Askew and Wilk, *The Anthropology of Media*. Critics who recognize audience agency tend, nonetheless, to subscribe to the belief that the "culture industry" remains more powerful (financially, narratively, ideologically) than any counter-narrative(s) that audience members may generate. See Larkin, *Signal and Noise*; Ambler, "Popular Films and Colonial Audiences"; Powdermaker, *Copper Town*; and Burns, "John Wayne on the Zambezi: Cinema, Empire, and the American Western in British Central Africa."

46. Jameson, *The Political Unconscious*, 9. Judith Butler talks of the challenge we

confront in our attempts to construct our subjectivities in the face of certain cultural-historical conditions that bind us to certain interpretive and social acts.

47. Barber, "Popular Arts in Africa," 25.

48. One early film critic "cast the interaction of ethnically and culturally diverse [immigrant] viewers with the cinema as a scenario of Americanization and upward mobility, conveying the impression 'that movie houses and nickelodeons were the back rooms of the Statue of Liberty. It is as if moving pictures had a well-defined role within the melting pot of American society, and immigrants went to the moving pictures as passive subjects eager to be integrated into the mainstream of American life.'" Quoted in Hansen, *Babel and Babylon*, 68.

49. Hansen, "Mass Production," 69.

50. Jaji, *Africa in Stereo*, 120.

51. Gordimer, "Living in the Interregnum," 265.

52. Biko, *I Write What I Like*, 22. Gordimer's assessment of white consciousness notably excludes the many, more intimate, everyday relationships between white and black South Africans that occurred because of the structures of labor conditions. This was particularly true on rural, white-owned farms and, more famously, in the mines.

53. Grey Street is now Dr. Yusuf Dadoo Street.

54. Ambler, "Popular Films and Colonial Audiences"; Burns, "John Wayne on the Zambezi: Cinema, Empire, and the American Western in British Central Africa."

55. Phillips, "Phillips News No. 5."

56. Reynolds, "Playing Cowboys and Africans," 421.

57. Gavshon, "Levels of Intervention in Films Made for African Audiences in South Africa," 15.

58. Gutsche, *The History and Social Significance of Motion Pictures in South Africa, 1895–1940*, 294.

59. Quoted in Gutsche, *The History and Social Significance of Motion Pictures in South Africa, 1895–1940*, 295, note 33.

60. Phillips, *The Bantu in the City*, 324.

61. Maingard, *South African National Cinema*.

62. Rancière, *Proletarian Nights*, ix; my emphasis.

63. Dovey, *African Film and Literature*, 30–31.

64. Morris, "Vernacular Modernism and South African Cinema," 652.

65. Quoted in Chapman, *The "Drum" Decade*, 186.

66. "African and European Scholars Debate," 35.

67. "African and European Scholars Debate," 35.

68. "African and European Scholars Debate," 35; my emphasis.

69. "African and European Scholars Debate," 35.

70. Quoted in Davis, *In Darkest Hollywood*, 10.

71. Quoted in Davis, *In Darkest Hollywood*, 25.

72. Quoted in Maingard, *South African National Cinema*, 71.

73. Phillips, *The Bantu in the City*, 326.

74. Phillips, "Phillips News No. 5," 3.

75. Quoted in Martin, *Cinemas of the Black Diaspora*, 481. Ntite Mukendi argues that "a certain censorship should be exercised against foreign films." Férid Boughedir writes that "the colonial cinema—especially that of the USA—has contributed myths, false values, misrepresentation of reality, a concept of world violence and frenzied individualism. Its films depict society and the masses as mediocre, stupid and hostile to the 'heroic individual.' The White is always superior to the African or the Indian must endeavor to be like him. It should also be noted that what differentiates the white hero from the African hero is that the latter is deeply attached to his community." Martin, *Cinemas of the Black Diaspora*, 483.

76. Martin, *Cinemas of the Black Diaspora*, 410.

77. Quoted in Martin, *Cinemas of the Black Diaspora*, 483. It continues: "A firm policy based on principle must be introduced in this field so as *to eliminate once and for all* the films which the foreign monopolies continue to impose upon us either directly or indirectly and *which generate reactionary culture and, as a result, thought patterns* in contradiction with the basic choices of our people."

78. For Teshome Gabriel, these filmmakers' "overriding concern . . . is not in aestheticizing ideology but in politicizing cinema." According to Gabriel, "the principal characteristic of Third Cinema is not so much where it is made, or even who makes it, but, rather, the ideology it espouses and the consciousness it displays." Quoted in Martin, *Cinemas of the Black Diaspora*, 483.

79. Martin, *Cinemas of the Black Diaspora*, 468.

80. Morris, "Vernacular Modernism and South African Cinema," 651.

81. Rancière, *Proletarian Nights*, x. "The equality of intelligences remains the most untimely of thoughts it is possible to nourish about the social order." Rancière, *Proletarian Nights*, xii.

82. Consider, for instance, the problematic gender politics in Frantz Fanon's writings. Chow, *Ethics after Idealism*.

83. Quoted in Maingard, *South African National Cinema*, 72.

84. Morris, "Vernacular Modernism and South African Cinema," 651.

85. Morris, "Vernacular Modernism and South African Cinema," 647.

86. Hansen, "Mass Production," 60.

87. Hansen, "Mass Production," 60.

88. Hansen, "Mass Production," 71–72; my emphasis.

89. Dlamini, *Native Nostalgia*, 130; my emphasis.

90. Appadurai, *Modernity at Large*, 1.

91. Hansen, "Mass Production," 69.

92. Morris, "Vernacular Modernism and South African Cinema," 647; my emphasis.

93. Hansen, "Tracking Cinema on a Global Scale," 605.

94. Hansen, "Mass Production," 68.

95. Hansen, *Babel & Babylon*, 112; my emphasis.

96. Stewart, *Migrating to the Movies*, 104; my emphasis.

97. Kracauer, "Boredom."

98. Snead, "Spectatorship and Capture in *King Kong*," 65.

99. Stewart, *Migrating to the Movies*, 1;00.

100. Davis, *In Darkest Hollywood*, 22. Mark Sanders's recent *Learning Zulu: A Secret History of Language in South Africa* importantly engages with the ethics of white South Africans and Zulu language learning.

101. Barber, "Popular Arts in Africa," 62.

102. Barber, "Popular Arts in Africa," 63.

103. Reynolds, "Playing Cowboys and Africans," 409.

CHAPTER 3

1. J. van Zyl Albert, owner of the company producing *Mighty Man*, also ran *To the Point*, a right-wing news magazine. Nonetheless, allegations that the comic was a propagandistic tool of white supremacists were adamantly denied. Mantlo, "Bill Mantlo's Column on South African Comics," 77.

2. Willenson, Younghusband, and Manning, "Africa: The Caped Crusader," 48.

3. Mantlo, "Bill Mantlo's Column on South African Comics," 75.

4. Quoted in Willenson, Younghusband, and Manning, "Africa: The Caped Crusader," 48.

5. Richard Manville, the U.S. consultant who had initially hoped that a success in South Africa would provide justification for a market in the United States as well, stopped publishing the comic in direct response to the burnings.

6. Attridge, *The Singularity of Literature*.

7. Photocomics' genealogy is not entirely clear, a generic instability reflected in the nomenclature used to describe them, which includes photonovels, photo-novellas, photo-novelettes, photostories, photoromans, photo soapies, picture comics, photo-comix, and "bookies."

8. In 1978 the photocomic is "omnipresent among the masses in Latin America, Northern Africa, France, and Italy," write Flora and Flora in "The Fotonovela as a Tool for Class and Cultural Domination," 135. Sylvette Giet provides some figures describing French consumption of *Nous Deux*, a popular romantic photocomic that debuted in 1947. In that year they printed 150,000 copies; 1950, 700,000 copies; 1957, 1.5 million copies; 1964, 1 million copies; 1971, 850,000 copies; 1977, 1 million. Giet, "Le Roman-Photo Sentimental Traditionnel Lu En France," 13. All translations are mine unless otherwise noted.

9. Krauss, "Reinventing the Medium," 300. Unlike the comic, "the photographic novel of the 1980s never has been taken seriously in all its aspects," writes Baetens in "The Intermediate Domain, or the Photographic Novel and the Problem of Value," 284–85. In Chile, *fotonovelas* were banned by Pinochet's government in the mid-1970s for

being "morally degenerate"; Flora and Flora, "The Fotonovela as a Tool for Class and Cultural Domination," 136.

10. Switzer and Switzer, *The Black Press in South Africa and Lesotho*, ix; my emphasis.

11. See recent work incorporating Paolo Freire's theories of teaching, especially Nimmon, *Photonovels through Critical Pedagogy*.

12. An exception to this is Matthias Kring's chapter on *African Film*, a photocomic starring "Lance Spearman: The African James Bond." Krings, *African Appropriations*.

13. The censorship board looked at publications as a matter of course if they were foreign imports. South African publications were examined only if they caused controversy. Nonetheless a "climate of self-censorship was encouraged by government statements of intent and a long-drawn-out process of investigation into 'undesirable publications' and the press." Merrett, *A Culture of Censorship*, 35. See also McDonald, *The Literature Police*; and J. M. Coetzee, *Giving Offense*.

14. Dates for the popular titles are based on the records of the National Library of South Africa. *Tessa* ran during the years 1975–85 and then merged with *Kid Colt* to form *Tessa and Kid Colt*; *Grensvegter*, 1972–95; *Swart Luiperd*, 1976–95; *Die wit tier*, 1977–95; *Young Love* (reincarnated as *Love Story* including *Charmaine*), 1974–95; *Ruiter in Swart & Kid die Swerwer* (the Afrikaans *Kid Colt*), 1985–90s; *Secrets plus Louise* (a merger of *Secrets* and *Louise*), 1984–93; *See: romantic adventures in photos*, 1963–95; *Verdwaalde Harte ("Ons Dominee Reeks") [en] Saal 10 Ongevalle*, 1984–95; *Eerste Liefde [en] Dr. Conrad Brand*, 1985–95. Photocomics also ran in *Drum*, the popular magazine for black South Africans, with local editions in Ghana, Kenya, and Nigeria. Dodson, "The Four Modes of Drum."

15. For representative examples, see Sampson, "One Last Picture Show," 83–88; Kruger and Shariff, "'Shoo—This Book Makes Me to Think!'"; and "In Praise of the Humble 'P*** Boekie' and Pinup Girls."

16. Altarriba, "Le Roman-Photo En Espagne," 43.

17. One reader's choice of words exemplifies the general way photocomics were viewed: "These trashy produced pieces of *literature* fascinated us because you did not need an imagination, and if you did not understand the text you could always look at the pictures." "In Praise of the Humble 'P*** Boekie' and Pinup Girls." Despite his initial dismissal of the form, the author, a former member of the South African Defence Force, nostalgically describes the role photocomics played in reinforcing troop morale.

18. Mda, *The Madonna of Excelsior*, 74–75.

19. "Photo Stories Make a Return."

20. Matthews, *The Party Is Over*, 21.

21. Peeters, "Le Roman-Photo: Un Impossible Renouveau?"; Flora and Flora, "The Fotonovela as a Tool for Class and Cultural Domination."

22. Giet, "Le Roman-Photo Sentimental Traditionnel Lu En France," 5.

23. Peeters, "Le Roman-Photo: Un Impossible Renouveau?" 16.

24. Barthes, *Image, Music, Text*, 66.

25. Taking this confusion of signification a step further, Altarriba distinguishes between the photoroman and the photoromance, while Flora and Flora insist that the photoroman is "a love story" and distinguish it from the *fotoaventura*. Altarriba, "Le Roman-Photo En Espagne," 52; Flora and Flora, "The Fotonovela as a Tool for Class and Cultural Domination," 135.

26. Peeters, "Le Roman-Photo: Un Impossible Renouveau?" 17.

27. Velde, "Le Roman-Photo Intérieur Et Son Reportage."

28. "The low cost of a romantic photoroman, the material banality of its presentation, its extra-library distribution and also its protocols of collective reading, are all contributing factors that seem to condemn the traditional photoroman to being nothing but a degraded object, less for reading than for consuming." Baetens, "Le Roman-Photo in Situ," 36.

29. This website is no longer accessible, although a reference to this statement can be found at "Model/Actress in Afrikaans Photo-Novels," *Hang Fire Books* blog, October 19, 2009. http://hangfirebooks.blogspot.com/2009/10/modelactress-in-af rikaans-photo-novels.html. "Actors" in the photocomics enjoyed some celebrity, although the work was not particularly lucrative. Sampson recalls: "Right up until the 1980s, pay was around R14 a day"—about $6 at the time. Sampson, "One Last Picture Show," 87.

30. The photocomic was also successfully adopted as a vehicle for pornographic content. Altarriba, "Le Roman-Photo En Espagne," 52.

31. Merrett, *A Culture of Censorship*, 60.

32. Flora and Flora, "The Fotonovela as a Tool for Class and Cultural Domination," 136–37.

33. Baetens, "Le Roman-Photo in Situ," 36.

34. Altarriba, "Le Roman-Photo En Espagne," 48.

35. Breyten Breytenbach writes that Afrikaans emerged from "the collision and coupling of culture—from domination and humiliation, ignorance and poetry, from the bible and the mosque and the bar and the shack and the veld, from death and adaptation." Quoted in Barnard, "Bitterkomix: Notes from the Post-Apartheid Underground," 752, note 27. The discourse of purity was not limited to whites; in a photo by *Drum* photographer Peter Magubane, a black male student wears a sign on his back in the 1976 Soweto riots that reads, "THE BLACK NATION IS NOT A PLACE FOR IMPURITIES AFRIKAANS STINKS." Magubane, *Magubane's South Africa*, 91.

36. Newell, *Literary Culture in Colonial Ghana*.

37. Artists who have engaged with the medium in their work include John Berger, James Coleman, Marie-Françoise Plissart (with commentary by Jacques Derrida), and Alain Robbe-Grillet. Baetens sees a place for the photocomic in the domain of the contemporary artist, drawing attention, perhaps overly optimistically, to a modern art concerned with anti-corporate expression, grounded in media that are readily available

to everyone, and to a rejection of the notion of the sublime, skilled artist and critic. Baetens, "Le Roman-Photo in Situ," 36.

38. Sampson, "One Last Picture Show," 83. *Sister Louise* was a photocomic about a nurse.

39. Flora and Flora oversimplify matters by dogmatically insisting the fotonovela is nothing but a tool of capitalist ideology. There is no room in such accounts for more nuanced discussions of reading practices.

40. Baetens, "Le Roman-Photo in Situ," 36–38.

41. "Photo Stories Make a Return."

42. Thaisi, "The Poetry of Job Mzamo in Kagablog." The "comics" referred to are actually photocomics.

43. "Photo Stories Make a Return."

44. Sampson, "One Last Picture Show," 87.

45. "Mweb Forums: Samson, Chunky Charlie and Battler Ben." This website is no longer available.

46. "Mweb Forums: Samson, Chunky Charlie and Battler Ben." "Poes" is "taboo slang" for "female genitals," translatable as "twat" or "cunt" in *Afrikaans-Engels Woorde-boek* (Cape Town: Pharos, 2005).

47. Van der Riet, "Photo Story Magazines."

48. Bhabha, *The Location of Culture*, 246.

49. Breytenbach, "Mandela's Smile," 46.

50. Bakhtin, *The Dialogic Imagination*, 13, 17.

51. This is now a commonplace assertion in most studies of the myth of the American West. See Slotkin, *The Fatal Environment*; Deloria, *Playing Indian*; and Huhndorf, *Going Native*.

52. Bazin, *What Is Cinema?* 148.

53. Borges, "Interview: The Art of Fiction No. 39," 123.

54. Clark and Holquist, *Mikhail Bakhtin*, 288.

55. Clark and Holquist, *Mikhail Bakhtin*, 77; my emphasis.

56. The background settings occasionally betray the impossibility of a North American setting with plant species or architectural styles particular to South Africa.

57. McCloud, *Understanding Comics*, 97.

58. McCloud, *Understanding Comics*, 100; my emphasis.

59. Bazin, *What Is Cinema?* 148.

60. Clark and Holquist, *Mikhail Bakhtin*, 287.

61. Bakhtin, *The Dialogic Imagination*, 13.

62. "Towards a People's History of South Africa?" 298–99.

63. Bhabha, *Nation and Narration*.

64. Altarriba notes, for example, that in Spain an attempt was made to market Western-themed photocomics to a male audience, without success: "At the peak of pho-toromans' success there was a decided effort to produce magazines for men (*Fotowest* or

Fotoaudacia that were founded on the western, spy stories, or adventures). The experience was a failure." Altarriba, "Le Roman-Photo En Espagne," 44.

65. Lamar and Thompson, *The Frontier in History*; Ford, "The Frontier in South Africa."

66. Explorations of the frontier as imaginative lodestar can be found in Keenan, *Fables of Responsibilty*; Crapanzano, *Imaginative Horizons*; Slotkin, *The Fatal Environment*; and Anzaldúa, *Borderlands*.

67. Van Niekerk, *Triomf*, 194. The term "the West" carries an ambiguous range of significations. On the one hand, the West is a conquerable territory, also known as the Wild West or the Old West; on the other, the West is the conquering force, which though mobile (through violence and territorial acquisition) is a fixed place. In the Derridean sense the conjoined signifiers "the West" are *sous rature twice*. First, the notion of the West as a superpower conglomerate of a certain set of shifting countries is always haunted by the East, which it requires for its self-definition. This is the first way the word is under erasure. Second, the West *means* the symbolic East when it is used to describe the place to be explored, the place to go to.

The way the article *the* is always used—recall it is almost always "*the* West," not merely the directional "West," that is invoked—works to solidify, concretize, and isolate a geographical entity that is unitary and fixed; there can only be one West, the article suggests, as there can only be one master race and one master gender. By affixing that article in English (as we do in French and German, but *not* in Zulu), the language attempts to make permanent a certain space as the solitary ruling space and to hide its instability and its dependence on a whole other set of Wests, including that West that means the unknown, that West that signifies precisely that which has yet to be incorporated into *the* West—*a* West, if we like, of the frontier.

68. This was frequently the case in the encounter between European whites and indigenous groups in places they were colonizing. The similarities have likely as much to do with Western concepts of rationality and Christianity as with anything they perceived upon arrival. Nonetheless, the relative synchronicity of the famous treks north and east with the American move west meant that the versions of white supremacy and religion both groups brought were similar.

69. Giliomee, *The Afrikaners*, 495–96.

70. Mellet, "Response to 'Identity Metamorphosis.'"

71. Agamben, *State of Exception*.

72. Bakhtin, *The Dialogic Imagination*.

73. Breytenbach, *A Season in Paradise*, 156. For a discussion of Breytenbach's concept of bastardy, see Sanders, *Complicities*.

74. In Marlene van Niekerk's monumental *Agaat*, the main character's husband gives her servant "a little bag of liquorice and a *See* magazine" to express his beneficence, underscoring the magazine's perceived harmlessness.

75. Nuttall, *Entanglement*, 2; and Van Onselen, *The Seed Is Mine*, 3–11. David Goldblatt's photographic chronicle of life under apartheid attests to the everyday "entangle-

ments" of blacks and whites, particularly in the retrospective. Goldblatt, *David Goldblatt Photographs*, 26, 31, 82–86, 89, 94, 101. Literary works also bear witness to such mixing, as I explore in chapter 4.

76. Mooney, "'Ducktails, Flick-Knives and Pugnacity,'" 754.

77. Mooney, "'Ducktails, Flick-Knives and Pugnacity,'" 761.

78. Hatred of the police was also a shared sentiment between the ducktails and many groups of South African blacks, as can be illustrated in a ducktail song: "Jolling on the corner with my razor and chain; Down came the ore [police], one took my name, / He grabbed me by the collar of my charcoal float [shirt], / Then out came the razor as I slit his throat, / Singing ducktail boogie." Mooney, "'Ducktails, Flick-Knives and Pugnacity,'" 759.

79. For a study of the influence of U.S. culture on black South African identity, see Nixon, *Homelands, Harlem, Hollywood*. Katie Mooney's piece is also a good, brief introduction to U.S. influence on white youth culture during apartheid. Mooney, "'Ducktails, Flick-Knives and Pugnacity.'"

80. "'Ducktails, Flick-Knives and Pugnacity,'" 761.

81. Quoted in Mooney, "'Ducktails, Flick-Knives and Pugnacity,'" 761; my emphasis.

82. Wicomb, "Shame and Identity."

83. Barthes, *Image, Music, Text*, 58.

84. Lott, *Love & Theft*.

85. Deloria, *Playing Indian*; and Huhndorf, *Going Native*.

86. Huhndorf, *Going Native*, 9. That signifiers like "Indian" in popular culture can carry multiple, even contradictory significations has been remarked upon by Jameson, who writes that "the vocation of the symbol . . . lies less in any single message or meaning than in its very capacity to absorb and organize all of these quite distinct anxieties together. . . . it is precisely this polysemousness which is profoundly ideological." Jameson, "Reification and Utopia in Mass Culture," 142.

87. John Lenihan argues that Westerns in the 1950s hid left-leaning racial sentiment in sympathetic portraits of Native Americans. Lenihan, *Showdown*, 55–89.

88. Freud, "The Neuroses of Defence," 92.

89. Freud, "Totem and Taboo," 499.

90. *Apache*, 41.

91. *Apache*, 98.

92. "Indian" characters in other photocomics of the period (figure 4) are also depicted as "noble savages."

93. Mooney explains that comics "played a significant role in the construction of masculinist subculture. These were read most avidly by boys on the edge of puberty but remained popular among older boys and young men imprinting themselves deeply on their notions of masculinity. The majority of prized comics were 'super-hero' comics where the main character embodies physical strength and competitive performance. Women were generally absent in comics except for the purpose of 'romance.' These

comics—like films and *other forms of media*—disseminated gender images which for boys stressed the need for them to be assertive, successful, to acquire physical strength, to compete with each other and to exert male dominance over girls, young women, 'weaker' boys and young men." Mooney, "'Ducktails, Flick-Knives and Pugnacity,'" 760; my emphasis.

94. For my thoughts on gender in these photocomics, see Saint, "Not Western."

95. Denning, *Mechanic Accents.*

96. Laden, "'Making the Paper Speakwell'"; McLoughlin, "Reading Zimbabwean Comic Strips."

97. Kaplan, *The Anarchy of Empire in the Making of U.S. Culture*, 94; my emphasis.

98. Denning, *Mechanic Accents*, 66.

99. Kaplan, *The Anarchy of Empire in the Making of U.S. Culture*, 101.

100. For Scott Simmon, nostalgic genres invent an ideal world separated both temporally and spatially from the present. Simmon, *The Invention of the Western Film*, 178–92. For Renato Rosaldo, "imperialist nostalgia" misleadingly bestows innocence—nostalgia is childlike, innocent—upon subjects who were actually complicit in creating the loss of the very thing now mourned. Rosaldo, *Culture & Truth.*

101. Kaplan, *The Anarchy of Empire in the Making of U.S. Culture*, 101.

102. Frederick Turner famously argued that the end of expansion in the United States created a crisis in American identity. Turner, *The Significance of the Frontier in American History.*

103. Lasch, *The True and Only Heaven*, 82.

104. Nixon, *Homelands, Harlem, and Hollywood.*

105. Modisane, *Blame Me on History*, 17.

106. Scott, *Domination and the Arts of Resistance: Hidden Transcripts.*

107. Fanon, *Black Skin, White Masks*, 147.

108. Because of this direct link between ideology and children's early reading practices, writers of the photocomic have more recently attempted to use it to disseminate a variety of "progressive" discussions of disease prevention and sexuality, for instance. Many studies of comic books and photocomics are indeed interested in how the genre itself is conducive to children's learning—focusing on how they can be used to disseminate information on important topics such as AIDs and child labor—and in how they can be employed in the service of getting young people interested in reading practices.

109. Quoted in Franklin, "After Empire," 74.

110. Freud, "Group Psychology and the Analysis of the Ego," 41.

111. Baetens, "Le Roman-Photo in Situ," 38.

112. The photocomics reached their peak successes in South Africa during the 1970s, which was, ironically, the most draconian decade in apartheid rule. In 1970 the Bantu Homelands Citizenship Act was passed with the express aim of revoking citizenship for all black South Africans, requiring them to relinquish South African citizenship for citizenship in one of the "independent" black Bantustans.

113. Baetens, "Le Roman-Photo in Situ," 38. "This pluralization valorizes the reader

without contest, thus contributing to affirming the success of the genre." Baetens, "Le Roman-Photo in Situ," 38.

114. While white children would also not have had access to becoming these figures either, the power they represented, through violence or less overt modes of dominance much more readily available to them, permitted them to transform their imaginative identifications beyond the realm of the fantastical into everyday interracial relations.

115. Modisane, *Blame Me on History*, 76.

CHAPTER 4

1. For debates on relationship between aesthetics and politics in South African writing, see Nkosi, "Fiction by Black South Africans"; Ndebele, "Rediscovery of the Ordinary"; and Sachs, "Preparing Ourselves for Freedom."

2. Nixon, "Aftermaths," 70.

3. Bewes, *The Event of Postcolonial Shame*, 127.

4. For a thoughtful reading of South African writers' thematics of disappointment in the post-apartheid moment, see Van der Vlies, *Present Imperfect*.

5. Wicomb, *October,* 237.

6. Kruger, *The Drama of South Africa.*

7. Bewes, *The Event of Postcolonial Shame*, 20–21.

8. Bewes's chronology situates writers' consciousness of writing's ethically compromised position in the mid-twentieth century. In South Africa, however, this came later, since before apartheid's demise many black South African writers explicitly saw writing as an instrument for political change.

9. In Zulu and other indigenous South African languages, there are separate words for people and white people: *abantu* and *abelungu*, respectively. This marked whites as radically different than the more universalizing *abantu*. The post-apartheid extension of the South African notion of *ubuntu* that includes whites within the category of *abantu* represented a fundamental act of generosity as well as a flexibility and expansion of South African languages in response to the dismantling of apartheid.

10. Dlamini and Jones, *Categories of Persons*, 11.

11. Quoted in Dlamini and Jones, *Categories of Persons*, 8–9.

12. Also known as "African humanism," its central premise is that we are who we are through others.

13. A version of de Kock's accounts of his crimes can be found in de Kock, *A Long Night's Damage*, 22.

14. *A Human Being Died That Night* was adapted for the stage by Nicholas Wright in 2013 and has been performed in Cape Town, Johannesburg, London, and New York.

15. Gobodo-Madikizela, *A Human Being Died That Night*, 6.

16. Arendt, *Eichmann in Jerusalem.*

17. Gobodo-Madikizela, *A Human Being Died That Night*, 16.

18. Gobodo-Madikizela, *A Human Being Died That Night*, 15.

19. Gobodo-Madikizela, *A Human Being Died That Night*, 128.

20. Krog, Mpolweni, and Ratele, *There Was This Goat*, 33.

21. Quoted in Gordon, "Foreword," xii.

22. Far less was apportioned to victims than recommended in the TRC's final report. About twenty-one thousand victims ended up receiving each a one-time payment of thirty-nine hundred dollars.

23. Gobodo-Madikizela recognizes that episodes such as this that demand a level of forgiveness from the victims "may indirectly bestow power back on the perpetrator instead of empowering the victim." *A Human Being Died That Night*, 100.

24. Peterson and Suleman, *Zulu Love Letter*, 20–21.

25. Another important instance of this refusal to forgive involved the mothers of "the Cradock Four," who filed a challenge to the National Prosecution Authority in 2004 to allow them to prosecute the killers of their sons.

26. Quoted in Hoffmann and Reid, *Long Night's Journey into Day*.

27. Biko includes, as I do, all "non-white" racial groups under the term *black*. The apartheid classifications were African, European, Coloured, and Indian.

28. Biko, *I Write What I Like*, 139.

29. Gordon, "Foreword," vii. Leela Gandhi writes of such separatist movements: "So it is that the most radical communities of difference, founded upon solidarities of class, gender, race, or ethnicity, lapse into a politics of similitude—privileging separation over relationality, demanding uniformity as the price for belonging." Gandhi, *Affective Communities*, 25.

30. Lewis Nkosi has argued that black writers lack a national referent because of the way apartheid made internal and external exiles of them. This seems less true for black political thinkers such as Biko or Mandela.

31. Mpumlwana and Mpumlwana, "Introduction," xxvii.

32. Biko, *I Write What I Like*, 21.

33. Breytenbach, *The True Confessions of an Albino Terrorist*, 36.

34. Mda, *The Madonna of Excelsior*, 215.

35. Attridge, *The Singularity of Literature*, 92.

36. Similarly, de Kock's imprisonment guaranteed a form of distance not always possible during that fragile transformation of interracial relation—the "interregnum." Gordimer, "Living in the Interregnum."

37. Attwell, Attwell, and Harlow, "Interview with Sindiwe Magona," 284–85.

38. Recognizing mutuality in motherhood is not, however, the cure-all to fix national trauma. As Samuelson insists, "This relationship is not romanticized. Though shared maternity provides the channel through which Mandisa is able to address Biehl's mother, maternity *per se* is not shown necessarily to create the conditions under which this dialogue can take place." Samuelson, "The Mother as Witness," 139.

39. Apartheid-era works include *To My Children's Children* and *Living, Loving, and Lying Awake at Night*. Since apartheid, she has published two additional works: a novel and a book of poetry.

40. Magona, *Mother to Mother*, 200.

41. Magona, *Mother to Mother*, 1.

42. Jennifer Wenzel refuses the ethical implications of the novel's dialogic structure, seeing instead that "the only image of sociality as sustaining community, rather than menacing, mindless crowd, is a nostalgic recollection of Blouvlei, where Mandisa lived as a child until the community was scattered by the 'whirlwind' of forced removal." Wenzel, *Bulletproof*, 166. For McHaney, however, "Magona gives Mandisa a voice that is at once stream-of-consciousness as well as conversational, suggesting throughout the novel that Mandisa is one mother speaking relentlessly and intimately with another mother and seeking a gendered, personal reconciliation." McHaney, "History and Intertextuality," 173.

43. Magona, *Mother to Mother*, 209.

44. Wenzel reads the novel's structure more pessimistically: "Magona's narrator can imagine the future only as an extension of an entropic present. Although we may want to assume that there is some distance between author and narrator, or that Biehl's optimistic presence enables a broader view than Mandisa's, Magona's own concern about the false hopes of 1994 reinforces Mandisa's pessimism, if not her melancholic ignorance (or dismissal) of current events." Wenzel, *Bulletproof*, 171.

45. Samuelson, "Reading the Maternal Voice in Sindiwe Magona's *To My Children's Children* and *Mother to Mother*."

46. Magona, *Mother to Mother*, 174.

47. Magona, *Mother to Mother*, 181.

48. Bakhtin, *The Dialogic Imagination*, 324.

49. Jay, *Force Fields*, 46–47.

50. Magona, *Mother to Mother*, vi.

51. Magona, *Mother to Mother*, 9.

52. McHaney, "History and Intertextuality," 171.

53. Attwell, Attwell, and Harlow, "Interview with Sindiwe Magona," 284. For a discussion of how Mandisa is a figure for Magona and also a figure for black South African women more generally, see Samuelson, "The Mother as Witness."

54. Attwell, Attwell, and Harlow, "Interview with Sindiwe Magona," 285.

55. Quoted in Schattemann, "The Xhosa Cattle-Killing and Post-Apartheid South Africa," 183.

56. Koyana, "Home at Last!" 195.

57. Dlamini, *Native Nostalgia*, 8.

58. Dlamini, *Native Nostalgia*, 18–19.

59. Magona, *Mother to Mother*, 147.

60. Magona, *Mother to Mother*, 148.

61. Magona, *Mother to Mother*, 148.

62. Ndebele, "Rediscovery of the Ordinary."

63. Dlamini, *Askari*, 79.

64. Nixon, "Aftermaths," 73.

65. Gandhi, *Affective Communities*, 187.

66. Quoted in Dlamini, *Native Nostalgia*, 98.

67. Dlamini, *Native Nostalgia*, 98.

68. Gandhi, *Affective Communities*, 189.

69. Quoted in Gandhi, *Affective Communities*, 19.

70. Jacobs, *Skirting the Ethical*, xvi.

71. Jacobs, *Skirting the Ethical*, xix.

72. Glissant, *Poetics of Relation*, 199.

73. Dlamini and Jones, *Categories of Persons*, 10.

74. Plaatje, *Native Life in South Africa*, 13.

75. A reviewer writing in the *Birmingham Post* surmises that Plaatje's book "may conceivably have an influence on future events in South Africa—and at home, for by no legal fiction can the Imperial power disassociate itself from *responsibility* for Native Affairs." In the *Bookseller's Record* a review argues: "Mr Plaatje is no firebrand; he writes with moderation, and his book should attract sympathetic attention." Quoted in Plaatje, *Native Life in South Africa*.

76. Gobodo-Madikizela, *A Human Being Died That Night*, 157.

77. Gandhi, *Affective Communities*, 31.

78. Gandhi, *Affective Communities*, 189, quoted in 20, 27.

79. Fanon, *The Wretched of the Earth*, 4.

80. Bataille, "The Big Toe," 22.

81. Bataille, "The Big Toe," 20–21.

82. Levinas, *Humanism of the Other*, 32–33.

83. Cohen, "Introduction," xxxii.

84. Taylor, *Buying Whiteness*, 1.

85. Cohen, "Introduction," xxiv. In the French, Levinas writes: "L'ouverture, c'est la dénudation de la peau exposée à la blessure et à l'outrage. L'ouverture, c'est la vulnerabilité d'une peau offerte, dans l'outrage et la blessure, au-delà de tout ce qui peut se montrer, au-delà de tout ce qui, de l'essence de l'être, peut s'exposer à la compréhension et à la célébration." Levinas, *Humanisme De L'autre Homme*, 92; my emphasis.

86. Levinas, *Humanisme De L'autre Homme*, 92; my translation.

87. Gobodo-Madikizela, *A Human Being Died That Night*, 32.

88. Gobodo-Madikizela, *A Human Being Died That Night*, 34.

89. Gobodo-Madikizela, *A Human Being Died That Night*, 40, 46; my emphasis.

90. Gobodo-Madikizela's awareness of hands' signifying potential is reflected also in the quotation that serves as the epigram of her book.

91. Bataille, "The Big Toe," 22. The cover of the U.S. edition of *Mother to Mother* depicts a black woman's hand spread out over an aerial photo of what is presumably meant to represent a South African township.

92. Magona, *Forced to Grow*, 38.

93. Gandhi, *Affective Communities*, 183.

94. Gandhi, *Affective Communities*, 188; my emphasis.

95. The Constitution of the Republic of South Africa, 1996.

96. Scholarly work, too, has taken interesting new directions in its consideration of the ethical, noticeable particularly in Mark Sanders's recent *Learning Zulu: A Secret History of Language in South Africa*, which explores the ethical minefield that is set live when white South Africans learn black South African languages after apartheid. His engagement with the homophobic and sexist defenses of Jacob Zuma that appeared in the Zulu press, particularly, and with a language learner's own ethical complicities in those unethical forms of relation, marks the complexity of post-apartheid ethical relations as a necessarily commonplace component of the present.

97. Farred, "The Not-Yet Counterpartisan," 596.

98. Farred, "The Not-Yet Counterpartisan," 596.

99. Barnard and van der Vlies, *South African Writing in Transition*.

100. See Jaji, "1994 as Frontier Myth."

101. Attwell, *Rewriting Modernity*, 27–50.

102. Mbembe, "Decolonizing Knowledge."

103. Non-Anglophone works might provide an interesting comparative case here— see, for instance, Mark Sanders's readings of contemporary Zulu novels and plays.

104. Desai, "Introduction: Teaching the African Novel."

105. Scott, *Omens of Adversity*.

Abrahams, Peter. *Mine Boy*. 1946. London: Heinemann, 1989.

Abrahams, Peter. *Tell Freedom*. 1954. Reprinted, London: Faber and Faber, 1990.

Achebe, Chinua. "The Truth of Fiction." In *African Literature: An Anthology of Criticism and Theory*, ed. Tejumola Olaniyan and Ato Quayson. Malden, MA: Blackwell, 2007.

Adichie, Chimamanda Ngozi. "The Danger of a Single Story." TED Conferences, 2009. Web.

Adorno, Theodor W. *The Culture Industry: Selected Essays on Mass Culture*. London: Routledge, 1991.

"African and European Scholars Debate: 'Is Bioscope a Disaster?'" *Drum* June 1952, 35.

Agamben, Giorgio. *Homo Sacer: Sovereign Power and Bare Life*. Trans. Daniel Heller-Roazen. Meridian: Crossing Aesthetics. Stanford, CA: Stanford University Press, 1998.

Agamben, Giorgio. *State of Exception*. Chicago: University of Chicago Press, 2005.

Ahmed, Siraj Dean. *The Stillbirth of Capital: Enlightenment Writing and Colonial India*. Stanford, CA: Stanford University Press, 2012.

Altarriba, Antonio. "Le Roman-Photo En Espagne." In *Le Roman Photo*, ed. Jan Baetens and Ana González, 41–54. Amsterdam: Rodopi, 1996.

Althusser, Louis. "Ideology and Ideological State Apparatuses (Notes towards an Investigation)." https://www.marxists.org/reference/archive/althusser/1970/ideology.htm

Ambler, Charles. "Popular Films and Colonial Audiences: The Movies in Northern Rhodesia." *American Historical Review* 106.1 (2001): 81–105.

Anderson, Benedict. *Imagined Communities: Reflections on the Origin and Spread of Nationalism*. London: Verso, 1983.

Ang, Ien. *Watching Dallas: Soap Opera and the Melodramatic Imagination*. New York: Methuen, 1985.

Anzaldúa, Gloria. *Borderlands/La Frontera: The New Mestiza*. San Francisco: Spinsters/Aunt Lute, 1987.

Apache. Vol. 28. Durban, South Africa: Republican Press.

Appadurai, Arjun. *Modernity at Large: Cultural Dimensions of Globalization*. Minneapolis: University of Minnesota Press, 1996.

Arendt, Hannah. *Eichmann in Jerusalem: A Report on the Banality of Evil*. New York: Viking Press, 1964.

Askew, Kelly, and Richard R. Wilk, eds. *The Anthropology of Media: A Reader*. Malden, MA: Blackwell, 2002.

Attridge, Derek. "Ethical Modernism: Servants and Others in J. M. Coetzee's Early Fiction." *Poetics Today* 25.4 (2004): 653–71.

Attridge, Derek. *The Singularity of Literature*. New York: Routledge, 2004.

Attwell, David. *Rewriting Modernity: Studies in Black South African Literary History*. Athens: Ohio University Press, 2005

Attwell, David, Joan Attwell, and Barbara Harlow. "Interview with Sindiwe Magona." *Modern Fiction Studies* 46.1 (2000): 282–95.

Auerbach, Erich. *Mimesis: The Representation of Reality in Western Literature*. Princeton: Princeton University Press, 1953.

Baetens, Jan. "The Intermediate Domain, or the Photographic Novel and the Problem of Value." *Critical Inquiry* 15.2 (1989): 280–91.

Baetens, Jan. "Le Roman-Photo in Situ." In *Le Roman Photo*, ed. Jan Baetens and Ana González, 36–40. Amsterdam: Rodopi, 1996.

Bakhtin, M. M. *The Dialogic Imagination: Four Essays*. Austin: University of Texas Press, 1981.

Balseiro, Isabel, and Ntongela Masilela. *To Change Reels: Film and Culture in South Africa*. Detroit: Wayne State University Press, 2003.

Barber, Karin. *Africa's Hidden Histories: Everyday Literacy and Making the Self*. Bloomington: Indiana University Press, 2006.

Barber, Karin. "Popular Arts in Africa." *African Studies Review* 30.3 (1987): 1–78.

Barber, Karin. "Preliminary Notes on Audiences in Africa." *Africa* 67.3 (1997): 347–62.

Barnard, Rita. "Bitterkomix: Notes from the Post-Apartheid Underground." *South Atlantic Quarterly* 103.4 (2004): 719–54.

Barnard, Rita, and Andrew van der Vlies, eds. *South African Writing in Transition*. Forthcoming, New York: Bloomsbury, 2018.

Barnes, Teresa. "'Am I a Man?': Gender and the Pass Laws in Urban Colonial Zimbabwe, 1930–80." *African Studies Review* 40.1 (1997): 59–81.

Barthes, Roland. *Image, Music, Text*. Trans. Stephen Heath. New York: Hill and Wang, 1977.

Bataille, Georges. "The Big Toe." In *Visions of Excess: Selected Writings, 1927–1939*, ed. Allen Stoekl, 20–23. Minneapolis: University of Minnesota Press, 1985.

Bazin, André. *What Is Cinema?* Trans. Hugh Gray. Vol. 2. Berkeley: University of California Press, 1972.

Belluck, Pam. "For Better Social Skills, Scientists Recommend a Little Chekhov." *New York Times*, October 4, 2013, A1. Web.

Benjamin, Jessica. *Like Subjects, Love Objects: Essays on Recognition and Sexual Difference*. New Haven: Yale University Press, 1995.

Benjamin, Walter. "The Work of Art in an Age of Mechanical Reproduction." *Illuminations: Essays and Reflections*, 217–52. New York: Harcourt, 1968.

Bewes, Timothy. *The Event of Postcolonial Shame*. Princeton: Princeton University Press, 2011.

Bhabha, Homi K. *The Location of Culture*. New York: Routledge, 2004.

Bhabha, Homi K. *Nation and Narration*. New York: Routledge, 1990.

Biko, Steve. *I Write What I Like: Selected Writings*. Chicago: University of Chicago Press, 2002.

Blumenthal-Barby, Martin. *Inconceivable Effects: Ethics through Twentieth-Century German Literature, Thought, and Film*. Ithaca: Cornell University Press, 2013.

Boltanski, Luc. *Distant Suffering: Morality, Media, and Politics*. New York: Cambridge University Press, 1999.

Bond, Patrick. "South Africa: Exploding with Rage, Imploding with Self-Doubt—but Exuding Socialist Potential." *Monthly Review* 67.2 (2015): 21–39.

Booth, Wayne C. *The Company We Keep: An Ethics of Fiction*. Berkeley: University of California Press, 1988.

Borges, Jorge Luis. "Interview: The Art of Fiction No. 39." *Paris Review* no. 40 (Winter-Spring 1967). http://www.theparisreview.org/interviews/4331/the-art-of-fiction-no-39-jorge-luis-borges

Botha, Martin. *South African Cinema 1896–2010*. Bristol, UK: Intellect, 2012.

Breckenridge, Keith. "The Biometric State: The Promise and Perils of Digital Government in the New South Africa." *Journal of Southern African Studies* 31.2 (2005): 267–82.

Breckenridge, Keith. "Verwoerd's Bureau of Proof: Total Information in the Making of Apartheid." *History Workshop Journal* 59 (2005): 83–108.

Breytenbach, Breyten. "Mandela's Smile." *Harper's*, December 2008, 39–48.

Breytenbach, Breyten. *A Season in Paradise*. Trans. Rike Vaughan. San Diego, CA: A Harvest Book, an imprint of Harcourt Brace, 1994.

Breytenbach, Breyten. *The True Confessions of an Albino Terrorist*. San Diego, CA: A Harvest Book, an imprint of Harcourt Brace, 1994.

Brooks, Peter, and Hilary Jewett. *The Humanities and Public Life*. New York: Fordham University Press, 2014.

Burns, James. "John Wayne on the Zambezi: Cinema, Empire, and the American Western in British Central Africa." *International Journal of African Historical Studies* 35.1 (2002): 103–17.

Butler, Judith. *Giving an Account of Oneself*. New York: Fordham University Press, 2005.

Caplan, Jane, and John Torpey. *Documenting Individual Identity: The Development of State Practices in the Modern World*. Princeton: Princeton University Press, 2001.

"Census 2011, Statistical Release (Revised)." Pretoria: Statistics South Africa, 2012.

Chapman, Michael. *The "Drum" Decade: Stories from the 1950s*. Pietermaritzburg, South Africa: University of Natal Press, 1989.

Chartier, Roger. *The Order of Books: Readers, Authors, and Libraries in Europe between the Fourteenth and Eighteenth Centuries*. Stanford: Stanford University Press, 1994.

Chatterjee, Partha. *Nationalist Thought and the Colonial World: A Derivative Discourse*. Minneapolis: University of Minnesota Press, 1993.

Chow, Rey. *Ethics after Idealism: Theory, Culture, Ethnicity, Reading*. Bloomington: Indiana University Press, 1998.

Clark, Katerina, and Michael Holquist. *Mikhail Bakhtin*. Cambridge, MA: Belknap Press of Harvard University Press, 1984.

Coetzee, J. M. *Elizabeth Costello*. London: Secker, 2003.

Coetzee, J. M. *Giving Offense: Essays on Censorship*. Chicago: University of Chicago Press, 1996.

Cohen, Richard A. "Introduction: Humanism and Anti-Humanism—Levinas, Cassirer, and Heidegger." In *Humanism of the Other*, by Emmanuel Levinas, vii–xliv. Trans. Nidra Poller. Urbana: University of Illinois Press, 2003.

Cole, Jennifer, and Lynn M. Thomas, eds. *Love in Africa*. Chicago: University of Chicago Press, 2009.

The Constitution of the Republic of South Africa, 1996. Department of Justice and Constitutional Development, Republic of South Africa, 1996. Web. www.justice.gov.za/legislation/constitution/SAConstitution-web-eng.pdf

Coplan, David B. *In Township Tonight! South Africa's Black City Music and Theatre*. Johannesburg: Ravan Press, 1985.

Couzens, Tim. "'Moralizing Leisure Time': The Transatlantic Connection and Black Johannesburg, 1918–1936." In *Industrialisation and Social Change in South Africa: African Class Formation, Culture, and Consciousness, 1870–1930*, ed. Shula Marks and Richard Rathbone, 314–37. London: Longman, 1982.

Crapanzano, Vincent. *Imaginative Horizons: An Essay in Literary-Philosophical Anthropology*. Chicago: University of Chicago Press, 2004.

Darwish, Mahmoud. "Identity Card." 1964. Web. http://www.barghouti.com/poets/darwish/bitaqa.asp. Accessed August 21, 2017.

Davis, Angela. "The Legacy of Slavery: Standards for a New Womanhood." In *Women, Race, and Class*, 3–29. New York: Vintage, 1981.

Davis, Peter. *In Darkest Hollywood: Exploring the Jungles of Cinema's South Africa*. Athens: Ohio University Press, 1996.

de Kock, Eugene. *A Long Night's Damage: Working for the Apartheid State*. Ed. Jeremy Gordin. Saxonwold: Contra Press, 1998.

de Kock, Leon. *Losing the Plot: Crime, Reality and Fiction in Postapartheid Writing*. Johannesburg: Wits University Press, 2017.

Deloria, Philip Joseph. *Playing Indian*. New Haven: Yale University Press, 1998.

Denning, Michael. *Mechanic Accents: Dime Novels and Working-Class Culture in America*. New York: Verso, 1987.

Derrida, Jacques. *Politics of Friendship*. London: Verso, 1997.

Desai, Gaurav. "Introduction: Teaching the African Novel." In *Teaching the African Novel*, ed. Gaurav Desai, 1–18. New York: Modern Language Association, 2009.

Dhlomo, R. R. R. *An African Tragedy: A Novel in English by a Zulu Writer*. Lovedale, South Africa: Lovedale Institution Press, 1928.

Dick, Archie L. *The Hidden History of South Africa's Book and Reading Cultures*. Toronto: University of Toronto Press, 2012.

Dlamini, Jacob. *Askari: A Story of Collaboration and Betrayal in the Anti-Apartheid Struggle*. Auckland Park, South Africa: Jacana, 2014.

Dlamini, Jacob. *Native Nostalgia*. Auckland Park, South Africa: Jacana, 2009.

Docker, John. *Postmodernism and Popular Culture: A Cultural History*. New York: Cambridge University Press, 1994.

Dodson, Don. "The Four Modes of Drum: Popular Fiction and Social Control in South Africa." *African Studies Review* 17.2 (1974): 317–43.

Dovey, Lindiwe. *African Film and Literature: Adapting Violence to the Screen*. New York: Columbia University Press, 2009.

Du Bois, W. E. B. "The Souls of Black Folk." In *W.E.B. Du Bois: Writings*, 357–548. Ed. Nathan Huggins. New York: Library of America, 1986.

Eco, Umberto. "Towards a Semiotic Inquiry into the Television Message." *Working Papers in Cultural Studies* 3 (1972): 103–21.

Fair, Laura. *Pastimes and Politics: Culture, Community, and Identity in Post-Abolition Urban Zanzibar, 1890–1945*. Athens: Ohio University Press, 2001.

Fanon, Frantz. *Black Skin, White Masks*. New York: Grove Press, 1967.

Fanon, Frantz. *The Wretched of the Earth*. Trans. Richard Philcox. New York: Grove Press, 2004.

Farred, Grant. "The Not-Yet Counterpartisan: A New Politics of Oppositionality." *South Atlantic Quarterly* 103.4 (2004): 589–605.

Febvre, Lucien, and Henri-Jean Martin. *The Coming of the Book: The Impact of Printing, 1450–1800*. London: N.L.B., 1976.

Flora, Cornelia Butler, and Jan L. Flora. "The Fotonovela as a Tool for Class and Cultural Domination." *Latin American Perspectives* 5.1 (1978): 134–50.

Ford, Richard B. "The Frontier in South Africa: A Comparative Study of the Turner Thesis." Ph.D. Thesis, University of Denver, 1966.

Foucault, Michel. *Discipline and Punish: The Birth of the Prison*. New York: Vintage Books, 1995.

Fouché, B. "Reading and Libraries in the Socio-Cultural Life of an Urban Black Community." *Mousaion Ii*. Vol. 10. Pretoria: UNISA, 1980.

Franklin, Ruth. "After Empire: Chinua Achebe and the Great African Novel." *New Yorker*, May 25, 2008, 72–77.

Freud, Sigmund. "Group Psychology and the Analysis of the Ego." In *The Freud Reader*, 626–28. Ed. Peter Gay. New York: W.W. Norton, 1989.

Freud, Sigmund. "Totem and Taboo." In *The Freud Reader*, 481–513. Ed. Peter Gay. New York: W.W. Norton, 1989.

Fugard, Athol. *Sizwe Bansi Is Dead*; and *The Island*. New York: Viking Press, 1976.

Gandhi, Leela. *Affective Communities: Anticolonial Thought, Fin-De-Siècle Radicalism, and the Politics of Friendship*. Durham, NC: Duke University Press, 2006.

Gandhi, Leela. *The Common Cause: Postcolonial Ethics and the Practice of Democracy, 1900—1955*. Chicago: University of Chicago Press, 2014.

Gavshon, Harriet. "Levels of Intervention in Films Made for African Audiences in South Africa." *Critical Arts* 2.4 (1983): 13–21.

Giet, Sylvette. "Le Roman-Photo Sentimental Traditionnel Lu En France." In *Le Roman Photo*, ed. Jan Baetens and Ana González, 3–14. Amsterdam: Rodopi, 1996.

Giliomee, Hermann Buhr. *The Afrikaners: Biography of a People*. Charlottesville: University of Virginia Press, 2003.

Giliomee, Hermann Buhr, and Lawrence Schlemmer. *Up against the Fences: Poverty, Passes, and Privilege in South Africa*. New York: St. Martin's Press, 1985.

Glissant, Édouard. *Poetics of Relation*. Trans. Betsy Wing. Ann Arbor: University of Michigan Press, 1997.

Gobodo-Madikizela, Pumla. *A Human Being Died That Night: A South African Story of Forgiveness*. Boston: Houghton Mifflin, 2003.

Goldblatt, David. "Audio Transcript." Jewish Museum. http://thejewishmuseum.org/exhibitions/south-african-photographs-david-goldblatt. Web. Accessed June 23, 2010.

Goldblatt, David. *David Goldblatt Photographs*. Rome: Contrasto, 2006.

Gordimer, Nadine. "Living in the Interregnum." In *The Essential Gesture: Writing, Politics and Places*, 243–310. London: Jonathan Cape, 1988.

Gordon, Lewis R. "Foreword." In *I Write What I Like: Selected Writings*, by Steve Biko, vii–xiii. Chicago: University of Chicago Press, 2002.

Gunner, Liz, Dina Ligaga, and Dumisani Moyo. *Radio in Africa: Publics, Cultures, Communities*. Johannesburg: Wits University Press, 2011.

Gutsche, Thelma. *The History and Social Significance of Motion Pictures in South Africa, 1895–1940*. Cape Town: H. Timmins, 1972.

Hale, Dorothy. "Aesthetics and the New Ethics: Theorizing the Novel in the Twenty-First Century." *PMLA* 124.3 (2009): 896–905.

Hall, Stuart. "Encoding, Decoding." In *The Cultural Studies Reader*, 2d ed., ed. Simon During, 507–18. London: Routledge, 1993.

Hansen, Miriam. *Babel and Babylon: Spectatorship in American Silent Film*. Cambridge, MA: Harvard University Press, 1991.

Hansen, Miriam. "The Mass Production of the Senses: Classical Cinema as Vernacular Modernism." *Modernism/Modernity* 6.2 (1999): 59–77.

Hansen, Miriam. "Tracking Cinema on a Global Scale." *The Oxford Handbook of Global Modernisms*, ed. Matt Eatough and Mark A. Wollaeger, 601–26. New York: Oxford University Press, 2012.

Higginson, Pim. "What Is and Where Is Francophone African Popular Fiction?" *Cambridge Journal of Postcolonial Literary Inquiry* 4.2 (2017): 207–21.

Hindson, Douglas. *Pass Controls and the Urban African Proletariat in South Africa*. Johannesburg: Ravan Press, 1987.

Hitchcock, Peter. "The Genre of Postcoloniality." *New Literary History* 34.2 (2003): 299–330.

Hofmeyr, Isabel. *Gandhi's Printing Press: Experiments in Slow Reading*. Cambridge, MA: Harvard University Press, 2013.

Hofmeyr, Isabel. *The Portable Bunyan: A Transnational History of the Pilgrim's Progress.* Princeton: Princeton University Press, 2003.

Hoggart, Richard. *The Uses of Literacy: Aspects of Working-Class Life with Special References to Publications and Entertainments.* London: Chatto and Windus, 1957.

Horwitz, Robert Britt. *Communication and Democratic Reform in South Africa.* New York: Cambridge University Press, 2001.

Huhndorf, Shari M. *Going Native: Indians in the American Cultural Imagination.* Ithaca: Cornell University Press, 2001.

Hume, David. "An Enquiry Concerning the Principles of Morals." In *Hume's Ethical Writings*, 22–156. Ed. Alasdair MacIntyre. Notre Dame, IN: Notre Dame University Press, 2003.

Hume, David. *A Treatise of Human Nature.* Oxford: Oxford University Press, 1978.

"In Praise of the Humble 'P*** Boekie' and Pinup Girls." Web. http://www.allatsea.co.za/army/pboek.htm. Accessed 16 March 16, 2010. No longer available.

Iser, Wolfgang. *The Act of Reading: A Theory of Aesthetic Response.* Baltimore: Johns Hopkins University Press, 1978.

Jacobs, Carol. *Skirting the Ethical.* Stanford, CA: Stanford University Press, 2008.

Jaji, Tsitsi. *Africa in Stereo: Modernism, Music, and Pan-African Solidarity.* New York: Oxford University Press, 2014.

Jaji, Tsitsi. "1994 as Frontier Myth: Reading, 'Future Memory' Across Borders." In *South African Writing in Transition*, ed. Rita Barnard and Andrew van der Vlies. New York: Bloomsbury, forthcoming 2018.

Jameson, Fredric. *The Political Unconscious: Narrative as a Socially Symbolic Act.* Ithaca: Cornell University Press, 1981.

Jameson, Fredric. "Reification and Utopia in Mass Culture." *Social Text* 1 (1979): 130–48.

Jay, Martin. *Force Fields: Between Intellectual History and Cultural Critique.* New York: Routledge, 1993.

Jones, Megan, and Jacob Dlamini. *Categories of Persons: Rethinking Ourselves and Others.* Johannesburg: Picador Africa, 2013.

Joshi, Priya. *In Another Country: Colonialism, Culture, and the English Novel in India.* New York: Columbia University Press, 2002.

Kaplan, Amy. *The Anarchy of Empire in the Making of U.S. Culture.* Cambridge, MA: Harvard University Press, 2002.

Keenan, Thomas. *Fables of Responsibility: Aberrations and Predicaments in Ethics and Politics.* Stanford, CA: Stanford University Press, 1997.

Khalip, Jacques. *Anonymous Life: Romanticism and Dispossession.* Stanford, CA: Stanford University Press, 2009.

Knapton, Sarah. "Great Novels Can Change Your Life . . . and Your Brain." *Telegraph*, January 6, 2014.

Knausgaard, Karl Ove. "I Am Someone, Look at Me." *T Magazine*, June 10, 2014: M294.

Koyana, Siphokazi. "Home at Last!" In *Sindiwe Magona: The First Decade*, ed. Siphokazi Koyana, 193–207. Scottsville, South Africa: University of KwaZulu-Natal Press, 2004.

Krabill, Ron. *Starring Mandela and Cosby: Media and the End(s) of Apartheid*. Chicago: University of Chicago Press, 2010.

Kracauer, Siegfried. "Boredom." In *The Mass Ornament: Weimar Essays*, ed. Thomas Y. Levin, 331–36. Cambridge, MA: Harvard University Press, 1995.

Krauss, Rosalind. "Reinventing the Medium." *Critical Inquiry* 25.2 (1999): 289–305.

Krings, Matthias. *African Appropriations: Cultural Difference, Mimesis, and Media*. Bloomington: Indiana University Press, 2015.

Krog, Antjie. *Conditional Tense: Memory and Vocabulary after the South African Truth and Reconciliation Commission*. London: Seagull Books, 2013.

Kruger, Loren. *The Drama of South Africa: Plays, Pageants, and Publics since 1910*. New York: Routledge, 1999.

Kruger, Loren. "Rev. of *Media and Identity in Africa*, and *Cinema in a Democratic South Africa*." *Research in African Literatures* 42.1 (2011): 192–94.

Kruger, Loren, and Patricia Watson Shariff. "'Shoo—This Book Makes Me to Think!': Education, Entertainment, and 'Life-Skills' Comics in South Africa." *Poetics Today* 22.2 (2001): 475–513.

Laden, Sonja. "'Making the Paper Speakwell,' or, the Pace of Change in Consumer Magazines for Black South Africans." *Poetics Today* 22.2 (2001): 515–48.

La Guma, Alex. *In the Fog of the Seasons' End*. New York: Third Press, 1973.

La Guma, Alex. *A Walk in the Night, and Other Stories*. London: Heinemann, 1967.

Lamar, Howard Roberts, and Leonard Monteath Thompson. *The Frontier in History: North America and Southern Africa Compared*. New Haven: Yale University Press, 1981.

Larkin, Brian. *Signal and Noise: Media, Infrastructure, and Urban Culture in Nigeria*. Durham, NC: Duke University Press, 2008.

Lasch, Christopher. *The True and Only Heaven: Progress and Its Critics*. New York: Norton, 1991.

Lenihan, John H. *Showdown: Confronting Modern America in the Western Film*. Urbana: University of Illinois Press, 1980.

Le Roux, Elizabeth. "Book History in the African World: The State of the Discipline." *Book History* 15 (2012): 248–300.

Levinas, Emmanuel. *Humanism of the Other*. Urbana: University of Illinois Press, 2003.

Levinas, Emmanuel. *Humanisme De L'autre Homme*. Montpellier: Fata Morgana, 1972.

Levine, Caroline. *Forms: Whole, Rhythm, Hierarchy, Network*. Princeton: Princeton University Press, 2015.

Locke, John. *An Essay Concerning Human Understanding*. New York: The Barnes & Noble Library of Essential Reading, 2004.

Long Night's Journey into Day: South Africa's Search for Truth and Reconciliation. Dir. Frances Reid and Deborah Hoffmann. San Francisco: California Newsreel, 2000.

Longman, Timothy. "Identity Cards, Ethnic Self-Perception, and Genocide in Rwanda." In *Documenting Individual Identity: The Development of State Practices in the Modern World*, ed. Jane Caplan and John Torpey, 345–57. Princeton: Princeton University Press, 2001.

Lott, Eric. *Love and Theft: Blackface Minstrelsy and the American Working Class.* New York: Oxford University Press, 1993.

Lukács, György. *The Theory of the Novel: A Historico-Philosophical Essay on the Forms of Great Epic Literature.* Cambridge, MA: MIT Press, 1971.

Magona, Sindiwe. *Forced to Grow.* 1992. Reprinted, New York: Interlink Books, 1998.

Magona, Sindiwe. *Mother to Mother.* Boston: Beacon Press, 1999.

Magubane, Peter. *Magubane's South Africa.* New York: Knopf, 1978.

Maingard, Jacqueline. *South African National Cinema.* New York: Routledge, 2007.

Mantlo, Bill. "Bill Mantlo's Column on South African Comics." *Comic's Journal* 43 (1978): 75–77.

Marinovich, Greg. *Murder at Small Koppie: The Real Story of South Africa's Marikana Massacre.* Cape Town: Penguin Random House South Africa, 2016.

Marks, Shula. "Southern and Central Africa, 1886–1910." In *The Cambridge History of Africa*, vol. 6, *From 1870 to 1905*, ed. Roland Oliver and G. N. Sanderson, 422–92. New York: Cambridge University Press, 1975.

Marks, Shula. "Towards a People's History of South Africa? Recent Developments in the Historiography of South Africa." In *People's History and Socialist Theory*, ed. Raphael Samuel, 297–308. London: Routledge, 1981.

Martin, Michael T. *Cinemas of the Black Diaspora: Diversity, Dependence, and Oppositionality.* Detroit: Wayne State University Press, 1995.

Mattera, Don. *Coming of Age in South Africa.* Boston: Beacon, 1989.

Mattera, Don. *Memory Is the Weapon.* Johannesburg: Ravan Press, 1987.

Matthews, James. *The Party Is Over.* Cape Town: Kwela Books, 1997.

Mbembe, Achille. "African Modes of Self-Writing." *Public Culture* 14.1 (2002): 239–73.

Mbembe, Achille. "Decolonizing Knowledge and the Question of the Archive." Wits Institute for Social and Economic Research, University of the Witwatersrand. 2015. Web.

Mbembe, Achille. *On the Postcolony.* Berkeley: University of California Press, 2001.

McCloud, Scott. *Understanding Comics: The Invisible Art.* Northampton, MA: Tundra Publishing, 1993.

McDonald, Peter D. *The Literature Police: Apartheid Censorship and Its Cultural Consequences.* New York: Oxford University Press, 2009.

McDonald, Peter D. "Semper Aliquid Novi: Reclaiming the Future of Book History from an African Perspective." *Book History* 19 (2016): 384–98.

McHaney, Pearl Amelia. "History and Intertextuality: A Transnational Reading of Eudora Welty's 'Losing Battles' and Sindiwe Magona's 'Mother to Mother.'" *Southern Literary Journal* 40.2 (2008): 166–81.

McHenry, Elizabeth. *Forgotten Readers: Recovering the Lost History of African American Literary Societies.* Durham, NC: Duke University Press, 2002.

McLoughlin, T. O. "Reading Zimbabwean Comic Strips." *Research in African Literatures* 20.2 (1989): 217–41.

Mda, Zakes. *The Madonna of Excelsior.* New York: Farrar, Straus and Giroux, 2004.

Mellet, Patric Tariq. "Response to 'Identity Metamorphosis.'" 2008. Web. www.sahistory. org.za

Merrett, Christopher. *A Culture of Censorship: Secrecy and Intellectual Repression in South Africa*. Macon, GA: Mercer University Press, 1995.

Mickenberg, Julia L. *Learning from the Left: Children's Literature, the Cold War, and Radical Politics in the United States*. New York: Oxford University Press, 2005.

Miller, J. Hillis. *The Ethics of Reading: Kant, De Man, Eliot, Trollope, James, and Benjamin*. New York: Columbia University Press, 1987. Modisane, Bloke. *Blame Me on History*. 1st ed. New York: Dutton, 1963.

Modisane, Bloke. "The Dignity of Begging." In *The "Drum" Decade: Stories from the 1950s*, ed. Michael Chapman, 10–17. Pietermaritzburg, South Africa: University of Natal Press, 1989.

Mogale, Arthur. "Crime for Sale: Another Escapade." In *The "Drum" Decade: Stories from the 1950s*, ed. Michael Chapman, 28–31. Pietermaritzburg, South Africa: University of Natal Press, 1989.

Mokoena, Hlonipha. *Magema Fuze: The Making of a Kholwa Intellectual*. Scottsville, South Africa: University of KwaZulu-Natal Press, 2011.

Mooney, Katie. "'Ducktails, Flick-Knives and Pugnacity': Subcultural and Hegemonic Masculinities in South Africa, 1948–1960." *Journal of Southern African Studies* 24.4 (1998): 753–74.

Moretti, Franco. *Atlas of the European Novel, 1800–1900*. New York: Verso, 1999.

Morris, Rosalind C. "Vernacular Modernism and South African Cinema: Capitalism, Crime, and Styles of Desire." In *The Oxford Handbook of Global Modernisms*, ed. Mark Wollager and Matt Eatough, 646–65. New York: Oxford University Press, 2012.

Mpumlwana, Malusi, and Thoko Mpumlwana. "Introduction." In *I Write What I Like: Selected Writings*, by Steve Biko, xvii–xxxi. Chicago: University of Chicago Press, 2002.

Muñoz, José Estaban. *Disidentifications: Queers of Color and the Performance of Politics*. Minneapolis: University of Minnesota Press, 1999.

Nancy, Jean-Luc. *The Inoperative Community*. Minneapolis: University of Minnesota Press, 1991.

Nandy, Ashis. *The Intimate Enemy: Loss and Recovery of Self under Colonialism*. Delhi: Oxford University Press, 1983.

Ndebele, Njabulo S. "Rediscovery of the Ordinary: Some New Writings in South Africa." In *South African Literature and Culture: Rediscovery of the Ordinary*, 41–59. Manchester, UK: Manchester University Press, 1994.

Newell, Stephanie. *Literary Culture in Colonial Ghana: How to Play the Game of Life*. Bloomington: Indiana University Press, 2002.

Newell, Stephanie. *The Power to Name: A History of Anonymity in Colonial West Africa*. Athens: Ohio University Press, 2013.

Newell, Stephanie. *Readings in African Popular Fiction*. Bloomington: Indiana University Press, 2002.

Nimmon, Laura. *Photonovels through Critical Pedagogy: A Consciousness Raising Health*

Literacy Project with ESL Speaking Immigrant Women. Saarbrücken, Germany: Verlag Dr. Müller, 2009.

Nixon, Rob. "Aftermaths." *Transition* 72 (1996): 64–78.

Nixon, Rob. *Homelands, Harlem, and Hollywood: South African Culture and the World Beyond*. New York: Routledge, 1994.

Nkosi, Lewis. "Fiction by Black South Africans." *Black Orpheus* 19 (1966): 48–54.

Nkosi, Lewis. "Postmodernism and Black Writing in South Africa." In *Writing South Africa: Literature, Apartheid, and Democracy, 1970–1995*, ed. Derek Attridge and Rosemary Jolly, 75–90. New York: Cambridge University Press, 1998.

Nussbaum, Martha Craven. *Love's Knowledge: Essays on Philosophy and Literature*. New York: Oxford University Press, 1990.

Nussbaum, Martha Craven. *Poetic Justice: The Literary Imagination and Public Life*. Boston: Beacon Press, 1995.

Nuttall, Sarah. *Entanglement: Literary and Cultural Reflections on Post Apartheid*. Johannesburg: Wits University Press, 2009.

Nxumalo, Henry. "The Birth of a Tsotsi." In *The "Drum" Decade: Stories from the 1950s*, ed. Michael Chapman, 18–23. Pietermaritzburg: University of Natal Press, 1989.

Onishi, Norimitsu. "Honoring a Filmmaker in the Shadow of Apartheid." *New York Times*, July 30, 2014, A4. Web.

Paleker, Gairoonisa. "The B-Scheme Subsidy and the 'Black Film Industry' in Apartheid South Africa, 1972–1990." *Journal of African Cultural Studies* 22.1 (2010): 91–104.

Palumbo-Liu, David. *The Deliverance of Others: Reading Literature in a Global Age*. Durham, NC: Duke University Press, 2012.

Pappe, Ilan. *Israel and South Africa: The Many Faces of Apartheid*. London: Zed Books, 2015.

"Pass Laws," 1957. Bailey's African History Archives. http://www.baha.co.za/search/preview/43_724

Paton, Alan. "To a Small Boy Who Died at Diepkloof Reformatory." In *A Book of South African Verse*, ed. G. Butler, 71–72. London: Oxford University Press, 1959.

Peeters, Benoît. "Le Roman-Photo: Un Impossible Renouveau?" In *Le Roman Photo*, ed. Jan Baetens and Ana González, 15–23. Amsterdam: Rodopi, 1996.

Peterson, Bhekizizwe. *Monarchs, Missionaries and African Intellectuals: African Theater and the Unmaking of Colonial Marginality*. Trenton, NJ: Africa World Press, 2000.

Peterson, Bhekizizwe, and Ramadan Suleman. *Zulu Love Letter: A Screenplay*. Johannesburg: Wits University Press, 2009.

Phillips, Ray E. *The Bantu in the City: A Study of Cultural Adjustment on the Witwatersrand*. Lovedale, South Africa: Lovedale Press, 1938.

Phillips, Ray E. "Phillips News No. 5." Ray and Dora Phillips Papers, Congregational Library and Archives. Johannesburg, 1920.

"Photo Stories Make a Return." *The Voice of the Cape*, May 23, 2009.

Plaatje, Sol T. *Native Life in South Africa: Before and since the European War and the Boer Rebellion*. 5th ed. London: P.S. King & Son, 1916.

Powdermaker, Hortense. *Copper Town: Changing Africa; The Human Situation on the Rhodesian Copperbelt.* New York: Harper & Row, 1962.

Rabinowitz, Peter J. *Before Reading: Narrative Conventions and the Politics of Interpretation.* Ithaca: Cornell University Press, 1987.

Rancière, Jacques. *Proletarian Nights: The Workers' Dream in Nineteenth-Century France.* New York: Verso Books, 2012.

Ranger, T. O. *Dance and Society in Eastern Africa, 1890–1970: The Beni Ngoma.* Berkeley: University of California Press, 1975.

Reed, Ishmael. "Cure the Canon of Literary Agoraphobia." *New York Times,* August 31, 2015. Web.

Reid-Pharr, Robert. *Once You Go Black: Choice, Desire, and the Black American Intellectual.* New York: New York University Press, 2007.

Reynolds, Glenn. "Playing Cowboys and Africans: Hollywood and the Cultural Politics of African Identity." *Historical Journal of Film, Radio and Television* 25.3 (2005): 399–426.

Rogosin, Lionel, and Peter Davis. *Come Back, Africa.* Johannesburg, South Africa: STE Publishers, 2004.

Rosaldo, Renato. *Culture & Truth: The Remaking of Social Analysis.* Boston: Beacon Press, 1989.

Rousseau, Jean-Jacques. *A Discourse on Inequality.* New York: Penguin, 1984.

Rousseau, Jean-Jacques, and Johann Gottfried Herder. *On the Origin of Language.* Chicago: University of Chicago Press, 1986.

Sachs, Albie. "Preparing Ourselves for Freedom: Culture and the ANC Constitutional Guidelines." *The Drama Review* 35.1 (1991): 187–93.

Said, Edward W. *Representations of the Intellectual.* New York: Pantheon Books, 1994.

Saint, Lily. "Not Western: Race, Reading, and the South African Photocomic." *Journal of Southern African Studies* 36.4 (2010): 939–58.

Sampson, Lin. "One Last Picture Show." In *Now You've Gone 'N Killed Me: True Stories of Crime, Passion, and Ballroom Dancing,* 83–88. Cape Town: Oshun, 2005.

Samuelson, Meg. "The Mother as Witness: Reading *Mother to Mother* Alongside South Africa's Truth and Reconciliation Commission." In *Sindiwe Magona: The First Decade,* ed. Siphokazi Koyana, 127–46. Scottsville, South Africa: University of KwaZulu-Natal Press, 2004.

Samuelson, Meg. "Reading the Maternal Voice in Sindiwe Magona's *To My Children's Children* and *Mother to Mother.*" *Modern Fiction Studies* 46.1 (2000): 227–45.

Sanders, Mark. *Complicities: The Intellectual and Apartheid.* Durham, NC: Duke University Press, 2002.

Sanders, Mark. *Learning Zulu: A Secret History of Language in South Africa.* Princeton: Princeton University Press, 2016.

Sandoval, Chela. *Methodology of the Oppressed.* Minneapolis: University of Minnesota Press, 2000.

Sandwith, Corinne. *World of Letters: Reading Communities and Cultural Debates in Early Apartheid South Africa.* Pietermaritzburg: University of KwaZulu-Natal Press, 2014.

Sartre, Jean-Paul. *"What Is Literature?" and Other Essays.* Cambridge, MA: Harvard University Press, 1988.

Schattemann, Renée. "The Xhosa Cattle-Killing and Post-Apartheid South Africa: Sindiwe Magona's *Mother to Mother* and Zakes Mda's *The Heart of Redness.*" *African Studies* 67.2 (2008): 275–91.

Scott, David. *Conscripts of Modernity: The Tragedy of Colonial Enlightenment.* Durham, NC: Duke University Press, 2004.

Scott, David. *Omens of Adversity: Tragedy, Time, Memory, Justice.* Durham, NC: Duke University Press, 2014.

Scott, James C. *Domination and the Arts of Resistance: Hidden Transcripts.* New Haven: Yale University Press, 1990.

Simmon, Scott. *The Invention of the Western Film: A Cultural History of the Genre's First Half-Century.* New York: Cambridge University Press, 2003.

Slotkin, Richard. *The Fatal Environment: The Myth of the Frontier in the Age of Industrialization, 1800–1890.* New York: Atheneum, 1985.

Smith, Adam. *The Theory of Moral Sentiments.* Oxford: Clarendon Press, 1976.

Snead, James. "Spectatorship and Capture in *King Kong*: The Guilty Look." *Critical Quarterly* 33.1 (1991): 53–69.

Sole, Kelwyn. "Authority, Authenticity and the Black Writer: Depictions of Politics and Community in Selected Fictional Black Consciousness Texts." Ph.D. Thesis, University of the Witwatersrand, 1993.

Soske, Jon, and Sean Jacobs, eds. *Apartheid Israel: The Politics of an Analogy.* Chicago: Haymarket Books, 2015.

Spivak, Gayatri Chakravorty. *A Critique of Postcolonial Reason: Toward a History of the Vanishing Present.* Cambridge, MA: Harvard University Press, 1999.

Spivak, Gayatri Chakravorty. "Ethics and Politics in Tagore, Coetzee, and Certain Scenes of Teaching." *Diacritics* 32.3–4 (2002): 17–31.

Stevens, Wallace. "The House Was Quiet and the World Was Calm." In *Wallace Stevens: Collected Poetry and Prose*, 358. Ed. Frank Kermode and Joan Richardson. New York: Library of America, 1997.

Stewart, Jacqueline Najuma. *Migrating to the Movies: Cinema and Black Urban Modernity.* Berkeley: University of California Press, 2005.

Switzer, Les, and Donna Switzer. *The Black Press in South Africa and Lesotho: A Descriptive Bibliographic Guide to African, Coloured, and Indian Newspapers, Newsletters, and Magazines, 1836–1976.* Boston: G. K. Hall, 1979.

Taussig, Michael T. *Mimesis and Alterity: A Particular History of the Senses.* New York: Routledge, 1993.

Taylor, Gary. *Buying Whiteness: Race, Culture, and Identity from Columbus to Hip Hop.* New York: Palgrave Macmillan, 2005.

Teitel, Ruti G. *Transitional Justice.* New York: Oxford University Press, 2000.

Ten Kortenaar, Neil. *Postcolonial Literature and the Impact of Literacy: Reading and Writing in African and Caribbean Fiction.* New York: Cambridge University Press, 2011.

Thaisi, Lebohang. "The Poetry of Job Mzamo in Kagablog." 2006. Web. http://kaganof. com/kagablog/2006/10/27/the-poetry-of-job-mzamo/

Themba, Can. *The Will to Die*. London: Heinemann, 1972.

Tomaselli, Keyan. *The Cinema of Apartheid: Race and Class in South African Film*. New York: Smyrna/Lake View Press, 1988.

Turner, Frederick Jackson. *The Significance of the Frontier in American History*. New York: Ungar, 1963.

Tutu, Desmond. *No Future Without Forgiveness*. New York: Doubleday, 1999.

Van der Riet, George. "Photo Story Magazines." *South African Comic Books*, March 29, 2011. Web. http://southafricancomicbooks.blogspot.com/2011/03/photo-sto ry-magazines.html

Van der Vlies, Andrew. *Present Imperfect: Contemporary South African Writing*. Oxford: Oxford University Press, 2017.

Van Niekerk, Marlene. *Triomf*. Trans. Leon de Kock. Woodstock, NY: Overlook Press, 2004.

Van Onselen, Charles. *The Seed Is Mine: The Life of Kas Maine, a South African Share-cropper, 1894–1985*. New York: Hill and Wang, 1996.

Velde, Roger G., van de. "Le Roman-Photo Intérieur Et Son Reportage." In *Le Roman Photo*, ed. Jan Baetens and Ana González, 181–96. Amsterdam: Rodopi, 1996.

Wasserman, Herman, and Sean Jacobs. *Shifting Selves: Post-Apartheid Essays on Mass Media, Culture, and Identity*. Cape Town: Kwela Books, 2003.

Weheliye, Alexander G. *Habeas Viscus: Racializing Assemblages, Biopolitics, and Black Feminist Theories of the Human*. Durham, NC: Duke University Press, 2014.

Weld, Kirsten. *Paper Cadavers: The Archives of Dictatorship in Guatemala*. Durham, NC: Duke University Press, 2014.

Wenzel, Jennifer. *Bulletproof: Afterlives of Anticolonial Prophecy in South Africa and Beyond*. Chicago: University of Chicago Press, 2009.

Wicomb, Zoë. *David's Story*. New York: Feminist Press at the City University of New York, 2001.

Wicomb, Zoë. *October*. New York: New Press, 2014.

Wicomb, Zoë. "Shame and Identity: The Case of the Coloured in South Africa." In *Writing South Africa: Literature, Apartheid, and Democracy 1970–1995*, ed. Derek Attridge and Rosemary Jane Jolly, 91–107. New York: Cambridge University Press, 1998.

Willenson, Kim, Peter Younghusband, and Richard Manning. "Africa: The Caped Crusader." *Newsweek*, June 14, 1976, 48.

Williamson, Sue. *Resistance Art in South Africa*. Cape Town: David Philip, 1989.

Yancy, George, and Cornel West. "Cornel West: The Fire of a New Generation." *New York Times*, August 19, 2015. Web.

Abrahams, Peter, 37–38, 50–52, 55, 60–61, 161
Achebe, Chinua, 15, 111–12, 148
Adichie, Chimamanda Ngozi, 2, 27
Adorno, Theodor, 64–65, 136, 163
Africa in Stereo (Jaji), 67, 157, 161, 164
African Tragedy, An (R.R.R. Dhlomo), 40
Agaat (van Niekerk), 170
Ahmed, Siraj, 19, 157
Altarriba, Antonio, 90, 168–69
alterity. *See* ethics and alterity
Althusser, Louis, 111, 159
Ambler, Charles, 152, 163–64
Americanization. *See* cultural imperialism
ANC (African National Congress), 28, 59, 71, 110, 115, 135, 145–46, 148, 155
Anderson, Benedict, 25, 152
Ang, Ien, 162
Anzaldúa, Gloria, 170
Apache, 104, 106–7
Arend, 92
Askari (Dlamini), 133, 135
Attridge, Derek, 5, 6, 11, 16, 33, 48, 127, 151, 153–54, 166
audience, 3, 5, 56–57, 60
　black audiences (*see* black spectatorship)
　encoding, decoding, 64–65
　film audiences, 56–58, 71
　theories of spectatorship (*see* Hall, Stuart; Hansen, Miriam; Stewart, Jacqueline)
Auerbach, Erich, 155
A Walk in the Night (La Guma), 46–47, 51–52

Baetens, Jan, 84, 112–13, 166, 168–69, 172–73
Bakhtin, Mikhail, 95, 98–100, 130
Balseiro, Isabel, 161
Barber, Karin, 56, 60, 66, 81–82, 152, 157
Barnard, Rita, 147, 154, 168, 177
Barthes, Roland, 49, 88, 103
Bataille, Georges, 140, 142–43
Bazin, André, 95, 97
Benjamin, Jessica, 131, 156
Benjamin, Walter, 77, 91
Bewes, Timothy, 116–17, 173
Bhabha, Homi, 12–13, 47–48, 50, 94, 155
"Big Toe, The" (Bataille), 140, 142
Biko, Steve, 15, 68, 118, 121–27, 144, 154, 174
Black Consciousness, 28, 33, 118, 123–24. *See also* Biko, Steve
black spectatorship, 58–59, 65–67, 79–80
　history in South Africa, 67–72
　on the mines, 68–69
Blame Me on History (Modisane), 37, 47–48
Blumenthal-Barby, Martin, 151
Bona, 93
bookies. *See* photocomics
Booth, Wayne, 4, 5, 25, 48, 137, 151, 157